The Malebranche Moment

SELECTIONS FROM THE LETTERS OF

ÉTIENNE GILSON & HENRI GOUHIER

(1920–1936)

The Malebranche Moment

Selections from the Letters of Étienne Gilson & Henri Gouhier (1920–1936)

TRANSLATED AND EDITED BY

RICHARD J. FAFARA

MARQUETTE STUDIES IN PHILOSOPHY

NO. 48

ANDREW TALLON, SERIES EDITOR

www.marquette.edu/mupress/

LIBRARY OF CONGRESS CATALOGING-IN-PUBLICATION DATA

The Malebranche moment : selections from the letters of Étienne Gilson & Henri Gouhier, (1920-1936) / translated and edited by Richard J. Fafara.
p. cm. — (Marquette studies in philosophy ; No. 48)
Includes bibliographical references and index.
ISBN-13: 978-0-87462-671-1 (pbk. : alk. paper)
ISBN-10: 0-87462-671-4 (pbk. : alk. paper)
1. Malebranche, Nicolas, 1638-1715. 2. Gilson, Étienne, 1884-1978—Correspondence. 3. Gouhier, Henri Gaston, 1898-1994—Correspondence. I. Fafara, Richard J., 1944-
B1897.M34 2006
194—dc22

2006031622

∞ The paper used in this publication meets the minimum requirements of the American National Standard for Information Sciences—Permanence of Paper for Printed Library Materials, ANSI Z39.48-1992.

MARQUETTE UNIVERSITY PRESS
MILWAUKEE

The Association of Jesuit University Presses

Contents

INTRODUCTION

St. Augustine, St. Bonaventure, St. Thomas Aquinas,
Pascal, Malebranche. Gilson loved these men;
he read and reread them, emulated them,
for they recognized the primacy of the
word of God and of theology.
—Armand A. Maurer[1]

Nicolas Malebranche,
the greatest metaphysician
France ever produced.
—Étienne Gilson[2]

A few weeks after the exam for my *agrégation*,
Étienne Gilson arrived in Paris.
I had read his works and was the
first Parisian student to find him and say,
"I want to do my thesis with you."
That was the start of a great friendship.
—Henri Gouhier[3]

The monumental work of Étienne Gilson (1884–1978), philosopher, historian, and man of letters, continues to be recognized and valued. New editions and translations of his works, as well as books and scholarly articles highlighting particular aspects of Gilson's thought, continue unabated. Many institutions have formally recognized Gilson's legacy. In 1978, the Pontifical Institute of Mediaeval Studies in Toronto established the *Etienne Gilson Lecture Series*. In 1995, as part of its centenary celebrations at UNESCO, the Institut Catholique in Paris created a Chair of Metaphysics, the *Chaire Étienne Gilson*. More recently, in 1999,

1 Maurer 1981, 43.

2 Gilson 1968, 240; Gilson 1979, 81.

3 Gouhier 1988, 9.

The Gilson Society was formed in the United States and published its inaugural volume, *A Thomistic Tapestry*, in 2003.

Recognition also has been accorded Henri Gouhier (1898-1994), Gilson's friend and one of his most famous students. From 1941 until 1968, Gouhier held the Chair of the Philosophical History of Religious Thought at the Sorbonne. In 1968, this philosopher and historian of French thought, expert on the seventeenth century and the Enlightenment, and philosopher of the theater entered the *Académie des sciences morales et politiques*. The year after Gilson's death Gouhier took his place at the *Académie française*. As with Gilson, Gouhier's varied and impressive *œuvre* has been the subject of conferences and colloquia,[4] and an intellectual biography of Henri Gouhier is projected along with the publication of his papers.

Gilson and Gouhier each engaged in extensive personal and professional correspondence during their long academic careers. Gilson, for example, wrote his wife, Thérèse, almost daily when away from her. He corresponded with philosophers, theologians, scholars throughout the world, religious leaders, and even politicians. Gouhier's friends included Jacques Maritain, Jacques Madaule, Robert Garric, Gabriel Marcel, Vladimir Jankélévitch, Gaston Bachelard, Charles Du Bos, Paul Ricoeur, Jean Starobinski, Jean Mouton, and Marc Fumaroli. The list of individuals with whom Gilson and Gouhier exchanged letters constitutes a veritable international and academic *Who's Who* of the twentieth century.

Although Fr. Laurence Shook integrated excerpts from Gilson's letters into his authoritative biography of him, only small portions of Gilson's correspondence have been published. These include Gilson's letters to Henri de Lubac, Jacques Maritain, P. Marie-Michel Labourdette, Bruno Nardi,[5] and Marie–Dominique Chenu.[6] Not long before his death in 1994, Henri Gouhier provided Géry Prouvost with a copy of the letters he received from Gilson during a period of almost 50 years (1919–1966). That same year Prouvost published extracts from the letters categorizing them according to nine themes ("the principal mo-

4 See Armogathe 1995; Leduc-Fayette 1999; and Sacquin 2002. Proceedings from a colloquium on "Henri Gouhier et le théâtre" held in Novembre 2002 at the Sorbonne have not been published.

5 de Lubac 1986; Prouvost 1991; Donneaud 1994; Dronke 1998.

6 Murphy 2005.

ments"), one of which was "Malebranche."[7] The remainder of Gouhier's correspondence remains unpublished. Mme. Marie-Louise Gouhier and Mme. Cécile Gilson have graciously agreed to allow 31 of the "early" letters (29 from Gilson and 2 from Gouhier) to be published. These letters have one central theme: Henri Gouhier's doctoral work on Nicolas Malebranche.

For Étienne Gilson and Henri Gouhier the 1920s through the mid 1930's were significant years. After being awarded a *licence* in 1905, his *Diplôme d'études supérieures* in 1906, and his *agrégation* (a nationwide civil service competitive exam for professional teaching positions in the public education system) in 1907, Gilson taught from 1907 to 1913 in several lycées outside Paris. In 1913, he defended his ground-breaking principal and supplementary doctoral theses on René Descartes: the "grande" thesis, *La liberté chez Descartes et la théologie* and the "petite" thesis, *Index scolastico-Cartésien*.[8] During Gilson's, and later Gouhier's, student days at the Sorbonne, philosophy consisted of a mixture of rationalism, positivism, and idealism. Gilson did not share the negative impressions of the Sorbonne as expressed by Charles Péguy. For his introduction to St. Thomas Aquinas, Gilson was forever indebted to Professor Lucien Lévy-Bruhl, a "great and honest man" and "sociologist of note." Lévy-Bruhl, "who never opened one of the works of Saint Thomas and never intended to," recommended that for his doctoral

7 Prouvost 1994b.

8 Gilson 1913 and 1912. At the time of Gilson and Gouhier, the first degree, called the *baccalauréat*, ended secondary education and allowed students to enter university. The *licence* was conferred upon completion of a three-to-four-year program of university study, the *Diplôme d'études supérieures* on the passing of advanced work/examinations, and the *Doctorat d'état* upon completion of several years of advanced academic studies. The older-style doctorates (now usually called "Higher Doctorates" in European countries) required two theses and took a long time to complete, since candidates had to show themselves to be leading experts in their subjects. These doctorates are now becoming rare, and are usually only awarded as honorary degrees. The old educational framework also allowed for a less demanding doctorate than the *Doctorat d'état* that required one or two years of research. Gouhier completed both the *Doctorat d'état* as well as a less demanding doctorate under Gilson's direction.

theses Gilson study Descartes's scholastic background. During nine long years of preparing his theses, Gilson learned two things: (1) to read St. Thomas and (2) to understand that "Descartes had vainly tried to solve, by means of his own famous method, philosophical problems whose only correct position and solution were inseparable from the method of Saint Thomas Aquinas."[9]

In reminiscing about his professors, Gilson made clear that, while he disagreed with much of their methodology, their conception of philosophy, and their teaching of philosophy as though metaphysics did not exist, he regarded the professors who taught him as just and kind. Gilson rejected Émile Durkheim's hostility to philosophy, but respected him as a scholar and a social scientist. Léon Brunschvicg, Victor Delbos and others may have protected "with care their philosophical thinking from all religious influence," but that did not preclude Gilson's being friends with them and defending the institution in which they taught. Gilson categorically denied he ever experienced the "fear of all that which pertains to thinking" with which Péguy taxed the Sorbonne of the first years of the twentieth century.[10]

Gilson's first university appointment at the University of Lille gave him a chance to teach the regular university courses and a public course on St. Thomas. After WWI erupted in August 1914, Gilson was drafted and fought the following year at the Verdun front. In February 1916, he was buried by an enemy shell and dug out under enemy guns. He spent the next two years as a prisoner of war. During these years he perfected his English and German, became fluent in Russian, studied St. Bonaventure, and even published an article on aesthetic judgments.

Following the war, Gilson returned to Lille and, on 12 April 1919, was appointed Professor of the History of Philosophy at the University of Strasbourg. Gilson's continued study of Descartes at Strasbourg made him keenly aware of the need to give prominence to medieval studies, which were lost in the university curriculum between the organized studies of antiquity and the Renaissance. At Strasbourg, while elaborating on Descartes's original doctrine, Gilson became increasingly convinced of the high quality of the thought preceding Descartes.

This discovery, which gained the respect of scholars in France and abroad, became the recurring dominant chord of much of what Gilson

9 Gilson 1941, xiii–xiv.

10 See Gilson 1962, 20–41.

said or wrote during the next twenty years. Gilson's genius consisted in breaking the traditional approach to the Middle Ages, which studied the period from the perspective of French rationalism, of the Renaissance, or of Thomism. Gilson studied the Middle Ages from within its own awareness. Just as he had done in his study of Descartes and his sources, Gilson went beyond the sources and placed himself in the position of one medieval writer after another to see those men as they saw themselves.

From 1921 until 1932, Gilson held appointments at the Sorbonne and the École Pratique des Hautes Études. During this period he completed an incomparable edition of Descartes's *Discours de la méthode* with its four hundred pages of "personal reflections" on Descartes's one hundred pages of text. Gilson also published a collection of crucial essays on the role of medieval thought on the formation of the Cartesian system, a two-volume study of philosophy in the Middle Ages, and works on St. Thomas, St. Bonaventure, and St. Augustine.

In 1926, the "*annus mirabilis*" (wondrous year) according to Gilson's biographer, Father Shook, Gilson visited North America for the first time and dominated two important philosophical congresses—a national one held in Canada and an international one at Harvard. He gave a summer course at the University of Virginia before the congress at Harvard and was Visiting Professor of Philosophy at Harvard during the fall following the congress and also for the fall of 1927 and 1928. In his courses during 1926 at Harvard and the University of Virginia, Gilson discussed Malebranche's thought. In 1929, Gilson agreed to spend three months a year at Toronto until he established the Institute of Medieval Studies that he had first dreamed of in Strasbourg. Although Harvard offered him a professorship, ultimately he accepted an offer from Toronto because it did not require him to leave Paris. In 1932, when Gilson was elected to the Collège de France, he resigned from the Sorbonne and the École Pratique, but chose to remain Director of Studies at the Institute of Mediæval Studies in Toronto.

The late 1920s and early 1930s were crucial for the development of Gilson's conception of Christian philosophy and his understanding of philosophy as found within philosophy's history. Criticism generated by Gilson's conception of Christian philosophy resulted in major expositions of this concept. The first took the form of a debate in 1931 between the famous historian of philosophy, Professor Émile Bréhier[11] and Gilson at a meeting of the French Society of Philosophy. The second exposition consisted of the Gifford Lectures that Gilson presented in 1931 and 1932 and published as *The Spirit of Medieval Philosophy*. In these lectures Gilson argued that: (1) we cannot explain the historical existence of some philosophies which are purely rational in their principles and methods without the existence of Christianity and (2) these philosophies are Christian as philosophies.

When debating Bréhier, Gilson maintained that modern philosophy's history from Descartes, Malebranche, and Spinoza onward would not have been what it is had there been no Christian philosophers. Gilson had occasion to discuss Malebranche again in the William James Lectures that he presented at Harvard in 1936 and subsequently published as *The Unity of Philosophical Experience*. While Gilson thought that philosophies do not exist independently of philosophers, he argued that philosophy consists of necessary, impersonal, sequences of ideas that have a life regarding their content and their relations independent of philosophers and their philosophies. By his examination of various philosophical experiences or experiments Gilson revealed the "abstract philosophical necessity," the "impersonal metaphysical determinism" that proceeds from the first principles of all authentic philosophies. Gilson located the difficulties and failures of Malebranche's philosophy, for example, in its following Descartes's substitution of the principles of mathematics for those of metaphysics.

Henri Gouhier became interested in philosophy while in secondary school in Auxerre. After passing his *baccalauréat* Gouhier attended the Lycée Henri IV in Paris. After only four months at the lycée, he was drafted in 1917. He took with him Book 2 of Malebranche's *La Recherche de la vérité*, which he found in a bookstore in Auxerre. Since Gouhier was only vaguely familiar with Malebranche, it was likely that the book's title impressed him. At war's end, Gouhier resumed his

11 Émile Bréhier (1876–1952) studied philosophy at the Sorbonne under Victor Brochard and Lucien Lévy-Bruhl. He taught at the Universities of Rennes (1909–1912), Bordeaux (1912–1914, 1919), and Paris (1919–1946). His most important work was his monumental *Histoire de la philosophie*. See Bréhier 1926–1932.

studies and, in 1919, entered the École Normale Supérieure in Paris. Under the direction of the famous historian of philosophy, Professor Bréhier, Gouhier completed a *mémoire* or term paper on "La foi et la raison chez Descartes" for the *Diplôme d'études supérieures*. In 1920, while Gilson was at Strasbourg, Gouhier sent him his *mémoire* in the form of an article (Letter 1). In August 1921, Gouhier passed the *agrégation*. Shortly afterwards, in October, Gouhier met with Gilson and asked him to direct his doctoral theses. Years later, in an interview given in 1990, Gouhier recalled his first conversation. It quickly took on a friendly tone when Gilson learned that Gouhier hailed from Auxerre. Since Gilson's family had a home in Vermenton, Gouhier said "we were almost compatriots."[12] Not long into their correspondence Gilson began addressing Gouhier as "my dear friend" (Letter 6).

Gilson's proposal to study Malebranche as the last great Augustinian scholastic (Letter 2) and Gouhier's acceptance of this thesis topic proved to be a fortuitous moment in the history of Malebranche scholarship. It resulted in the creation of a dream team—two quite capable scholars, each among the best of their generation, who studied Descartes and focused their talents on better understanding the thought of Père Malebranche, the great seventeenth-century Oratorian.

Gilson's exposure to Malebranche dated back to his student days at the Sorbonne (1904–1907) when he attended Professor Victor Delbos's lectures on Malebranche. As an assignment for Delbos's course he submitted an essay on "La polémique de Malebranche contre Aristote et la philosophie scolastique."[13] Gilson's essay attempted to explain Malebranche's violent rejection of Aristotelianism and scholasticism. Professor Delbos found the essay to be "done with intelligence and exactitude," but thought that it offered no explanation of the intensity of Malebranche's polemic against the scholastics. In 1921, Gilson characterized Malebranche as a "scholastic" in the Augustinian tradition. This reflected his more mature thought on the solution to the problem that had eluded him earlier in his student essay. Years of study of medieval thought, and of Augustinianism in particular, allowed Gilson to situate Malebranche's thought in a context that allowed for an accurate account of its inherent anti-Aristotelianism and antischolasticism.

---

12 Belgioioso and Gouhier 2005, 17–20, 36–38.

13 Gilson's essay can be found in its entirety in Appendix 1.

Gilson's writings and his seminars at the École Pratique included two areas that he recommended Gouhier explore to interpret Malebranche's thought adequately: (1) Augustinianism and its differences from Thomism, and (2) the notion of Christian philosophy. Gilson came to understand that Malebranche's vehement opposition to Aristotle and his scholastic followers was much stronger than that of Descartes's precisely because Malebranche was, in his own way, a scholastic—an Augustinian, exactly like St. Bonaventure.

Malebranche's occasionalism with its attendant denial of the reality and efficacy of secondary causes was the antithesis of St. Thomas's robust and intrinsically causal created world. This is why Malebranche equated Aristotelianism with paganism (Letter 4). Aristotle and his scholastic followers endowed creatures with a nature that in Malebranche's eyes conceded too much sufficiency to creatures. Gilson clearly expressed this difference as follows: "In St. Augustine, God delegates His gifts in such a way that the very insufficiency of nature constrains it to return toward Him; in St. Thomas, God delegates His gifts through the mediacy of a stable nature which contains in itself—divine subsistence being taken for granted—the sufficient reason of all its operations."[14]

In his undergraduate *mémoire* on Descartes, Gouhier had already studied Augustinianism, Thomism, and Christian philosophy and had his own ideas as to how they applied to Descartes. Under Gilson's guidance Gouhier deepened his understanding of these areas, and expanded the *mémoire* into a doctoral thesis that he submitted to the École Pratique in 1923. Gouhier's work played a key role in Gilson's modifying the interpretation of Descartes that he originally put forth in his thesis of 1913 (Letters 6–9). In 1926, before an audience of eminent academics, Gouhier brilliantly defended his two magisterial theses for the *Doctorat d'état*. The theses interpreted Malebranche as a Christian philosopher influenced by St. Augustine, sharing similarities with St. Bonaventure, and never separating philosophy from the religious experience that he lived. In his "small" thesis, *La vocation de Malebranche*, and "great" thesis, *La philosophie de Malebranche et son expérience religieuse*,[15] Gouhier employed the same biographical-historical method he used in his earlier study of Descartes: "Malebranche's life is his work; his history is the history of his mind." Gouhier focused on the history of Malebranche's

---

14 Shook 1984, 397.

15 Gouhier 1926a and b.

mind, not on impersonal concepts or on philosophy divorced from the person who thought them. Going beyond the scholarship to date, Gilson hailed Gouhier's work as penetrating the heart and mind of this great seventeenth century thinker (Letters 19-22).

Gilson and Gouhier did not share the same understanding of philosophy or philosophy's history. Gilson thought philosophy's history involved more than the biographies of philosophers or accounts of their philosophies. It traced the development of philosophy itself. In his works, Gilson approached Malebranche's Christian philosophy from the perspective of his own philosophical history of philosophy and unity of philosophical experience. Making precise Malebranche's deviations from Augustine's thought and his inability to deal successfully with problems inherent in Descartes's metaphysical experiment, Gilson concluded that Malebranche's thought constituted an excellent example of a philosophy that is thoroughly Christian and philosophically inadequate.

Gouhier, who considered himself a historian, always had difficulty conceiving doctrines that would subsist independently of the beings that think them. Gouhier's historical method allowed no divorce of Malebranche's life from his thought and assumed from the outset the internal coherence of that thought. This method posited Malebranche's philosophy and religious experience as one and remained completely within Malebranche's vision of the world. For Gouhier, philosophy's history consisted of the histories of philosophies because no concept or essence of "philosophy" existed that fits all philosophers or that transcends philosophers. Only philosophers existed. And they defined philosophy within their philosophy. This resulted in a sympathetic interpretation of Malebranche, noncritical in the sense that it refused to evaluate Malebranche's thought from a viewpoint other than his own. Gouhier viewed Malebranche as a classic example of a philosopher of reality elaborating his lived experience of the divine.

Gilson and Gouhier also did not share the same view of Christian philosophy. Gilson posited Christianity's influence as remaining exterior to philosophy considered in itself. He viewed Christian philosophy as one that stressed religious dogma as coming to the aid of reason and allowing reason "to attain a fuller comprehension of its own deepest truths." Gouhier adopted more of an Augustinian position and argued for Christian philosophy as one allowing for religious experience as interior to philosophy.

Both Gilson and Gouhier spent much of their philosophical careers elaborating and refining their thinking on Christian philosophy and the relationship between history and philosophy. And over time, both men also refined their interpretations of Malebranche.[16]

Those familiar with Gilson will find in his early letters to Gouhier many of the themes that characterized his published writings—a high standard of scholarship, sense of humor, remarkably distinctive style, and serious Catholicism. The letters reveal aspects of Gilson's personality privy primarily to his students—the capable and demanding teacher at work: suggesting books, shepherding his student through doctoral work and a thesis defense, arranging seminars to benefit academic work and enhance career, and providing practical advice on positions and publications. The letters also provide glimpses into the initial stages of a friendship between student and professor that ripened into a deep relationship between two colleagues and lasted more than half a century.

Gilson's letters, all handwritten, have a characteristic handsome appearance. My transcription of Gilson's letters remains faithful to the original, except for instances where I have added accent marks that Gilson omitted or forgot. Words and book titles underlined by Gilson in the original have been italicized. For consistency, I have changed the case of the initial letters of some words (for example, sometimes Gilson wrote "École pratique," and sometimes "École Pratique"). Where necessary, for clarity, I have expanded Gilson's abbreviations. Square brackets [ ] denote my editorial additions. I provide footnotes to identify people or matters mentioned in the letters on the first occasion they occur. Footnotes from the original French texts are not included in the English translation.

I am grateful to Mme. Marie-Louise Gouhier, Mme. Cécile Gilson, Mr. Bernard Gilson, and the Pontifical Institute of Mediaeval Studies for their support in publishing this correspondence.

16 For a fuller discussion of these issues, see Fafara 2003.

I wish to acknowledge the following individuals for their generous and prompt assistance with my requests for archival, research, and biographical materials: the late Fr. Frederick Black, C.S.B., archivist of St. Michael's College and the Pontifical Institute of Mediaeval Studies at the University of Toronto, and Ms. Evelyn Collins, his successor; Mrs. Judith McManus, Reference Librarian, Georgetown University; Mr. Kevin O'Hagan, Library Assistant, Northern Virginia Community College; and Professors André Motte and Paul Gochet, University of Liège, and Mathieu Marion, University of Quebec at Montreal.

Thanks to the *Revue Thomiste* for permission to publish one of Gilson's previously published letters. My thanks also to Mr. Ralph Nordenhold for digitally editing photographs, and to Liz and David Hayes who provided an ideal setting nestled in the Appalachian Mountains in which to combine leisure and work on this project.

I owe a deep debt of gratitude to Mme. Gouhier; Dr. Michel Florian and Fr. Armand Maurer, C.S.B.; Dr. Francesca Murphy; Professors Peter Redpath and John Catan; Dr. Andrew Tallon; Ms. Anne Sellmansberger; and my wife, Anne, for their helpful comments on draft versions of the text. All remaining imperfections are mine.

I

Strasbourg
7 November 1920

Dear Sir,

Thank you very much for the interesting article you sent me and for all the nice things in it about me.[1] I have never studied the question of the relationship of reason and faith in Descartes as closely as you have, so it is rather you who ought to be teaching the rest of us. In no way can I pretend to tell you what the shortcomings of your work are, if indeed there are any. Apart from the real pleasure I had in reading it, I just want to mention a few qualms I had about your way of handling the question.

1. You attempt to define the nature of Descartes's faith. Are you sure that this problem is capable of an historical solution?[2] Father Laberthonnière considers it an "arid faith"[3]; Espinas makes it the ardent faith

---

1 Gouhier 1920. The article was his *mémoire* for Professor Bréhier published under a slightly different title.

2 Gouhier gained deeper insight into the complexity of this issue during his career: "L'histoire d'une âme... la formule est paradoxale dans la mesure où il y a peut-être une âme de l'âme qui échappe à l'histoire, surtout lorsque cette âme vit en présence de Dieu, cette présence seraitelle dans le sentiment d'une absence. Ici est le grave problème de toute histoire religieuse: ce qui c'est passé dans l'âme de Paul sur le chemin de Damas échappe à l'histoire mais l'histoire ne serait pas ce qu'elle fut s'il ne s'était rien passé dans l'âme de Paul sur le chemin de Damas. Telle est la situation dont il faut s'accommoder. Dans la perspective d'une biographie intellectuelle et spirituelle, il faut reconnaître que, si l'érudition est nécessaire, elle n'est pas suffisante: pour suivre Henri Bremond jusqu'à cette question: qui suis-je? ou, ce qui est ici la même chose: quelle est ma foi? le critique doit avoir la possibilité de lire en lui-même ce qu'il lit sous les mots du texte chargé non plus seulement de transmettre un message mais de faire revivre ce qui a été vécu" (Gouhier 1975).

3 Father Lucien Laberthonnière (1860–1932), a French priest of the Oratory, professor of philosophy at the Collège de Juilly, and Director of the *Annales de philosophie chrétienne* (1905–1913), interpreted Descartes as, above all else, a scientist who turned to metaphysics only in order to make his science palatable to believers. See Laberthonnière 1935. Laber-

of a "knight—errant"[4]; you believe that it is something spontaneous and connatural to Descartes's personality. It would undoubtedly be necessary to distinguish among the different periods in time; his faith could have been all of these successively. In any case, the documents that would clarify the issue for us seem to me extremely sparse; unless, of course, you might provide something new in your work. I do not doubt Descartes's faith, but I really do not know what particular nuance it presents. If I had to characterize it, to save my life, for example, I would say it was a kind of a *loyalism*; I would say it and believe it, but I know nothing about it.[5]

2. One does not solve the problem by showing that Descartes conceives the relationship of faith and reason as Saint Thomas did.[6] Descartes can

---

thonnière participated in the discussion of Gilson's landmark thesis, *La liberté chez Descartes et la théologie* (See Gilson 1914).

4 Alfred Espinas (1844-1922) completed the first *Doctorat d'état* in sociology in France and played a key role in the introduction of the human sciences into the French university system. Espinas's thesis studied animal societies, with the avowed intent to extract from this study some laws that were common to all societies, not in order to govern them but simply in order to better understand them, and in order to show that, sociology is possible. In 1892, he obtained the chair of social economy at the Sorbonne, considered the first chair in the social sciences in France. He retired from teaching in 1907. Based on the general law that the product of all human thought strictly depends on the place in which it was born and the conditions in which it develops, Espinas interpreted Descartes as an ardent apologist for the Catholic faith. Gilson was impressed and influenced by Espinas's interpretation. See Espinas 1925; Gilson 1913, 434; and Gouhier 1924a, 24-30.

5 See Gilson 1935b, 235–236.

6 In his article, Gouhier argued that the problem of the relationship of faith and reason never arose for Descartes. According to Gouhier, Descartes remained faithful to St. Thomas's doctrine on the relation of faith and reason even though this doctrine acquired a different meaning in Descartes's thought. Some religious interpreters of Descartes, such as Fr. Laberthonnière, had viewed Descartes's faith as "expedient," "solitary and static," "cold," and "dry" only because they mistakenly interpreted Descartes's "tranquil assurance" and "confident optimism" as indifference. On the other hand, rationalists whose method condemns them to change the history of philosophy into a philosophy of history, considered Descartes as one glorious stage in the liberation of reason from faith. Such interpretations dismissed, reinterpreted, or failed to take into account Descartes's character and psychology: "Les

subscribe to Saint Thomas's formulae or even adopt them, but the fact remains nonetheless that the *historical* relationship between these two elements can be quite different in the two theories. And I believe it is. For both philosophers, there is, at one and the same time, agreement and independence of the two elements. In fact, Saint Thomas's philosophy seems to me to have been born within, and for, his religion; Descartes's seems to me to have been born from nonreligious interests. What a profound difference there is with Malebranche, for example.[7]

3. I believe you are correct in insisting on the biased nature of the history of philosophy. On this point, I am more in agreement with you than on the rest.[8] One must hope things will change.

---

rapports qui uniront sa raison et sa foi s'établissent dans son esprit en même temps que sa pensée s'éveille ... c'est moins une théorie qu'une disposition d'âme, et l'attitude religieuse de Descartes s'explique par cette sorte de parti pris intellectuel" (Gouhier 1920, 20). With his intense desire for unity, his need for clarity and his passion for order, faith and reason never constituted an antinomy in Descartes's mind (ibid., 29).

7 Under the direction of Lucien Lévy-Bruhl (1857–1939), Professor of the History of Modern Philosophy at the Sorbonne, Gilson developed two doctoral theses that explored the scholastic sources of Descartes's thought. This placed Gilson in an excellent position to assist Gouhier in bridging the gap between the Middle Ages and Descartes, and other Cartesians such as Malebranche. Gilson agreed with Lévy-Bruhl's interpretation of Descartes. Like Charles Adam (1857–1940), Laberthonnière, Maurice Blondel (1861–1949), and, later, Jacques Maritain (1882–1973), Lévy-Bruhl followed Louis Laird (1846–1917) in maintaining that Descartes subordinated his metaphysics to physics. See Gilson 1913, 95n.1, and Gilson 1914, 219–220.

8 Although Gilson and Gouhier were historians, they arrived at quite different conceptions of the history of philosophy and of philosophy itself. In 1925, Gilson characterized his approach to philosophy as similar to that of Gouhier's; Gilson was interested in philosophers in their historical contingency. "Je crois, en effet, que s'il importe dans certains cas de réduire les hommes à des idées, il est beaucoup plus important encore d'essayer de comprendre les idées par les hommes .... Les idées pures, prises dans leur rigueur abstraite, sont, généralement, irréconciliables, et les hommes que l'on réduit à de telles idées semblent, par une conséquence toute naturelle, l'être ou l'avoir été. De là naissent des oppositions dans une certaine mesure peut-être factices qui, une fois introduites dans l'histoire, peuvent exercer leur répercussion jusque sur le temps présent" (Lefèvre 1925, 71–72). Afterwards, when trying to clarify the notion of Christian philosophy, Gilson began looking at "pure positions" that

If you will allow me one piece of advice, I would recommend you reexamine the history of medieval philosophy to fill in the gap between Descartes and Saint Thomas.[9] Afterwards, go back to Descartes and you will have a better sense of how far removed he is from the Middle Ages on this point, at least from Thomism. Malebranche, however, is, in his own way, a scholastic.

---

transcended time and place rather than the philosophers in their contingency. See Gouhier 1993b, 40–58. Gilson maintained that philosophical systems appear as conditioned uniquely by the necessary relations that tie ideas together. See Gilson 1927 and the later, classical formulation of this position, Gilson 1937a.

Gouhier denied that philosophy, as such, had a historical existence. "L'historien de la philosophie commence à s'apercevoir qu'il est impossible de séparer la vie intellectuelle de la vie religieuse. On a trop longtemps cru que la raison pouvait subsister par ses propres forces et on l'a étudiée comme si elle s'était développée toute seule, mais le 'splendide isolement' n'a jamais réussi à personne; la raison et la philosophie ont vécu parce qu'elles ont été portées à travers les siècles sur deux ailes de poésie et de prière. La tâche de l'historien est de renouer les liens qui unissent les concepts aux sentiments, le système à l'âme" (Gouhier 1926c, 3–4). For Gouhier only philosophers existed, and they defined philosophy within their philosophy. Every definition of a philosophy, as philosophy, is relative to a particular philosophy, a unique "vision of the world." Gouhier disliked the term "history of philosophy" or "history of ideas" because of the intellectual resonance associated with it. According to Gouhier "visions of the world" included concepts, but concepts that are imbued with feelings and imagery. Central to Gouhier's method was the biographical, the way in which an individual saw the world. The history of philosophy is the history of philosophers who created these philosophies. See Henri Gouhier 1978b. Gilson accounted for the difference between Gouhier's way of writing history and his own to the fact that Gouhier was interested mainly "in the philosophers" while Gilson was "interested particularly in philosophy" (Prouvost 1994b, 476–478).

9 Gouhier did not follow Gilson's injunction to bridge the gap between Descartes and the Middle Ages. Instead, Gouhier decided to look forward. He concentrated on the modern period beginning with Descartes and continuing to Auguste Comte and even Henri Bergson.

But I believe you have more pressing things to do this year. I am always available if you think I can be of any assistance to you.

Ét. Gilson

❦

2

Strasbourg
3, allée de la Robertsau
17 September 1921

Dear Sir,

First of all, allow me to congratulate you upon your success with the *agrégation*—the key to your intellectual life—and for your good idea to take advantage of the remaining year you have left in Paris by beginning work on your doctoral theses.[10]

The subject you submitted to me is certainly interesting, but it has two disadvantages for you.[11]

1. It will not qualify you for teaching the history of philosophy, at least not *indisputably*. It will qualify you for "The History of Religious Ideas" and it will be difficult for you to find a position.

2. It is a subject on which you can work a long time without any certainty of success. I am not sure that the diverse, detailed research on the libertines that you will have to pursue will lead you to interesting

10 Gouhier passed the *agrégation* (a highly competitive examination for teaching positions) in August 1921. He ranked first of all the candidates.

11 Although we do not have the letter to Gilson in which Gouhier proposed a thesis topic, he provided details in his 29 September 1921 letter to Jacques Maritain (unpublished, Maritain Papers): "J'avais proposé à Gilson quelque chose se rapprochant de ce dont nous avions parlé: il s'agissait d'étudier le mouvement libertin au XVII, et à propos de cela, d'examiner la fin de la scolastique en France, cédant la place au cartésianisme et impuissance à combattre la libre-pensée naissante." It is certainly possible that Gouhier "s'était d'abord adressé à Maritain en vue d'un sujet de thèse, avant de se tourner vers Gilson qui l'orienta vers un travail d'histoire de la philosophie, voie plus sûre pour 'avoir une chaire de faculté'" (Chenaux 1997, 155). In his letter to Maritain, Gouhier repeated what most likely became one of the deciding factors in selecting a topic, i.e., Gilson's practical comment about the proposed topic limiting Gouhier to teaching the history of religious ideas: "Gilson m'a fait, entre autres objections, une remarque dont je dois tenir compte pour mon avenir...."

findings; as for Descartes, there would be no reason to isolate him from a movement much broader than the Catholic Renaissance in which he might get a little lost.

But it goes without saying that if you really like that subject you can try it at your own risk and peril. My advice to you would be to hold it in reserve and note what can be of use in your later research on the same period. If you see it taking shape in this way by doing something else, nothing prevents you from taking it up later without having lost one or two years to uncertain research.

As for subjects to work on in this period, I can see many which would be genuine subjects, and which could become very attractive. Here are a few which you can think about.

1. *The History of Latin Averroism from the XIII to the XVII Century.*

Renan's book has to be completely redone.[12] A broad topic, sometimes calling for painstaking inquiry; but it will lead you to some strange Italian milieus not well studied, ultimately arriving at a movement that you might want to analyze.

2. *Gassendi.*

To be taken up again completely after P.F. Thomas's book,[13] which is just a 'review' of Gassendi's works; situating him in his own era, putting together the history of the development of his ideas; presenting him as a man of the Renaissance—which Thomas did not see. Why has G[assendi], who was Descartes's equal in the XVIIth century, disappeared? Gass[endi], and corpuscular physics (note that Descartes and Gassendi are two different representatives of this movement).

Moreover, I want to call your attention to an unedited manuscript edition of an important part of the *Syntagma philosophicum*, certainly earlier than what has been printed. Thomas knew of its existence and did not use it! It is in the Municipal Library of Tours and the School Library would undoubtedly know about it. Municipal Library of Tours, Manuscripts, numbers 709–710.

3. *Mersenne's Correspondence.*

Its publication is urgent but, first, it is necessary to make a sort of analytical inventory of it to make it ready for publication. An *excellent complementary thesis*; it would put you at the very heart of the period you want to study.

12 Renan 1852.

13 Thomas 1889.

4. *Leibniz.*

Leibniz *as a Renaissance philosopher* and studied from the perspective of the evolution and formation of his philosophical ideas. Look in Blanchet's thesis for points of similarity with Campanella;[14] it is the key to Leibniz about whom we no longer understand anything because of not knowing that the XVIth century lasted until at least the XVIII (sorry to put it so badly, but you know what I mean). Even Leibniz's religious preoccupations, which have been so well studied by J. Baruzi,[15] go back to the XVIth century.

5. *Malebranche: the last of the great Augustinian Scholastics.*[16]
The resurrection, in the case of Malebranche, of the struggle in the XIIIth century between Aristotelian Thomism and traditional Augustinianism.[17] There you would have the key to all the instances of *Modernism*, up until Father Bautain and including Father Laberthonnière.[18]

---

14 Blanchet 1920; see Gilson 1921c.

15 Baruzi 1907.

16 Gilson's doctoral theses and subsequent publications demonstrated that "far from coming after the Greeks almost as though there had been nothing between itself and the Greeks, the philosophy of the seventeenth century is inexplicable both in content and form if one does not take into consideration, along with the Jewish-Christian revelation, the fourteen centuries of theology which have relentlessly tried to achieve some understanding of the faith on which they were founded. This use of reason within faith, and for it, but finally assuming the shape of a science, is exactly what is called scholasticism" (Gilson 1962, 193).

17 Gilson's two important seminars offered at the École Pratique, "Études des textes de Saint Augustin relatifs à l'illumination divine" (1921–1922) and "Saint Thomas critique de saint Augustin" (1922–1923) contributed greatly to his later interpretation of Malebranche which was much more adequate than the earlier one he presented to Professor Delbos. See Appendix 1, pp. 126-131 below. For Gilson's summaries of these seminars, see Shook 1984, 395–397.

18 Modernism, a general movement in religion in the late 19th and 20th centuries, tried to reconcile historical Christianity with the findings of modern science and philosophy. This movement placed importance on God's immanent, not transcendent, nature and on the subordination of dogma to practice. The movement as a whole was influenced by the pragmatism of William James (1842–1910), the intuitionism of Henri Bergson (1859–1941), and the philosophy of Maurice Blondel (1861–1949). Among the leaders in France was Alfred Loisy (1857–1940). Gilson was familiar with Loisy's work and impressed by his "profonde sincérité et par l'honnêteté intellectuelle absolues."

I am, of course, only indicating starting points here. It's up to you to

See Gilson 1919a, 130. Ordained a Roman Catholic priest in 1879, Loisy was dismissed in 1893 from his teaching position at the Institut Catholique in Paris for his views about the Old Testament canon. In December 1903, Pope Pius X approved a decree of the Holy Office that placed five of Loisy's works on the *Index auctorum et librorum prohibitorum*. He was excommunicated in 1908 and taught at the École des Hautes Études (1900–1904) and at the Collège de France (1909–30).

In England George Tyrrell (1861–1909), an Irish-born Jesuit priest, was dismissed from his teaching post and from the Jesuits for his views on papal infallibility and for a doctrine that minimized the intellectual element of revelation and thus appeared to contradict the teachings of the first Vatican Council. His theories influenced others, notably the French layman and noted pupil of Bergson, Édouard Le Roy (1870–1954).

In his encyclical *Pascendi* (1907) Pius X condemned modernism as the "synthesis of all heresies." Gilson reviewed two of Loisy's books (Gilson 1919a and b), was sympathetic towards him, and thought that theology should be permeated with scientific history and philosophical speculation. "[L]ike St. Thomas himself, Gilson believed theology to be a science and felt that the force and impulse of scientific thinking ought in some sense to purify faith. Ultimately, Gilson would become critical of Pius X" (Shook 1984, 32 and 115; see also Boyer de Sainte Suzanne 1968).

The extreme reaction to rationalism by Abbé Louis Eugène Bautain (1796–1867) made him one of the principal representatives of fideism. He sustained the Augustinian thesis that "philosophy which is the study of wisdom is nothing else but religion." After modestly submitting to censure from Rome, he died in communion with the Church. For Gilson's interpretation of Bautain, see Gilson, Langan, and Maurer 1966, 222–226. At one point, arguing that Catholic philosophies such as Bautain's were inferior to that of St. Thomas and the secular philosophies of their own day, Gilson recommended deleting the section on French traditionalists that he developed for the collaborative work on *Recent Philosophy* (ibid.). For the contention that Gilson's recommendation caused between Gilson and his friend and colleague Anton Pegis (1905–1978), see Shook 1984, 356–358.

Although he appreciated the high quality of Laberthonnière's interpretation of Descartes—"analyses les plus remarquables que l'on ait consacrées à Descartes"— Laberthonnière's incomprehension of traditional theology and misunderstanding of Thomism troubled Gilson. Gouhier considered much of Laberthonnière's work on Descartes decisive, but disagreed with the book's fundamental thesis, Laberthonnière's definition of the Christian God. Both Gilson (1935j) and Gouhier (1935–36) reviewed Laberthonnière's *Études sur Descartes*. Gilson felt that his friend Abbé Laberthonnière, though in philosophical error,

give this some thought and carve out in each question an area that will suit you and force you to work more in depth than breadth. Needless to say, I am always available to discuss with you whatever questions might be of interest to you.

Very truly yours,[19]

Ét. Gilson

❦

3

Strasbourg
26 September 1921

Dear Sir,

I'm afraid that when I wrote you I may have forgotten one of the most interesting starting points for studying the beginning of the XVIIth century. I have often wondered when and where the Augustinian movement that goes through Descartes and blossoms in Ambrosius Victor and Malebranche began.[20] This movement itself warrants further study;

---

deserved, at most, a sympathetic reprimand by the Church instead of having several of his books placed on the *Index*, "followed by the cruel interdiction to teach and to publish" (Gilson 1962, 56). For impressions of Laberthonnière and the Oratorians from one of Gilson's contemporaries who attended the Oratorian grammar school in Juilly and whose family Laberthonnière visited regularly, see Fumet 1978, 18-26.

19 French closing formulas do not always translate well into English, so I have tried to provide usable equivalents, rather than literal translations.

20 Malebranche cited passages from St. Augustine as found in the 1667 edition of *Philosophia christiana*, edited by the Cartesian Oratorian André Martin (1621–1695, pseud. Ambrosius Victor). Gouhier provided the authoritative discussion of the influence of Martin's collection on Malebranche's thought and a collation of passages from St. Augustine cited or quoted by Malebranche. See Gouhier 1926b, 279–311, 411–420, 78–79; see also Gouhier 1978a, 284–293.

Augustinianism is transmitted by great men. Here, I believe, you will find answers to some of the questions you are asking.

Best wishes,

Ét. Gilson

4

Strasbourg
27 September 1921

Dear Sir,

You are not bothering me at all; just the opposite. I do hope we will have an opportunity during the next academic year to discuss the topic that interests you. My nomination will not occur until the end of October, but it appears certain.[21] We will proceed more quickly discussing this than writing about it. In the meantime, here is exactly what I think of the questions you are asking me.

(1) Blampignon's book[22] is sound. He provided Ollé-Laprune his starting point.

(2) Ollé-Laprune's book, dated in some respects, remains quite remarkable.[23] I believe that he has understood the essentials of Malebranche.

---

21 Gilson accepted the invitation to replace François-Joseph Picavet [1851–1921], *chargé de cours* for medieval philosophies in the University of Paris who died suddenly in April. "The ministry's official appointment of Gilson to the Faculty of Letters, University of Paris was dated 16 November 1921. A month later the further appointment followed to the École Pratique des Hautes Études; lectures at the École, discontinued since the war years, were scheduled to resume April 1922" (Shook 1984, 103).

22 See Blampignon 1861–62. Despite the limitations of Abbé Émile-Antoine Blampignon's (1830–1908) work—"beaucoup de réflexions, quelques appréciations inexactes, pas de conclusion pratique, mais un vague rationalisme"—his paleographical discoveries resulted in a rich series of publications on Malebranche "sur lesquelles nous vivons jusqu'à ce jour." See Easton, Lennon, and Sebba 1992, 58no.253. See also Robinet 1967, 334.

23 See Ollé-Laprune 1870. Contemporary scholars share Gilson's favorable appraisal of Léon Ollé-Laprune's (1839–1898) work. They regard it as the "best work of the nineteenth-century M[alebranche] scholarship, still read and considered." See Easton, Lennon, and Sebba 1992, 136.

There also exists—in the hands of Mr. D. Roustan, I believe—an unedited work of Delbos on Malebranche[24] that certainly completes Ollé-Laprune's two volumes. Henri Joly's book is absolutely worthless.[25] But with Ollé Laprune and Delbos there is enough to prevent you from thinking of doing a thesis purely and simply on Malebranche.

(3) It is necessary to begin with Malebranche taken as the preferred case of the Augustinian renaissance. There again you have before you Blampignon and Ollé-Laprune: the latter, in particular, (Volume I, Part I, chap. 1) has pointed out the importance of Malebranche's Augustinian predecessors, but his very clear-sighted chapter gives only indications and will show you very precisely the directions your initial research can take. Above all, Ollé-Laprune's weakness is that he ignores the Middle Ages; in spite of his quotations from Saint Thomas, he does not see that Malebranche, precisely as an Augustinian, is an anti-Thomist; he is an Augustinian type of scholastic, exactly like Saint Bonaventure.[26] What is

24 After Victor Delbos (1862–1916) died, his philosophical papers were entrusted, not to Désiré Roustan (1873–1941), but to Delbos's friend, Maurice Blondel. See Delbos 1924, ix–xiv and p. 124 n. 47 below.

25 See Joly 1901. Joly (1839–1925) taught at the Sorbonne and Collège de France. In 1903 he became a member of the Académie des sciences morales et politiques. Others shared Gilson's assessment of Joly's work: ". . . il ne semble pas que M. Joly ait le goût de la métaphysique, car son analyse, remarquablement consciencieuse, est aussi remarquablement froide: on n'y sent bouillonner ni l'enthousiasme pour une œuvre qu'on repense à son tour, ni la résistance passionnée à une doctrine qu'on ne peut adopter. Il en résulte que nous considérons la lecture de ce chapitre [on Malebranche's metaphysics] comme dangereuse pour celui qui n'a pas pris contact direct avec Malebranche; elle ne peut que détourner, en fait, de la pensée d'aborder l'étude directe du grand méditatif" (Lechalas 1900–1901, 623). "M. Joly glisse volontairement sur certaines doctrines qui lui paraissent dangereuses. Tout esprit, un peu familiarisé avec la pensée de Malebranche, s'étonnera de voir traiter ainsi des théories aussi importantes que la vision en Dieu et les causes occasionnelles . . . . Nous terminerons ces notes . . . par un vœu. Puisse Malebranche, trouver enfin un historien de sa pensée, qui sache s'en pénétrer assez et assez l'aimer, pour en présenter une analyse fidèle, émue et communicative" (Sayer 1901–02, 593 and 596). Gouhier's works on Malebranche would fulfill Sayer's wish.

26 Gilson's interest in St. Bonaventure began during his student days at the Sorbonne. While a prisoner in the La Courtine Army Camp in Germany, Gilson continued reading St. Bonaventure. Gilson's seminars at the École Pratique, which focused on Thomistic thought and the Augustinian tradition,

interesting about Malebranche is that, contrary to Descartes, he revives right in the middle of the seventeenth century the Augustinianism of the thirteenth; it is an episode in a secular struggle, which still persists, between two different scholastic orientations. When you have studied the thirteenth-century Augustinians you will be surprised to see to what extent Malebranche is just one of them; then, you will be able *to interpret*, give the precise and historically demonstrable meaning, to so many aspects of his doctrine which are *known*, but *not understood*.

Examples: Ollé-Laprune says: it is "a religious philosophy." This is true, but vague. Precisely: it is "Augustinian *Wisdom*," that is, the faith which seeks understanding. (On this point Malebranche *copies* the Augustinian Saint Anselm.)

Malebranche's critique of Aristotelianism is that of all Augustinians, for whom Aristotelianism = paganism.

You will find a lot of other things by looking in this direction. Ambrosius Victor should be an inexhaustible source of connecting links.[27] But to situate Malebranche precisely in history it is necessary to determine the course of the Augustinian movement, the reasons for its existence, if possible, and its true significance. It is the false notion of a break between the XVIIth century and the Middle Ages which makes a man like Malebranche unintelligible. I believe that the history of Augustinian philosophy in France in the seventeenth century or, at least the part of this movement that immediately affects Malebranche, deserves to be written.

It is Mr. D. Roustan who is responsible for the edition of Malebranche.[28] His work is very advanced but I don't know exactly where they are with regard to printing.

Best wishes,

Ét. Gilson

deepened his understanding of St. Bonaventure and culminated in a book (Gilson 1924a). For bibliographical details on Gilson's seminars at the École Pratique, see Edie 1959, 18–34.

27 See n.20, above.

28 Roustan's project, initiated by Lucien Lévy-Bruhl, had as its advisor Gilson's former professor and friend, Professor Victor Delbos. The war precluded the completion of the proposed sixteen-volume edition of Malebranche. See Roustan 1938a and 1938b; see also Gouhier 1938b. For Gouhier situating

5

[Undated][29]

Observations that I would like to make:

(1) If *philosophy* consists in *metaphysics* Malebranche did not have to learn it and will never learn any of it from Descartes; he derives his own from Saint Augustine.
(2) The *Augustinian* Malebranche is asleep; he does not philosophize for himself. When will he philosophize? When he discovers the Cartesian *physics* of extension and movement.
(3) Having found it, he becomes a philosopher because his interior equilibrium is broken; he will find it when he completes Augustine's metaphysics with Descartes's physics.
(4) It seems to me that it is the strict mechanism of the *Treatise on Man* which triggered his personal philosophical pursuit.
(5) Consequently, the preface in question is to be put into the foreground because it sets forth this mechanism with such rigor that it calls for occasionalism.[30]

Roustan's project in the context of the Centre Nationale de la Recherche Scientifique's decision in 1956 to publish a definitive edition of all texts by Malebranche, see Malebranche 1958–67, 1:i–iv. Since the publication of the complete works there has been an explosion of interest in Malebranche in France and in other countries. The *renaissance Malebranchiste* has been sustained by English translations of Malebranche's works. See Malebranche 1980, xxix.

29 It is unclear which of Gilson's early letters to Gouhier contained these "observations."

30 Gouhier masterfully developed these points in his detailed examination of "Malebranche's conversion to philosophy." In 1664, while walking on the rue St. Jacques and happening upon a copy of Descartes's *Treatise on Man* in a bookstall, Malebranche discovered in Descartes a philosophy that enabled him to understand better the Christian truth that he was living. On 20 September of the same year that he discovered Descartes's *Treatise* and four years after he had entered the Oratory, Malebranche was ordained a priest. Thus, his religious vocation preceded his philosophical one and, no doubt, guided and directed it.

In the posthumous edition of Descartes's *Treatise on Man* that Malebranche read, a preface by Clerselier developed the agreement between this work and the thought of St. Augustine; the notes by La Forge praised the work for having destroyed the scholastic verbalism, and the preface by Schuyl concluded that,

6

6, Rue Ponthierry
Melun (S-et-M)
28 July 1922

My dear friend,

You have my sincere congratulations on your nomination to the Thiers Foundation,[31] all the more so because you owe it to no one but yourself. If your qualifications had not been judged adequate, what qualifications would have?[32] I am also glad that you have an idea of the main points of your thesis and, because of the situation in which you will find yourself, you will be able to actively pursue it. You know that in my opinion a dissertation should be completed without delay; it is not a "*Lebenswerk*." As for a diploma from the École Pratique des Hautes Études, this also is an excellent idea; I even believe it might be advantageous to do it. This is a milieu which is not as lively as it might be, but it will become so; I was able to ascertain in many instances that it was already a force more powerful

---

while invincibly demonstrating the spirituality of the soul and the existence of God to atheists, it demonstrated the absolute dependence of creatures on their Creator and conserver of their existence. This provided the stimulus for Malebranche to develop a Christian philosophy which, according to Gouhier, had as its essential theme "the glory of God." By ridding the world of substantial forms and all the other small entities that are supposed to reduce the mystery of causality, the new physics left only one agent, one efficacious cause, just as in Christianity; the new physics provided the means of overthrowing the pagan gods and left man in the presence of one God. The principle of occasional causes allowed the victory of the Christian spirit over the pagan intelligence. See Gouhier 1926b, 7–8, 49–79. Descartes's *Treatise on Man* excited Malebranche to such an extent that he was forced at times to stop reading the book because of heart palpitations. Gilson cited Malebranche's experience as a classic example of intellectual pleasure. See Gilson 1965, 23–24.

31 Gouhier was a "pensionnaire de la Fondation Thiers" from 1922–1925. The Thiers Foundation was housed in a private mansion constructed in 1892 as a memorial to Adolphe Thiers, President of the French Republic. The foundation provided housing and funding to some of France's most brilliant students. In the early 1990s, it was converted into a luxury residential hotel.

32 Gouhier had two prestigious titles. He was a student at the École Normale Supérieure (a "*Normalien*") from 1919 to 1922. He also was "agrégé," having passed the agrégation in philosophy in 1921 (see n.10, above).

É. Gilson, Toronto, 1929

than one assumes. For one of my two seminars I submitted: *Descartes and the religious thought of his time*. I did it in the hope that you would still be in Paris. I would appreciate your opening this set of seminars with three or four lessons (although that's not the right word for it) in which you would present your conception of the relations of reason and faith in Descartes according to your earlier research. No need to tackle this question again; afterwards, we will attempt to do so together if you wish.[33] Moreover, I believe you could turn your work for the diploma into a work for the Hautes Études, unless, of course, you've found another topic.[34] (Your note in the *Revue de métaphysique* was very amusing; it is amazing that no one noticed that Descartes was a *conservative*).[35] I will discuss this with you again at the beginning of the school year; right now I am preparing for a trip. As a good disciple of Descartes I am going to shut my books for five or six weeks to read the "book of the world" and renew myself by doing something. I leave almost certainly on the 12th of August for the regions in Russia where there is famine; when I return I hope that my testimony will save a few poor wretches and, who knows, perhaps a few thousand. I

33 During the first part of Gilson's seminar, Gouhier collected, classified, and interpreted texts from Descartes on the subject of faith and reason. Gouhier then established an intellectual biography of Descartes in terms of his metaphysical, scientific, and apologetical preoccupations and submitted it as his doctoral thesis. See Gilson 1923a. The Practical School of Higher Studies where Gilson taught was destined by its founders to be a sort of school of lay theology. The Sorbonne's faculty of theology, revived after the French revolution by Napoleon I's reform of the university, disappeared with the law of 21 March 1885 that laicized higher education. In its place, one year later, on 30 January 1886, was born the fifth section of the École pratique des hautes études devoted to the study of religious science. See, Marchand-Thébault 1973, 92–96. The fifth section of the École pratique was not favorably viewed by the clerical faculty of the Institut Catholique, a bastion of clerical Thomism not up to date on the latest thinking of the time. See Thieulloy 2005, 50.

34 Gouhier received the *Diplôme d'École Pratique des Hautes Études, Sciences Religieuses* in 1923 and dedicated his thesis (Gouhier 1924a) to Gilson. In the preface to the second edition, Gouhier provided an account of the history of this thesis.

35 See Gouhier 1922. On 2 October 1793, the Convention Nationale ordered that Descartes's remains be transferred to the Pantheon. Three years later, because of the politics of the day, the unimplemented decree was revoked. See also Rodis-Lewis 1984, 96–98.

H. Gouhier at the Thiers Foundation.

intend to focus especially on the children of intellectuals; I prefer that to a month of boredom at the beach.[36]

Thank you for sending the list of candidates for the *agrégation*; I was pleased to see many of the names there and I hope they will remain on the final list.

Best wishes,

Ét. Gilson

❦

7

[post card]
21 October 1922

My dear friend,

We will discuss this question again the first chance we get. But my impression is that it is better to eliminate the historical question, i.e., the [Part] II, [chapter] 3 and stay with the doctrinal reconstruction whose main lines you have shown me. This II, 3 actually can be one or more theses: you will have more than enough with a "Christian Philosophy of Malebranche" and your thesis will have a perfect unity. At the Hautes Études I scheduled: *Descartes and the Religious Thought of His Time*—a title that is vague and will allow us complete freedom. I will give an introductory lecture and will call upon you for three or four lectures as you wish: afterwards, we will take up the question together. I definitely think you should eliminate: *The Origins of Christian Philosophy*, much too broad a subject, and go from: *Faith and Reason* to *The Glory of God*.[37]

---

36 Gilson was involved in the Association for Aid to Russian Children, a private program formed by professional people in Paris that worked in cooperation with the Nansen Committee of the League of Nations. Because he spoke Russian, Gilson was placed in charge of this mission. See Shook 1984, 109–111. During his stay in Russia, Gilson profoundly experienced the universality of the Catholic Church. See Gilson 1957.

37 Although Gilson's letters contain insufficient detail to determine the precise results that his recommendations had on the structure of Gouhier's theses, the published versions seem to be accord with Gilson's advice. See Gouhier 1926b, which devoted an entire chapter to "Le principe de la philosophie chrétienne" and another to "La notion de 'Philosophie chrétienne.'" Likewise,

Sincerely yours,

Ét. Gilson

8

[post card]
Revue d'histoire Franciscaine
17 April 1924

My dear friend,

Your book is very attractive, and since it is good I can only wish it success.[38] You have organized reviews for your book so remarkably well that you would make an excellent 'prime minister'.[39] For England, send a copy to *Mind* and another to the *Hibbert Journal*. For Italy, a copy to the *Critica*, and another to the *Rivista di Filosofia neo-scolastica*. Then, let's wait. Besides, these two countries are not very inquisitive, especially England.[40] Rest up and if the vision in God offers resistance, adjust your discussion of it; perhaps it means *several* things and serves, perhaps, several functions. I leave on Wednesday morning; see you soon, in May.

Your friend,

Ét. Gilson

---

the entire first part of his "grande thèse" (Gouhier 1926a) discussed "La gloire de Dieu."

38 The reference is to Gouhier's *La pensée religieuse de Descartes* published in 1924.

39 France's Third Republic (1871–1940) had 87 prime ministers. The "président du conseil" and the prime minister were one and the same. Gilson humorously made the point that Gouhier's abilities would allow him to "run the country."

40 For details concerning the reviews of Gouhier's book, including those that appeared in England and Italy, see Sebba 1964, 36–37, no. 168. Sebba acknowledged his debt to the scholarship of Gouhier—one of the "three Cartesian G's—Gilson, Gouhier, Gueroult" (ibid., x, xiv).

9

[post card]
23 May 1924
Revue d'histoire Franciscaine

My dear friend,

I believe you are wise in devoting all of your time next year to your thesis,[41] unless you wish to give a course and find it profitable. But it seems to me that it is better for you to concentrate on your writing. I will try to see you as soon as I get back into my normal routine, to discuss all of this with you; but keep yourself free. Needless to say, I am happy to see you seeking precision in your work; a danger sensed is one halfway avoided. See you soon.

Your friend,

Ét. Gilson

On second thought, if you can come next Tuesday to 91 Port-Royal Boulevard, at 8:15 p.m., you will certainly find me at home and even do me a favor by coming.

❦

10

[post card]
15 June 1924

My dear friend,

I do not see anything at all to change in the pages you returned to me. The entire conclusion is very good. The meeting at which I will submit your thesis[42] will be held next Wednesday, June 20, at 4:30; all you have to do is be there at that time; I will arrive about fifteen minutes late. Draft a letter to the President of the École Prat[ique] des H[autes] É[tudes], Sciences Religieuses, asking for permission to give a provisional course next year, in conjunction with my courses and

41 For the *Doctorat d'état.*

42 For the *Doctorat d'état.*

with my permission, and specifying the topic (the word "religious" will appear there, of course).[43]

Mr. McKeon gave an *excellent* analysis of Malebranche.[44]

Your friend,

Ét. Gilson

---

43 During the 1923–1924 academic year Gilson arranged for Gouhier to present a series of lectures at the École Pratique on "La vision en Dieu chez Malebranche et ses sources théologiques." Gouhier devoted the first semester to an analysis of texts; he devoted the second to a study of Malebranche's sources. See Gilson 1924f. During the 1924–1925 academic year, Gilson presented two courses: "Études sur la doctrine d'Albert le Grand" and "Études sur la philosophie de Duns Scot." I have found no reference to a course given by Gouhier during that year (Gilson 1925d and e).

44 McKeon's presentation likely occurred during Gouhier's lectures on Malebranche (Gilson 1924f). Richard McKeon (1900–1985) was born in Union Hill, New Jersey. After a stint in the Navy during World War I, McKeon returned to graduate work at Columbia University in 1919 and completed an M.A. in philosophy in 1919. During a stay in Paris from 1922–1925, he studied under Léon Robin, Brunschvicg, and "studied Descartes, Malebranche, and medieval philosophy with Gilson." Both McKeon and Gouhier regularly attended Gilson's seminars. Under Gilson's direction, McKeon wrote a thesis for the *Diplôme d'études supérieures* on the problem of the universal in twelfth-century philosophy. It was also in Paris that McKeon acquired a taste for "perennial philosophy." He "learned from Gilson to trace the basic patterns and unity of philosophic thought through the diversity of philosophic systems and expressions" (McKeon 1990, 6–9) even though he later criticized Gilson's approach to "doctrines" in the Middle Ages and found little in them that was "directly relevant to modern problems" (McKeon 1936).

In July 1926, when Gilson arrived in New York for the first time and visited Columbia University, he carried a letter of introduction from McKeon (Shook 1984, 140). McKeon completed his Ph.D. in 1928 and began teaching history of philosophy at Columbia. In 1935, he was summoned to the University of Chicago at the behest of its president, Robert Maynard Hutchins, who had been introduced to McKeon by their mutual friend, Mortimer J. Adler. McKeon taught there until his retirement in 1974. As Gilson's oldest American friend, McKeon became "the dean of Gilson's North American students" dining with Gilson whenever possible or visiting dockside with him in New York when

II

28 June 1924
Revue d'histoire Franciscaine

My dear friend,

Congratulations on the fine and gratifying success you just achieved.[45] I am, need I tell you, very pleased with it and I see this as just the beginning. If you can spare a few minutes on Tuesday about four o'clock, I will be at the office in Vrin's bookshop (the branch on the Rue St. Jacques; formerly Mulot).[46] I would like to determine with you the provisional titles of your theses so they can appear in the catalogue of the series

---

Gilson would arrive or set sail for France. See Shook 1984, 107, 140, 147, 231, 263, 311.

Gilson and McKeon corresponded during their long careers. In his letters to McKeon, Gilson commented on McKeon's doctoral thesis on Spinoza, provided McKeon recommendations for a book of selections of medieval texts and suggestions on specific points of translation, discussed playing tennis with students at Harvard, insisted that the McKeons use his apartment and library when McKeon returned to Paris in 1951 on a Fulbright Scholarship, and mentioned having read almost all of McKeon's works. See the *Richard McKeon Papers*, Box 36, folder 11 and Box 76 folder 23. When Gilson resigned from Harvard in 1928 to go to Toronto, he recommended that McKeon replace him. In a 3 March 1928 letter to Ralph Barton Perry (1876–1957), Professor of Philosophy at Harvard, Gilson wrote that "if our Department of Philosophy decided to secure Richard McKeon, all that I have done in Harvard would be done, and much better, by my young friend and 'alter ego'" (Perry Correspondence). McKeon dedicated his work, *Thought, Action, and Passion* "[t]o Étienne Gilson who has explored, as few philosophers have, the subtle relations that join poetry, philosophy, and history in the varied meanings and values men have found in speculation and sought in action" (McKeon 1954).

45 In 1924, the French Academy awarded Gouhier's *La pensée religieuse de Descartes* the Prix Trubert.

46 Gilson developed a close relationship with Joseph Vrin, who became Gilson's friend, adviser, and publisher. See Belgioioso and Gouhier 2005, 76. Because of differences in temperament and Gilson's continual revisions of manuscripts, Vrin referred facetiously to Gilson as "*mon calvaire.*" Vrin's sudden death in 1957 was very hard on Gilson. "Their careers had risen together and their affection for one another had withstood the trials of forty years" (Shook 1984, 335, 112–113, 139).

that we are preparing; this is the time to insert them. I even took the first steps by proposing, without any commitments:

(1) *The intellectual biography of Father Malebranche, Oratorian.*

(2) *The Philosophy of Malebranche and His Religious Inspiration.*

We will discuss this again, if you have the time.
See you soon, I hope.
Your friend,

Ét. Gilson

❦

12

6, Rue de Ponthierry
Melun (S-et-M)
9 October 1924

My dear friend,

Thank you for the trouble you have once again taken on my behalf; this is a friendship that ends up costing you dearly.[47] I decided to subscribe (at no cost) to the *Vie Catholique*, precisely because this journal seems to me to meet a real need. Up until now I can hardly find fault with it, except for a fairly strong editorial, especially for a first issue. I wasn't expecting to be introduced so quickly to its readers, and especially not by you.

I would like to call your attention to the following paragraph in P. Souday's[48] (*Temps*, 9 Oct. 1924) column: "But I thank them (scil. Messrs. Maritain and Massis) for having categorically repudiated Descartes; I prefer this straightforward anathema against the founder of modern philosophy to the efforts of some others to disguise this great and free

47 Gouhier developed an article defending Gilson against O. Habert and then agreed with Gilson's request not to publish it so as to leave space for Gilson to defend himself. See Letter 13.

48 Paul Souday (1868–1931) was a well-known literary critic whose articles appeared in *Les Temps* from 1912 to 1929. During this period, Souday was the most spectacular and even the most popular figure in criticism. He provided the form, battlefield, and publicity for the conflict between right and left in literature and, especially, in criticism.

spirit as an orthodox thinker."[49] *Es galt Ihnen!* as the Krauts say. This is for you. We are going to keep an eye on Paul Souday and, as soon as he mentions a specific person, we will have to do him in. It is a pity he did not name you; the subject-matter was fine; but he will come back to it.[49]

The Rabelais seems to have amused you.[50] So much the better! I doubt very much that I will participate in a subsequent edition, because, even if they should offer it to me, I would hesitate to be part of a team whose captain is Pierre Benoît of the history of ideas![51] We are not

---

49 In his 9 October 1924 "Feuilleton du *Temps*," Souday reviewed Frédéric Lefèvre's famous series which appeared in the *Nouvelles littéraires, Une heure avec...* . In commenting on both Lefèvre's opinions and the individuals he interviewed, Souday criticized Jacques Maritain's and Henri Massis's unreserved admiration for St. Thomas's philosophy and summarily dismissed the view that St. Thomas, a "theological compilator of the thirteenth century," had anything to contribute to modern thought and science. This is the context in which Souday paid Maritain and Massis a backhanded compliment. He expressed his preference for Maritain's and Massis's straightforward repudiation of Descartes, the father of modern philosophy, rather than attempts (such as Gouhier's whose work on Descartes was published in 1924) that try to make Descartes "orthodox," i.e., a "*conservateur*." In 1925, Gilson made the point that Maritain's "méthode consiste à ramener les hommes à des idées pures afin d'être mieux à même de les juger. Sous sa main, les philosophes deviennent des thèses abstraites dont il s'empare et qu'il exécute avec une verve admirable" (Lefèvre 1925, 71).

Mme. Gouhier kindly provided me a copy of Souday's article as found in Henri Gouhier's papers. Just below the article Gouhier wrote two sentences clarifying his position on this matter: "Cela n'a rien à voir: Maritain et Massis lancent l'anathème contre le cartésianisme. Moi, je m'occupe de Descartes lui-même." See also Gouhier 1978b. On Maritain and Massis, see Doering 1983, 6–59.

50 Gilson 1924d; see also Gilson 1925b, 113. Gilson sought "to illustrate through Rabelais the indebtedness of Renaissance and modern French literature to the scholastic thought of the Middle Ages." This subject provided Gilson with an impromptu lecture before the Alliance Française in Boston in January 1927. See Shook 1984, 130–132.

51 Gilson's remark is directed against Abel Lefranc (1863-1952) who with a team of researchers authored the first critical edition of Rabelais in the 20th century. Lefranc argued for Rabelais being an atheist. Gilson, and Lucien Febvre who amplified Gilson's position, argued the opposite. See Gilson 1932b,

free spirits, my dear friend; it can't be helped. ...We work too hard to have that liberating ignorance which would allow us to affirm anything whatsoever.

See you soon.
Your friend,

Ét. Gilson

P.S. I just rediscovered an astonishing Franciscan humanist of the thirteenth century, author of a *De virtutibus philosophorum* (!), who cites the ancients as often as Montaigne.[52] I fear my Catholic prejudices are not the cause of this discovery, which I would have judged unlikely eight days ago. That's how people are...

230, 236 and Febvre (1942). Pierre Benoît (1886–1962), a novelist elected to the French Academy in 1931, was not held in great esteem by intellectuals and critics, or considered a first-rate author by the general public. A letter from Benoît that appeared in Souday's 9 October 1924 "Feuilleton du *Temps*" triggered Gilson's sarcastic comment. In an earlier review of Benoît's novel, *La châtelaine du Liban,* Souday expressed serious doubts that the location and description of Lady Stanhope's tomb as found in the novel was anything more than pure literary fabrication. In his letter, Benoît tried to make the case that he had seen the tomb and provided details as to its location. Souday presented details to the contrary, rejected Benoît arguments, and concluded that "il y a presque toujours quelque chose de peu satisfaisant, de suspect et de truqué dans les histoires que raconte M. Pierre Benoît ... . Malheureusement pour lui, ce petit supplément de publicité ne rendra pas son roman meilleur" (Souday 1924).

52 The reference is to Johannes Guallensis (J. Vallensis, John of Wales, Jean de Galles) (ca. 1220–1285), an important British Franciscan scholar who arrived in Paris from Oxford about 1270. He probably attended the Paris sermons, and perhaps lectures, by his fellow Franciscans John Pecham and St. Bonaventure and Dominicans such as Thomas Aquinas. John of Wales wrote his quota of biblical commentaries, but devoted most of his time and energy to encyclopedic preaching aids that proved of value during the thirteenth and fifteenth centuries. The *Breviloquium de virtutibus antiquorum principum et philosophorum sive de quattuor virtutibus cardinalibus,* one of John's earliest preaching aids that appears to predate 1270 and postdate 1260, is a collection of exempla illustrating the virtuous behavior of ancient princes and philosophers. For a discussion of the significance and influence of the Breviloquium, see, Swanson 2002.

13

Sunday, 26 October 1924

My dear friend,

Thank you again for your article so full of understanding, and, still more, for your reply to the aforementioned O. Habert.[53] But I ask you to leave room for me because mine has been sent in as well. Mine agrees with yours, except on the point (in which I otherwise follow your view) that there is no Catholic history. This is a point which you will be able to come back to sometime; it is definitely worth doing. The outline of my response is simple: (1) I re-establish the texts. (2) I dissociate my *review* of Delacroix from the *books* in which I present my own position. (3) I declare that I am Catholic. (4) I also declare that I do not know from what chapel he excludes me, and I give him the address of my own: *Saint François—Saint Dominique,* refusing to suppress either of the two names.

The more this goes on, the more I am convinced the planet has the choice between religion and savagery, and that God is in Catholicism. But if it is good to be Catholic to avoid Guignebert,[54] it is just as important to avoid Habert. By definition Catholicism excludes all sects.

---

53 In a virulent anti-Gilson article, Abbé O. Habert "strongly resented the dabbling of a wicked Sorbonne professor in the delicacies of Christian mysticism and Christian thought." Habert attacked Gilson's interpretation of St. Thomas as "distorted" and Gilson's interpretation of St. Bonaventure as nothing more than a forerunner of Pascal and pragmatism. Habert also expressed shock that Gilson's book review (Gilson 1922a) had shown only praise for Delacroix's *La raison et la foi*. See Habert 1924. Gilson responded by stating that he had "presented his [Delacroix's] ideas without criticizing them, a procedure unacceptable to the abbé whose method is, rather, to criticize my ideas without presenting them" (Shook 1984, 130).

54 The reference is to Charles Guignebert (1867–1939), the great rationalist historian, student of Renan, and Professor of the History of Christianity at the Sorbonne from 1919 to 1937. Guignebert authored many works on the history of Catholicism (Guignebert 1907; 1910; 1927; 1933; 1935; 1943). He argued that the writers of the Gospels were not interested in recording history, but only in proving a doctrinal system. Three influential French scholars, Maurice Goguel, Guignebert, and Loisy, all agreed in interpreting Christianity as a syncretistic religion formed under the influence of Hellenistic mystery religions.

What I regret, and what my reply will not have, is your fluid style. The title is the following: *To Work Peacefully.*[55]

Your friend,

Ét. Gilson

❦

14

6, Rue de Ponthierry
Melun (S-et-M)
2 June 1925

My dear friend,

I delivered your manuscript to the secretariat, along with my report, and requested the permission for you to publish.[56] So you should be able to proceed right away.

Here are my general impressions. The third part is good (the vision in God). I think eliminating a certain number of pages from it that are only citations, in order to condense the ideas into brief statements, will be fine. The comparative tables [of Augustine] with Ambrosius Victor should be retained but moved to an appendix (in small print) to gain space and not interfere with the flow.[57]

The second part contains a good chapter on the connections between Malebranche and Saint Augustine. All the others did not come out very well, especially with regard to editing. So your effort should focus on the whole of *The Union with God through the Will*; it will be necessary to try and rethink that and obtain a more solid, less wordy, construction.

I recommend you remove the very substandard chapter on Malebranche's *ethics* from it, recast it, and, in reworking it, use it as the basis for your conclusion to the second volume (*The Union with God*). There you will find ideas on the interior life as an abridgement of the union with God; on metaphysics as orientation toward God and detachment from bodies; on efficacity reserved for God, the bond of all spiritual society and goal of our society since He is its principle; on the sacred character (because it is divine) of efficacity whose distributors we are

55 Gilson 1924c.

56 Gouhier's *Doctorat d'état* was published before he defended it. See Letter 17.

57 Gouhier 1926a.

and which forbids us from every purely *secular* conception of life (VII *Dialogues [on Metaphysics and Religion]*, 14. *Treatise on Morals*, II, ch[apter] 10 ff.).[58]

Finally, I think—leaving this up to you—your thesis would gain much in prominence by contrasting very clearly Malebranche and the scholastic Thomists. The elements of this opposition are to some extent all over the place, in a colloidal state. This is stronger in Malebranche, who has complete and terrifying chapters on that which you do not have: scholasticism is idolatry. It is necessary—it seems to me—to condense this somewhere into a brief table of his critique of the scholastics. I was expecting to hear about the philosophy of the serpent;[59] this is not entirely successful.

I see no objection to the plan which you currently have in mind to make two theses out of your manuscript.

Sincerely yours,

Ét. Gilson

P.S. Above all, convince yourself that a concise editing and a scrupulously accurate exposition of your subject will enable you to gain not only space but even richness in terms of intellectual content.

Make sure you have strong transitions to link the paragraphs; *you know what they are*, now formulate them.

58 Ibid. Gouhier's approach to Malebranche in terms of "l'union à Dieu par la raison" (Part 2) and "l'union à Dieu par la volonté" (Part 3) corresponded to the general approach of Gilson's presentation of St. Augustine's thought: "la recherche de Dieu par l'intelligence et par la volonté." See Gilson 1929a.

59 Malebranche considered any philosophy teaching that God communicates His power to creatures as making them into gods and undermining the worship of the true God. Such a philosophy is essentially pagan, the correct philosophy of fallen nature—"it is not the philosophy received from Adam that teaches these things; it is that received from the serpent" (Malebranche 1980, 451 and xxxiii–xliii). See paragraphs 12–14 of Gilson's essay in Appendix 1 below and Gilson and Langan 1963, 477–478.

15

Jacques Band Residence
Morzine (Hte Savoie)
31 July 1925

My dear friend,

I understand your uncertainty about the choice of a position; it is certain this choice won't in any way influence your career in higher education, in any case not in any appreciable way; your personal preferences are not a suitable topic for debate, and, consequently, I believe you alone can make the decision. It seems clear to me that your being in Evreux would be a "utopia"; and since your theses will very likely be printed in Poitiers (French Printing and Bookshop Company, rue Oudin), it might be very beneficial for you to be there in order to move things along quickly. That said, only you can decide.[60]

Mr. Brunschvicg, whose report I read, said nothing as precise to me as he did to you since I only barely spoke with him in between two oral examinations. His impression, which dovetails with your original design, appears to me *decisive* for the layout of your work.[61] Rightly there can be

60 Gouhier accepted a teaching position at a lycée in Troyes (1925–1928) and went on to teach at the Universities of Lille (1929–1940) and Bordeaux (1940–1941). Later he was Professor at the Sorbonne (1941–1968).

61 Léon Brunschvicg (1869–1944) along with Henri Delacroix, Léon Robin, André Lalande, and Jean Laporte served as members of the jury for Gouhier's doctoral thesis defense in 1926. See Garric 1926. Gouhier dedicated his "small" thesis on Malebranche to both Bréhier and Brunschvicg and paid tribute to Brunschvicg after his death (Gouhier 1945, 19). Brunschvicg held the Chair of the History of Modern Philosophy at the Sorbonne from 1927 until World War II, when he was forced into exile and Gouhier replaced him. When the Germans occupied Paris in 1940, Brunschvicg fled. Under the alias of Mr. Brun, he settled in Aix-en-Provence and finally in Aix-les-Bains where he died.

Gilson considered Brunschvicg his "formidable maître et ami" (Shook 1984, 170). A founding member of the *Revue de métaphysique et de morale* (1893) and the Société française de philosophie (1901), Brunschvicg participated in the session devoted to Gilson's thesis on Descartes (Gilson 1914). Brunschvicg also suggested that Gilson prepare his edition of Descartes's *Discours de la méthode*. See Gilson 1924e, 135. At a subsequent meeting of the Société, Gilson tangled with Brunschvicg on the question of atheism (Brunschvicg 1928). A connoisseur of Malebranche, Brunschvicg assisted at the famous debate between Gilson

no possible wavering and it is necessary to go back to the first solution. How the publication and the sale will go are points that we will settle after the printer's estimate. Until then continue to *condense* as much as possible, you gain on all fronts by doing so. Chin up, my dear friend; my family joins me in sending you our best regards.

Sincerely yours,

Ét. Gilson

16

19 August 1925

My dear friend,

I find myself so far from Malebranche right now that I fear suggesting some foolishness to you in advising you. At this point in your work, you are the only person from whom you can expect sound advice; finish it off based on what other people have told you; among the contradictory opinions which you have received, you will always find one that will suit you. I am generally on the go from 7 o'clock in the morning until 7 at night, and at altitudes which vary from 1,000 to 2,600 meters. My mind is completely blank and for this I congratulate myself. You can see I would be giving very bad advice right now.

Courage and best wishes,

Ét. Gilson

and Bréhier on the existence of Christian philosophy hosted by the Société; Brunschvicg characterized Malebranche as "le représentant typique et essentiel d'une philosophie chrétienne" (Gilson 1931a, 77). See also Gilson 1962, 29–34. The Société française de philosophie provided a forum for dialogue among French intellectuals, especially from the faculties of the university and École normale supérieure. It met approximately eight times a year and based most of its debates on the recent publications of its members.

17

6, rue Ponthierry
Melun (S-et-M)
29 oct. 1925

My dear friend,

I know about your negotiations with the publisher; it is expensive, and yet these are the best terms that one can hope for. You have already realized a substantial gain by reducing the length of your manuscript . . . . I will do my best so that you meet your deadline and I am confident we will succeed. Your manuscript is already in Poitiers; I would like to follow the printing closely and request that you return all your galley proofs, corrected, to Vrin's bookstore where I will see them. This detour can actually avoid a lot of wrong moves and gain time. I hope all will go well, and I am sure it will.

I would like to be as optimistic about the immediate future of our country. There are moments when one wonders who its fellow country-men are and how many of them there are.[62]

Sincerely yours,

Ét. Gilson

18

Revue d'histoire franciscaine
28 November 1925

My dear friend,

I will be happy to see you Wednesday; but come at the end of my lecture at the Hautes-Études, at 3:15 p.m.; we will have a minute or two before my class at the Faculty of Letters,[63] which begins at 4 o'clock.

62 On 16 October 1925, Germany signed a mutual security pact with Britain, France, Belgium, and Italy at Locarno. The pact also affirmed the postwar frontiers set out in the Versailles Treaty and accepted Rhineland demilitarization.

63 The reference might be to a course on Malebranche. It is known that Gilson took extensive notes, apparently during 1924–1925, from Malebranche's *Entretiens sur la métaphysique*. Included in the notes is Fr. Shook's handwritten comment that these materials seem to have been used for a course on

I have just read your preface; it is *very good;* I am very satisfied; it is good Gouhier.

As to the affair Malebranche, you, of course, are free. From my point of view, this for you is a deadly, unavoidable exploitation, with no compensation. If I were you, I would say I didn't have the time.[64]

See you soon; your friend,

Étienne Gilson

❦

19

6, Rue de Ponthierry,
Melun (S-et-M)
December 30, 1925

My dear friend,

It seems utterly impossible to me that the person who interviewed me so quickly is the one you spoke to me about. That lady emphatically maintained she did not live in Paris which is why she could not even set up a meeting with me.

As for the thesis, from now on there is no need for you to send me your proofs; your corrections are sufficient, although not always perfect (whose corrections are?). Nevertheless, beware of references to your first volume, whose pages you don't have (p. 56, note 1). They will print your second volume before the first, and leave you a blank. It would be better to refer to the chapters, as you usually do.

The *s*'s which bother you, and which you indicate like an "s" looked at differently are actually s's turned around. It is sufficient to correct them

---

Malebranche's metaphysics that Gilson gave at the Sorbonne in 1924. Shook added that the notes must have been pulled together for Gilson's lecture notes at Harvard. See Gilson Papers, "Early Lecture Notes from the 1920s, Harvard and the Sorbonne, Mostly on Malebranche." See n.81, below.

64 The reference might be to a proposal to develop a book or present a course. Finances concerned Gilson (see Letter 23) and finance interested him. "Gilson is a man interested in everything that is interesting—in literature, drama, fine arts, politics, social problems, and even in sports, business and the financial page . . . . I have heard businessmen comment upon his ability to estimate and forecast movements in international finance and the money markets" (Lyons 1936).

this way s, and draw a line in the margin /. [See the excerpt below from a copy of the original letter.]

6, RUE DE PONTHIERRY
MELUN (S.-ET-M)

30 Décembre 1925

Mon cher ami

Il me paraît tout à fait impossible que la personne qui m'a si rapidement interviewé soit celle dont vous me parlez. Cette dame m'a formellement affirmé qu'elle n'habitait pas Paris et c'est même pourquoi elle n'a pu prendre avec moi aucun rendez-vous.

En ce qui concerne la thèse, inutile de m'envoyer désormais vos épreuves ; vos corrections sont suffisantes (quoique non toujours parfaites (quelles corrections le sont ?). Méfiez-vous toutefois des renvois à votre tome I, dont vous n'avez pas les pages (p. 54, note 1). On va tirer votre tome II avant le tome I, et vous laisser un blanc. Mieux vaudrait renvoyer aux chapitres, comme vous faites le plus souvent.

Les s qui vous gênent, et que vous indiquez comme d'un autre œil (s), sont en réalité des s retournées. Il suffit de corriger ainsi s, et en marge S/.

Vous aurez en effet Laporte, si vous ne vous y opposez pas. Vous savez de quoi il vous parlera, et c'est vous qui aurez commencé la conversation.

Je serai content de vous voir lancer une série d'Essais et verrai avec plaisir votre projet. Mais D. Halévy est de meilleur conseil en ces matières. Merci de vos bons vœux ; transmettez les nôtres à vos parents, et gardez en d'abord une bonne part. Votre doctorat se passera très bien et vous ne devrez rien à personne ; on dit à Melun : Bel oiseau se fait de lui-même. C'est assez vrai, et vous le constaterez au cours de votre enseignement.

Excusez le décousu de ma lettre (je le sens), et ne croyez pas que, dans mon cœur, je vous expédie ; mais

Copy of the letter that refers to the old French letter s.

Sure enough, you will have Laporte if you don't object to it. You know what he will discuss with you, and it is you who will have begun the conversation.[65]

65 Jean Laporte (1886–1948), Professor of the History of Philosophy at the Sorbonne, developed a number of important studies on various aspects of Malebranche's thought. Gilson's attempt to anticipate how Gouhier could best deal with Laporte at the thesis defense failed. See Letter 22.

I will be happy to see you launch a series of *Essays* and will be pleased to examine your project. But D. Halévy is the best person to advise you on these matters.[66] Thank you for your good wishes; give ours to your parents, and, first and foremost, keep a good part for yourself. Your doctorate will go very well and you will owe nothing to anyone; as we say in Melun, a beautiful bird is its own creation. That is true enough, and you will observe it during your own teaching.

Excuse the rambling nature of my letter (I sense it), and do not think I am really trying to get rid of you; right now I have so much work to do preparing my lectures that I am truly overwhelmed. I hope to see my way more clearly two or three months from now.

Sincerely,

Ét. Gilson

❦

20

6, Rue de Ponthierry,
Melun (S-et-M)
10 January 1926

My dear friend,

I am happy that my article did not displease you. I thought it would be best to present your book publicly and seriously.[67] Actually, I have

---

66 D. Halévy (1872–1962), historian, essayist, and friend of Péguy collaborated with him from 1898 on the *Cahiers de la quinzaine*. Halévy and Gouhier corresponded from 1921 to 1931. In the autumn of 1925 Gouhier asked Halévy (unpublished letter) whether he would be interested in publishing a volume containing Gouhier's "bons petits articles de revue." Gouhier added that if the articles could not be published in timely fashion he would be willing to reduce the size of the volume by limiting it to two "essential" articles. "Je crois en effet que les deux morceaux de résistance sont ma 'Note sur l'intellectualisme' [see Gouhier 1922b], qui est un essai historique sur la littérature et la philosophie du dernier demi-siècle, et 'le Point de départ de M. Barrès' [Gouhier 1924b] que je n'ai pas voulu retoucher parce que Barrès l'a vu et approuvé, et parce que ces lignes m'ont valu une de mes plus vives joies, une visite boulevard Maillot et des attentions infiniment délicates de la part de Barrès à la veille de sa mort."

67 The reference is to the review of Gouhier's thesis for the École Pratique des Hautes Études. See Gilson 1925c. Gilson remained unconvinced by some of Gouhier's particular claims (e.g., Descartes's alleged affinities with

the impression that these pages received much more attention than I expected. My good teacher is a little surprised at this and I tried to explain to him that previously we made a mistake in interpretation; I do not think I convinced him. Can it be that he is at that age where one no longer makes such mistakes; I believe, however, that he is one who would recognize our mistake if he had the time to tackle the question again.[68]

Thomism instead of, as scholarly convention held, the Augustinianism of the seventeenth-century French Oratory). Nonetheless, he praised his student's method as Aristotelian as well as properly historical. Gouhier's biographical rather than systematic focus moves from Descartes's concrete actions to cautious speculations about Descartes's hidden motives.

68 The publication of Gouhier's thesis triggered a modification in Gilson's interpretation of Descartes. As early as 1923, Gilson spoke of an "intériorité, nous dirions presque de l'immanence de la métaphysique à la physique cartésienne." See Gilson 1930d, 176. In 1924, in his review of Gouhier's thesis, Gilson admitted that the interpretation of his former teacher, Lévy-Bruhl, i.e., that Descartes's metaphysics was developed for, and subordinated to, his physics (see Letter 1, n.7), could be validly challenged by a different reading of Descartes. Gilson maintained that Gouhier's thesis definitively interpreted the formative years of Descartes's thought as consisting of physics and metaphysics developing simultaneously in an organic progression: "M. H. Gouhier a tout à fait raison de dire que nous n'avons pas assez insisté sur le parallélisme très réel des deux conceptions, si bien que l'on croit, à nous lire, que Descartes a construit la métaphysique pour la mettre au service de la physique. Tel ne fut certainement pas le cas pendant les années décisives qui sont celles de la formation du système, et où nous voyons ses diverses parties croître simultanément d'une croissance organique; les pages où M. Gouhier le prouve resteront certainement et nous apportent un résultat définitif" (Gilson 1930a, 295). Gilson admitted that since it may be an oversimplification to maintain that Descartes's physics did not inspire his metaphysics, Descartes's radical and new physics should also be recognized as a metaphysics.

Afterwards, Gilson's interpretation of Descartes evolved further. The final, and most important, stage of the evolution occurred between the years 1936–1947 with the publication of *The Unity of Philosophical Experience*, *God and Philosophy* and *L'Être et l'essence* (Gilson 1937; 1941; 1948). In these three works, two of which were published directly in English, Gilson considered Descartes as a metaphysician who followed Suarez by placing a primacy on essence as metaphysically pure of all trace of existence and interpreting existence as a simple realization of essence, not the irreducible act of existing. Gilson argued that

Don't regret your novels;[69] your whole person will be in your books, regardless of the subject.

I believe you will be presented in the second tier (for the sake of form) as assistant of philosophy in the Sorbonne (new position; 1 hour per week; to correct dissertations; 3,000 francs). Baruzi[70] will be presented in the first tier. In brief, we thought about you; it is Lévy-Bruhl[71] who mentioned you and Lalande[72] seems to think highly of you.

Descartes's innovations were seriously deficient because of a misguided metaphysics that substituted for being as the object of this science one particular aspect of being studied by diverse sciences of nature. In brief, Gilson initially underestimated Descartes's innovations (ca. 1913), then recognized and situated them (ca. 1923–1930), and finally judged them (ca. 1937–1948). Referring to the final stage of this evolution, Sebba noted Gilson's "merciless critique" and "astounding change of attitude towards Descartes." See Sebba 1964, 36 and Marion 1980. For a broader discussion of Gilson's moving increasingly during 1926 to 1946 toward a basically metaphysical interpretation of philosophy's history, see Pegis 1946.

69 During this period the novels of Maurice Barrès (1862–1923) greatly influenced Gouhier: "Barrès m'enseigné la sympathie qui fait l'histoire; il m'a appris le secret de faire vivre en moi des personnalités qui n'étaient point la mienne. Il m'a conseillé de réserver le 'je' pour les préfaces et de disparaître le plus vite possible. Il m'a donné l'ambition et l'illusion de ressusciter des morts." See Belgioioso and Gouhier 2005, 30–32. "Ma conception de l'histoire de la philosophie se situe dans la ligne de Barrès" (ibid., 115).

70 Gilson was a member of the jury for Jean Baruzi's (1891–1953) doctoral defense of a thesis on Saint John of the Cross (Baruzi 1924). In March 1925, Baruzi agreed to substitute for Alfred Loisy, who held the Chair of the History of Religion at the Collège de France. In addition to two courses at the Collège de France, Baruzi gave a weekly lecture at the Sorbonne from March 1926 until July 1928. For a summary of Baruzi's life and a chronological bibliography of his works, see Vieillard-Baron 1985, 221–225.

71 Exposure to Lévy-Bruhl's teaching resulted in Gilson adopting his master's approach to philosophy—"seeing facts in an impartial, cold, and objective light, just as they were" (Gilson 1941, xiii). Lévy-Bruhl and Gilson's other professors at the Sorbonne told students "*how*, in their opinion, we should think, but not one of them ever presumed to tell us what we should think" (Gilson 1962, 27–28, 87; see Gilson 1939; and Synan 1991, 57–58).

72 André Lalande (1867–1963) served as a member of the jury for both Gilson's and Gouhier's thesis defense. See Canivez 1974, 3:473–76.

I will have some off prints and I will give you almost all, if not all, of them. I usually place my reviews in the furnace; besides, they are very bad fuel.

Will you have some galley proofs for L. Brunschvicg?[73] He is kind and tormenting himself over writing an anti-Gilsonian (*sic*) book. There's nothing I can do about it, he sighs. I believe it really distresses him. As for me, I couldn't care less! What other people think belongs to them so completely that I cannot conceive how that could affect what I think.[74]

Did you read Maritain in the *Chronicles*?[75] It is excellent and I think that for the first time I completely agree with him.

Your friend,

Ét. Gilson

❦

21

6, Rue de Ponthierry
Melun (S-et-M)
23 March 1926

My dear friend,

I am adding this letter to the one that I put in the packet, to tell you that I just re-read your two theses while preparing the few questions that we will discuss on the 15th of May exactly as we usually do.

---

73 Gouhier's two doctoral theses were to be published before his defense. See Belgioioso and Gouhier 2005, 51n.2.

74 The reference is to Brunschvicg's great rationalist interpretation of the history of philosophy in which he harshly and pointedly denied Gilson's contention that St. Thomas was a philosopher in the modern sense of the term even though he presents his philosophy within a theology. See Brunschvicg 1927, 113, 122 and Gouhier 1927. For Brunschvicg, the development of science was not autonomous: philosophy is not separated from science and should not pretend to attain a superior and distinctive kind of truth. Gilson considered Brunschvicg's philosophy as "an invitation to absolute idealism" (Gilson, Langan, and Maurer 1966, 326–329).

75 The reference is to Maritain's "Grandeur et misère de la métaphysique" in which he reproached Baruzi for confounding metaphysical and mystical knowledge. See Maritain 1982–1999, 4:287–90.

Your first thesis is perfect; this is your best product and it is a real pleasure to read you. Furthermore, the general balance of the two theses is now excellent and the editing of the second has become quite satisfactory. So my impression is extremely favorable and I am certain all will go very well; one will, without any trouble, be able to find something to congratulate you about cordially without having to flatter you. As for the points to be discussed, it would be unnecessary to tell you we will find some. But I don't see on what I can disagree with you or cite as mistakes; I might reproach you for not having gone into sufficient depth on certain points if I did not think you intended to accentuate the structural design of the system. Also, we can talk without having anything at all on which to reproach you.[76]

When will I ever see a thesis like this again....

Rest up, my dear friend, and give my regards to your parents.

Yours sincerely,

Ét. Gilson

76 During Gouhier's thesis defense Gilson cited the efficacy of the idea in Malebranche as one issue warranting further explanation. This complicated and controversial topic has drawn much attention from Malebranche scholars ever since Gilson raised it. "J'ai toujours pris plaisir à faire remarquer que la réédition de 1948 de *La philosophie de Malebranche* ... comportait une Addition décisive à propos de l'efficace de l'idée. L'origine s'en trouve dans la théâtralité de la vie philosophique française: l'événementiel a conduit Henri Gouhier à discerner l'essentiel. Voici ce qu'il écrit à propos de la page 275 de son édition de 1926: 'A la soutenance de cette thèse, M. Étienne Gilson fit très justement remarquer que le thème de l'efficacité de l'idée n'avait pas été nettement mis en lumière. C'est ici sans doute qu'il conviendrait de le développer. La substance de Dieu est seule efficace: les idées étant la substance même de Dieu sont efficaces.' Les commentateurs de Malebranche, pas même Delbos, n'avaient jamais abordé ce problème précis, ce qui justifiait l'intervention de Gilson" (Robinet 1999, 199).

Robinet cited the lack of a critical edition of Malebrance's works as one reason why scholars did not clearly see or understand this difficulty. Robinet also considered Gilson's remark as emanating not from an understanding of Malebranche's corpus but from Gilson's familiarity with St. Augustine. According to Robinet, Gilson, during this same period, provided no satisfactory explanation of how, according to St. Augustine, God illuminates the human intellect. Gilson simply posed the problem of how the divine light can be

22

6, Rue de Ponthierry
Melun (S-et-M)
21 May 1926

My dear friend,

The "Samuel evening"[77] has no importance if that is its only claim to fame. For the rest, it is important that you take the matter into your own hands; if the sketches by Texcier[78] I saw in the room can be avoided, that would be even better. And if there were no sketches or text, it would be perfect.

Everything turned out well. As you know the situation was horribly unpleasant for me; at two o'clock in the morning, the following night,

---

introduced in us without ceasing to be divine: "A cela Augustin n'a répondu que par une métaphore: la lumière divine nous 'touche'; mais c'est la nature et la possibilité même d'un tel contact qu'il eût été nécessaire d'expliquer' [Gilson 1929a] (p. 147). Ainsi, et c'est flatteur, la remarque émise lors de la soutenance d'Henri Gouhier avait été addressée à Augustin lui-même! C'est donc à Augustin que Gilson posait sa question avant de la répercuter sur le cas Malebranche. Au demeurant, Gilson ne répondait pas plus à ce problème augustinien que ne le faisait Gouhier à propos de Malebranche. Il se contentait de renvoyer à son article d'hommage à de Wulf de 1934 [Gilson 1934e] sans amender sur ce point sa seconde Préface de l'*Introduction à Augustin* (1943)" (Robinet 1999, 202).

Robinet's study of the idée efficace in Malebranche as it appears in the context of "system and existence" in Malebranche's work (Robinet 1965, 259–284) remains the starting point for contemporary discussions of this notion (e.g., Alquié 1974; Fafara 1978; Jolley 1990; Nadler 1992). Robinet sought and valued Gilson's opinion of *Système et existence*, a meticulous study of the evolution of Malebranche's thought: "Pour toutes sortes de raisons, je désire profondément que ce livre soit soumis à votre jugement" (Robinet 1964). Gilson regarded Robinet's *Système et existence dans l'œuvre de Malebranche* as "one of the two best books I know of on Malebranche (the other one is by Henri Gouhier)" (Gilson 1969).

77 Mr. Samuel organized a reception the previous evening in honor of Gouhier receiving the *Doctorat d'état* with distinction. Gouhier's personal papers include Jean Soulairol's account of the thesis defense, "Malebranche en Sorbonne," which mentioned Samuel's reception. Unfortunately, Soulairol's account, which seems to have appeared in a French newspaper, lacks a precise source and date. Gouhier's personal files also contain a letter from the University of Paris setting his thesis defense for 20 May 1926.

78 Jean Texcier (1888–1957) was a famous graphic portrait artist.

I had to take a drug (Didial Ciba to be precise) to escape at last from that obsession. The harshness based on error, and that anger which works itself up, with arguments that recur like refluxes of bile, and all of that leveled against you, literally upset me. In short, life goes on, and work goes on too; but there remains something in all this that I do not understand.[79]

I am the one who must write the account of your thesis defense.[80]

Take a break, my dear friend, and ease back into work as soon as you can. The more I think of this, the more I believe once you have finished Malebranche, the nineteenth century will be a favorable field for you. I see only one subject to compete with this: Voltaire and his times. To get

---

79 See Garric 1926, 548 and de Gandillac 1998, 104: "A la soutenance de Gouhier, le 25 juin [incorrect date, see note 77 above], je retrouve Laporte, dont la sévérité me surprend à l'égard d'un cadet qui sera bientôt son collègue (il insinue que, hormis quelques pages au début, sa *Philosophie de Malebranche* n'apporte guère plus que ce qu'on a pu lire chez Ollé-Laprune). Sur un tout autre ton parlent non seulement Gilson, ami personnel du nouveau docteur, mais aussi Robin, Lalande et—encore ici—Delacroix." Gouhier followed the example of the latter examiners and became known for his polite, almost apologetic, manner when questioning students during oral exams and doctoral defenses. See Tilliette 1994.

Joseph Vidgrain suggested to Gouhier that Laporte wanted to use the influence of Christianity on Malebranche's thought as undermining any interpretation of him as a rationalist. Belgioioso and Gouhier 2005, 143n.2. In addition, Laporte considered Gilson's interpretation of freedom and liberty in Descartes "radicalement fausse." Laporte also argued against Gilson that Descartes's preoccupation with physics did not prevent him from developing a genuine, original, defensible doctrine of freedom. See Laporte 1937, 101. All or some of this may have played into Laporte's severe reaction to Gouhier. In his "Corrections et Additions de la Deuxième Édition" to *La philosophie de Malebranche*, Gouhier cited Laporte's studies of Malebranche's conceptions of freedom and intelligible extension. See Gouhier 1926a, 443–440.

80 The French press hailed Gouhier's defense of his *Doctorat d'état* on 20 May 1926 as "a philosophical event." Gilson applauded Gouhier as the only interpreter of Malebranche to have developed a synthesis of Malebranchism as Malebranche would have conceived it. See Gilson 1928.

to the root of the disease and draw from it an anti-toxin, with sincerity as its principal ingredient.[81]

81 Gilson was being ironic in stressing sincerity, very unlike Voltaire's frequent sarcasm often laced with insult and hatred. See Gilson and Langan 1963, 532. According to Gouhier, Gilson also suggested another area of study: "Ensuite, Gilson m'a suggéré de travailler sur Auguste Comte qu'il aimait beaucoup et auquel peu de travaux avaient été consacrés. Cela m'a séduit parce que c'était une philosophie de l'histoire. Ici encore il faut parler de hasard: parti pour écrire un livre, j'ai fini par en écrire trois" (Gouhier 1998, 12). See Belgioioso and Gouhier 2005, 52–55.

After Gouhier's defense, Gilson continued to study and write about Malebranche. In a summer course on the "Evolution of French Thought from the Sixteenth Century to the Present" given at the University of Virginia during August and September of 1926 Gilson discussed Malebranche. See University of Virginia 1926. Afterwards, he went to Boston where he taught at Harvard and Radcliff during the fall semester. He continued to teach during the fall at Harvard until 1929, when he decided to base his activities in North America in Toronto. During the first half of the academic year 1926–1927, Gilson taught a graduate course on "The Conflict between Augustinianism and Thomism in the Philosophies of Descartes and Malebranche" (Harvard University 1926–1927, 78). Gilson also took aspects of Malebranche's thought into account in his book on St. Augustine (1929a), his famous debate with Bréhier in 1931, articles on Christian philosophy, and the William James Lectures (1937a).

Shook cited two separate incidents that turned Gilson toward teaching in America. The first was a meeting of the *Société Française de Philosophie* at which Léon Brunschvicg argued that good professors of philosophy were too thinly spread out and that concentration of teaching strength in a limited number of centers was required. Gilson disagreed. He maintained that the problem was the lack of properly prepared students for existing professors to teach. See Brunschvicg 1926. "Gilson could not put this problem out of his mind and took it to North America with him." While at Harvard Gilson seriously considered immigrating to the United States, which seemed to possess so many more appreciative students.

The second incident was a conversation with Albert Georg Adam Balz, Corcoran Professor of Philosophy at the University of Virginia, who invited Gilson to give a summer course. See Shook 1984, 139. Born in Charlottesville, Balz received undergraduate and graduate degrees from Virginia in 1908 and 1909, and a Ph.D. from Columbia in 1916. He returned to the University of Virginia as a university professor and longtime chairman of the Philosophy Department (1929–1955). During the 1920s and 1930s, Balz published a number of articles on Descartes, important Cartesians, and the development of Cartesian doctrine. Balz was especially interested in the derivation of Cartesian

My wife joins me in sending you our best wishes.

Ét. Gilson

❦

23

6, Rue Ponthierry
Melun (S-et-M)
17 January 1928

My dear friend,

I am getting back to my correspondence, my soul racked with remorse. To have left your letter three days without a reply a sort of illness was needed, and, in fact, I understood Saint Augustine's proof of the existence of God, which is what made me unsociable to my friends for all this time. The result, it is that I have a framework of sorts for Saint Augustine, etc., etc.[82] But let's move on to the urgent business.

If Morize is to meet you, it would be better to take the boat that he suggests. Besides, no where else will you be better than on that one, even in second class, and you will complete the crossing in five days, 15 hours and some minutes. So take it; but put down only a deposit on the price of

---

philosophy from Scholastic and Thomistic thought; see Balz 1951 and, his most important work, 1952. Balz viewed Descartes's philosophy not as a revolt, but as a continuation of Thomism derived from it and wholly intelligible within it. In 1937, when Gilson returned to the University of Virginia to deliver the Richard Lectures on *Reason and Revelation in the Middle Ages* he dedicated them to Balz. See Gilson 1938 and Levine 1998.

82 After Gilson returned from North America early in 1927, he was determined to learn more about St. Augustine. "Ever since he had composed an article ... on 'Why St. Thomas criticized St. Augustine' [Gilson 1926a], Gilson had been furiously revising all his writings on Augustine. In the future he planned to devote as many courses and lectures as possible to Augustine's ideas." During the 1927–1928 academic year at Harvard, Gilson presented a course on "The Philosophy of Saint Augustine," and "attempted to revise what he had written on Augustine in the first volume of his *La philosophie au moyen age* [Gilson 1922a], and planned to make Augustine the subject of his next major book" (Shook 1984, 169, 174–175).

the passage. After your marriage[83] you will go to the Ministry of Foreign Affairs to see Jean Marx,[84] on my behalf; he will send you with a recommendation to Mr. Hémard, who will provide you with purchase orders from the Ministry to the C.G.T. (Comp[agnie] Gen[erale] Trans[Atlantique]!!!) and, when you pick up your ticket, they will deduct 30% of the price of the crossing. On no account pay them; you will never see them again. As for Morize, he has nothing to gain in this. It is really the C.G.T. which gives the discount on the purchase order from the Ministry of Foreign Affairs. Foreign Affairs will also pick up your two passports if you so instruct them.

So, for now, reserve a cabin for two, as close as possible to the center (what I mean is as far away as possible from the stern), pay the deposit, and...get married. The rest will sort itself out later.

I, too, would be very happy to see you, but I never go to Paris on Monday or Thursday, the day before and day after my courses. Don't go to any trouble to come; an occasion will present itself.

On a different subject, my friend Father Baudin asks if you would be so kind as to accept writing the *Malebranche* volume in the series: *Christian Moralists*, where I did one on Saint Thomas (publisher, Gabalda).[85] Financially, it is interesting, since the author receives 10% of the full price paid in advance for every 1,000 copies placed on sale. The task will not be very hard for you since it is essentially a collection of texts; but Father

---

83 Gouhier married Marie-Anne Moyse, who died of cancer in 1948. In 1950, Gouhier married Marie-Louise Dufour, *agrégée* in philosophy.

84 In 1928 Jean Marx (1884–1972), a paleographer, medievalist, and specialist in Celtic mythology and literature, was a Director of Studies at the École Pratique and also Director of Cultural Relations in the Ministry of Foreign Affairs. Marx and Jacques Maritain were classmates at the Lycée Henri IV. Marx converted to Catholicism after World War II. He was Maritain's godson and remained one of Maritain's oldest friends. See Michel 2003, 53– 54. Marx contributed to the *festschrift* in honor of Gilson's 75th birthday; see Marx 1959.

85 L'abbé E. Baudin and Gilson had great esteem for each other. Baudin was most favorably impressed by Gilson's work (see Baudin 1922 and 1923) and Gilson took Baudin's work and comments very seriously (see Gilson 1925a; Gilson 1935b, 298, 478–485; and Shook 1984, 122–123). Gilson agreed to Baudin's request to place a volume on St. Thomas's moral teachings in a series on Christian moralists. For Maritain's comments on Gilson's *Saint Thomas d'Aquin* and Gilson's reaction to them, see Prouvost 1991, 24–31.

Baudin hardly sees anyone but you who can link these texts according to their authentic metaphysical relationships, as they exist in Malebranche. It has to do with showing Malebranche's practical ethics while at the same time having it bathe in its metaphysical milieu (what style!). I sincerely hope you will want to accept. If you think you are able to do it, please reply directly to Father Baudin, Professor at the University of Strasbourg, at All Saints, All Saints Street, Strasbourg, Bas-Rhin.[86]

Nevertheless, see you soon, I hope.

Your devoted friend,

Ét. Gilson

❦

10 Elmsley Place, Toronto, built (1896) as a private residence, became the first home of the Institute for Mediæval Studies in 1929. The building was demolished in 1962.

86 Gouhier agreed to abbé Baudin's request. See Gouhier 1929. For an account of Baudin's project, see Gouhier 1926c, 6–7.

24

The Institute of Mediaeval Studies
St. Michael's College
University of Toronto
Toronto 5

10 November 1930

My dear friend,

Your letter gave me the greatest pleasure because those in exile sometimes feel that even when there is nothing to complain about one is still not happy.[87] I am noting your new address in Lille; you are evolving normally and completely in accord with the sane traditions of the place! As for your "little Comte"[88] I understand your feeling because I forget my books as soon as they are born. I remain unchanged in regretting the introduction on Saint-Simon;[89] I fear you might have imagined that

87 In the summer of 1929, Gilson left Paris for the official founding of the Institute of Mediaeval Studies in Toronto. Gilson's plans for the Institute can be found in Gilson 1929b. For a brief history of the Institute, see Synan 1989 and 2000. During much of the remainder of his career, Gilson taught half the year in Paris and half in Toronto. Gilson's decision to base his North American activities in Toronto was regretted in two places: "[Ralph Barton] Perry and his colleagues would like to have held Gilson at Harvard, and Gilson's friends in Montréal, Ottawa and Québec would have liked to see him set up his institute in French Canada." See Shook 1984, 192, 180. In his 18 December 1933 letter to Professor Perry (Perry Correspondence, unpublished) declining his invitation to join the Harvard Philosophy Department, Gilson wrote, "I feel it as an honor but as something much more intimate and rare: the mark of a friendship and affection that gave me more pleasure than anything else ever did during the course of an already long career."

88 Gouhier 1931a.

89 Ibid. Gouhier's "Prologue: Le Précurseur" was devoted to Saint-Simon (1760–1825), a utopian reformer. In his letters to Gouhier during the period 1926–1933 that dealt with his work on Comte, Gilson repeatedly advised Gouhier to delete the Prologue: "C'est très bien mais il faut [underlined twice] amputer votre manuscrit de son Prologue, qui fait mal puisque c'est un petit livre avant le grand. Vous n'aurez pas à revenir à Saint-Simon dans la suite, ce que vous dites de ses relations avec Comte étant suffisant" (extract from Gilson's 12 May 1930 letter to Gouhier as cited in Petit 2002, 67–68). "Je ne vous *conseille pas un livre sur Saint Simon*; pour plusieurs raisons que je vous

just because one has certain intentions while writing they incorporate themselves into the text. My experience is that only a small part of what we think passes into our text, and what we do not write at all does not

---

expliquerai un jour. Faites votre Comte . . . ." (extract from Gilson's 19 June 1931 letter to Gouhier as cited in Prouvost 1994b, 466). Gouhier retained the Prologue and Gilson favorably reviewed Gouhier's book (Gilson 1931b).

Subsequent rethinking of the relationship between Saint-Simon and Comte resulted in Gouhier's greatly minimizing Comte's debt to Simon and denying Saint-Simon the role of inspiring Comte's philosophy. "Devant ses [Saint-Simon's] écrits informes et sa physique fantaisiste, personne ne songe à faire de Saint-Simon un penseur . . . . [L]incohérence de ses écrits et l'extravagance de son imagination," Gouhier argued, were obvious. "En réalité, il n'y a aucune évolution de Saint-Simon, mais un voyage en zigzag au cours duquel les idées emportés au départ n'ont justement pas changé" (Gouhier 1933–41, vol. 2, 2 and 345; vol. 3, 405).

Gilson agreed with Gouhier's conclusions. In 1937 Gilson maintained that although Saint-Simon, like de Bonald, de Maistre, and Fourier, was concerned about building a new social order according to new principles, only Comte "approached the situation as a born philosopher for whom the whole problem was essentially a problem of ideas, [the] solution of which must necessarily be a philosophical solution" (Gilson 1937a, 250). Years later, Gilson devoted less than one page to Saint-Simon who "considered himself a prophet destined to found a new Christianity . . . . Saint-Simonism was an active religious formation of little philosophical significance." Gilson intentionally limited his discussion of Saint Simon in order to get to "one disciple of Saint-Simon [who] was to organize a religion of his own. His name was Auguste Comte, the founder of philosophical positivism and of the positivist cult of Humanity." See Gilson, Langan, and Maurer 1966, 266.

The study of Comte flowed from Gouhier's understanding of philosophy based on his work on Descartes and Malebranche. This led Gouhier to conclude that philosophy had its source outside of itself: philosophers developed a particular "vision of the world" because of changes brought about by science or religious inspiration. Early in his career, Gouhier was impressed by the example of Henri Bremond's *Histoire littéraire du sentiment religieux en France* (Bremond 1916-33) and considered systematizing his work under the rubric, "Histoire philosophique du sentiment religieux." See Neveu 2002, 19–38 and Gouhier 1926a. Comte fit very nicely into this schema. "Même si, parce que je m'intéressais à la pensée française, j'envisageais surtout le catholicisme, je devais aussi prendre au sérieux la religion naturelle de Jean-Jacques Rousseau ou la religion de l'humanité d'Auguste Comte . . . . j'ai montré qu'Auguste Comte; . . . faisait lui aussi une religion nouvelle, avec un nouveau calendrier" (Gouhier 1998, 10–11; and 1988, 17).

pass into it at all. But once the book is born, it will live its life without you or me and perhaps some people will even like it for its shortcomings, if it has any.

Nothing could be more accurate than what you wrote me on the gap between teaching and publishing; this is true even when one succeeds in focusing teaching on the same subject as one's research. Yet when it is necessary to choose, I believe publishing should come first, because if one puts teaching first, one kills the publishing and lowers the level of the teaching. The lectures of someone who publishes, even on something other than what he teaches, differ *toto genere* from the lectures of a professor who is only a professor. At least that is how it seems to me.

I saw none of the critiques of Saint Augustine which you told me about, but I will find them, no doubt, at J. Vrin.[90] P. Archambault[91] is a courageous fellow who believes the books of others contain only what he understands and that other people's thought changes or evolves according to what he understands. You, on the contrary, push your friends forward and want to make them believe they have more richness in them than they believe. That is more encouraging. Your two volumes on Descartes will perhaps see the light of day,[92] but right now

---

90 Gilson dedicated his work on Saint Augustine (Gilson 1929a) written shortly before his last trip to Harvard as a visiting regular professor, "Aux maîtres et aux étudiants du Département de Philosophie de l'Université Harvard: É. G. celui qui reste un des leurs." Despite Gouhier's sympathetic review (Gouhier 1930b) which acknowledged Gilson's characterization of his work as an introduction to the central theses in St. Augustine's work that required more refining, the book drew criticism from secular and Catholic philosophers. In perhaps the most thorough analytical critique of the book, Fernand Van Steenberghen rejected Gilson's thesis that St. Augustine's doctrine is a philosophy. Shook (1984, 189–191) cited this criticism as, in part, explaining "why Gilson now began to develop his thesis of Christian philosophy in earnest and would spend most of the 1930s demonstrating it in a variety of ways."

91 Paul Archambault (1883–1950), founder of the Blondelien review *La Nouvelle Journée* in 1914, was considered a modernist. Gilson's bibliography makes no mention of a review by Archambault of Gilson's work on Augustine (McGrath 1982, 13, no. 73), but Gilson and Archambault were familiar with each other's work. See Gilson 1932a, 20–21 and Archambault 1926; see also Gouhier 1928 and 1932b.

92 Gouhier 1937.

I am far from them, totally wrapped up in my *Gifford Lectures*,[93] which are in their third draft—but that is good. The first two refused to go anywhere or even yield to violence, whereas this one now generates its own chapters with the spontaneity of a living being. But what a story! What won't they say! Brunschvicg and Father Mandonnet[94] will join forces in anathematizing me. By the way, do you know what Father Mandonnet calls me? "A little ladybird." Ah! If only I had the wings and the agility! I would gladly lose half of my weight to be anything like those pretty creatures.

Yesterday I went to Ann Arbor, Mich[igan], where I met the young Schwob who is here as a Rockefeller Foundation traveling-fellow. That is a nice title. We spoke of you and Mrs. Gouhier, and you should have heard it. He is a charming young man; for me it was most pleasant

---

93 On 21 August 1885, Adam (Lord) Gifford (1820–1887), a Scottish jurist with literary and philosophical interests signed a will that left eighty-thousand pounds for a lectureship in natural theology at major Scottish universities such as Edinburgh, Glasgow, Aberdeen, and St. Andrews. The Gifford Lectures, which rotated unevenly through the Scottish universities, began in 1888. Since then approximately 215 lecture series have taken place. The lectures have become the foremost intellectual event in the matter of religion. See Jaki 1986 and Pullen 2005.

94 In these lectures, delivered and originally published in French (Gilson 1932a and 1934b), Gilson argued that: (1) the Judeo-Christian revelation was a religious source of philosophical development and (2) the Latin Middle Ages is the historical demonstration *par excellence* of that development. Specifically, Gilson contends that, historically, the theology of the medievals reveals itself as the seedbed of authentically philosophical notions subsequently incorporated into religiously neutral systems of modern Western philosophers. Whereas Brunschvicg maintained that theology could only contaminate philosophy, the great historian, Father Pierre Mandonnet, O.P. (1858–1936), "every inch a Dominican," disagreed with Gilson's application of the term "philosophy" to the thought of various medieval theologians. "Father Mandonnet did not intend to deny that the Middle Ages had and been able to conceive a precise notion of philosophy. On the contrary he maintained that there had been one philosopher and one philosophy worthy of the name, St. Thomas Aquinas, O.P., and Thomistic philosophy … . So the Christian middle ages had had one philosopher, but only one." Gilson wondered whether Mandonnet's "loyalty to the Dominican Order was … carrying him outside history." See Gilson 1962, 92–94. On Gilson and Mandonnet, see Prouvost 1994a, 413–417.

to meet this Parisian in the middle of Michigan.[95] My old professor Lévy-Bruhl came through here eight days earlier[96] and I'm sorry to have missed him. As for Father Gillet, I saw him in Ottawa, always simple, good, intelligent, and kneading the Dominican dough with admirable energy.[97] He is the Foch of the Dominicans; he makes decisions with the resolute ease of a true leader. The American O.[rder of] P.[reachers] will know he has come through. For openers, he is sending 40 of them to Rome, just like that, and will install them at Saint Sabina. He is creating a general commissioner for Central America, reorganizing their studies everywhere, etc., etc. All that in a frock coat and overcoat. This is a true leader.

You know that the university does not yet want our little Cécile.[98] We will try to keep her busy this year and if that doesn't work, I will do my best to convince her to abandon a project where she is ruining

95 The reference is to Philippe Schwob (1905–). In 1929, he received his undergraduate degree in law from the University of Paris and successfully passed the *agrégation* in philosophy. Appointed from French military service, Schwob received a fellowship from the Rockefeller Foundation to study economics in the United States from 1930 to 1931. He was in Ann Arbor from October 1930 through February 1931 and then traveled to New York City, Washington, Chicago, Boston, and Montreal (Rockefeller Archive Center). He used the results of his study for his doctor's degree in law (Schwob 1934). No doubt, Schwob's study of philosophy provided the occasion for his coming to know Professor and Mme. Gouhier.

96 Lévy-Bruhl traveled widely, especially during the later part of his career. He came to the United States under the auspices of the Alliance Française and served as a brilliant ambassador for French culture. He preceded Gilson as an Exchange Professor at Harvard (1919–1920), participated in the fiftieth anniversary proceedings of Johns Hopkins University (1926), and lectured at the Academy of Arts and Letters of New York (1930).

97 Martin Stanislas Gillet, O. P. (1875–1951) was professor of philosophy in the Dominica studia; "in 1921, he occupied the chair of moral philosophy at the Institut Catholique, Paris. In 1927 he became provincial of the Dominican province of France and, in 1929, he was elected master general of the order, a post he held until 1946, when he was named titular archbishop of Nicaea by Pius XII." Gillet also belonged to an elite group of contributors to *La vie intellectuelle*. It replaced the old *Nouvelles religieuses* and tried to reach a wider audience of Catholic intellectuals. See Coffey 1967 and Shook 1984, 216–127.

98 Gilson and his wife, Thérèse, had three children: Jacqueline (1912–1991), Cécile (1913–), and Bernard (1928–).

her health for naught. I believe Jacqueline is getting on well enough, and even very well. As for Bernard, it is pointless to begin singing his praises; I would never finish.

An edition of Descartes will indeed soon be needed, and if you want to do it, I am certain it will be done well.[99] As for the *Commonplace Book*, you would do well to ask your collaborator if he knows *Johnston's, The Development of Berkeley's Philosophy*.[100] This book will draw his attention to the problem of the order to follow in the edition of the text. Fraser misarranged everything and I believe Johnston's hypothesis, also proposed by others before him, is good.[101] All your other projects seem interesting and reasonable to me; you are right that the curricula are a poison. The university is just an exam factory, but that is what it has always been since the twelfth century; the real work will be done more and more outside of the universities.

Remember me to Mrs. Moyse,[102] all my regards to your children and to their mother. From now on we are going to be able to see one another without depending on chance meetings and I believe, despite everything, that Paris will suit me. I am sending you my regards and

---

99 In 1930 Gouhier published an edition of the *Regulae*. See Descartes 1930.

100 See Johnston 1923.

101 See Berkeley 1901. The *Philosophical Commentaries*, edited by Luce (see Berkeley 1948–1957, vol. 1) definitively replaced the editions of Berkeley's two notebooks, the "Commonplace Book," offered by Fraser (1901, vol. 1) and by Johnston (Berkeley 1930). Fraser, who located the notebooks, found them bound in the wrong order and read and published them in the wrong order. According to Luce, Fraser "never understood them, and his name for them, *Commonplace Book*, is a complete misnomer" (Luce 1934, Preface to 2d ed., x–xi). Determining the structure, purpose, and date of the *Commonplace Book* is important for interpreting Berkeley's thought. Scholars "take quotations from the *Commonplace Book* to adorn their tale, much as theologians of the old school used quotations from Scripture. A serious use of the work in a study of the sources and the growth of Berkeley's system is nearly impossible while its date remains uncertain and its purpose obscure" (ibid., 178).

102 Mme. Moyse, the mother of Gouhier's first wife, was deported and died in 1944.

my best wishes for success in your projects, including the "big Comte" whose publication we will do well to see.

Your friend,

Ét. Gilson

❦

25

20 February 1931

Dear friend,

On Tuesday Vrin told me that you were already in England! I thought it was for the spring. I know that you are playing a big part over there—both for you and for that which you love. I understood that it is the meditation of several years that will take shape.[103] Rest assured that my thoughts faithfully accompany you, with a confidence all the more sure since I sense behind these lectures something like the profound I, which Bergson discusses at the end of the *Essay*, ready to realize itself in a free act....[104]

---

103 Gilson delivered his Gifford Lectures on "The Spirit of Medieval Philosophy" in four five-lecture series at the University of Aberdeen, Scotland on 16–20 February and 29 May–2 June of 1931, and on 8–12 February and 30 May–3 June of 1932. Like many others, Chenu considered the lectures to be "le plus bel ouvrage de Gilson" (Chenu 1980, 45). During his third year as a student at Seton Hall University, *The Spirit of Medieval Philosophy* provided Edward Synan his first indirect contact with Gilson. Synan would go on to become one of Gilson's students and, eventually, the President of the Pontifical Institute of Mediaeval Studies. See Synan 1991, 51–52. During Gilson's absence in 1932 Gouhier substituted for him and presented a series of lectures at the Sorbonne on Thomistic epistemology. See Gouhier 1932a.

104 See Bergson 1959. To the "superficial I" which looses itself in the dispersed diversity of its states, Henri Bergson (1859–1941) opposed the "profound I" which endures and creates.

Here we live in an awful tragedy, with fears that one cannot express.[105]

With our affection,

Henri Gouhier

26

St Michael's College
Toronto 5.
21 November 1931

My dear friend,

Thank you for your letters, for the trouble you have taken for my book[106] and, above all, for your faithful friendship. I was not in a hurry to see my *Gifford Lectures* published; they are so schematic that I do not like them very much. Every lecture should be a book. I want to hope with you, however, that they will do some good. I also believe that it is time to build something, for we are in a void; what we need is constructive teaching. Before being able to give it, it is necessary to grasp the essence of principles, for it is the possession of fundamental truths which gives the mind its liberty.[107] I will get there only after the last of

---

105 The reference is to the long and painful illness of Gouhier's father who died in July 1931.

106 Although Gilson makes no formal mention of it, Gouhier may have helped Gilson prepare his book, *Etudes sur le rôle de la pensée médiévale* (Gilson 1930a) that consisted of a reprinting of previously published book chapters, articles, and lectures.

107 Gilson wanted to furnish Catholic philosophers and intellectuals with a positive means by which to combat the errors of modernism. In providing the context for one of Gilson's letters to Maritain during this same time frame, Gouhier wrote that Gilson "est à la fois intransigeant sur les principes en ces questions mais peu disposé à jouer le rôle de procureur. Le Roy est sans aucun doute dans l'erreur mais une fois l'erreur dénoncée, les mises à l'*Index*, les condamnations trop voyantes sont vaines. Ce qui est important, ce n'est pas de critiquer Édouard Le Roy (see note 18 above) mais de dire ce qu'il faut penser à la place de ses erreurs. Si l'on rejette Le Roy en invoquant l'argument d'autorité, que diront les jeunes philosophes catholiques? Ce ne sont pas les condamna-

my *Gifford Lectures*. They open the doors; then one only has to enter. Right now, I am at grips with epistemology and ethics;[108] I would have made more progress had I not been overwhelmed with correspondence about affairs of the Collège de France,[109] but soon I will be able to make up for the lost time.

Things turned out much better than I expected and I believe from now on everything will go smoothly. L. Rougier, no doubt, will be a candidate, if he is not one already. That is why, among other reasons, I prefer not to reply to his article. Despite my modicum of optimism in temporal matters, I cannot believe that between the plagiarist and the plagiarized, they will select the plagiarist.[110] Besides, the example

---

tions qui importent mais les constructions" (Prouvost 1991, 71–72n.3). In June 1931, Le Roy's works were placed on the *Index*.

Murphy thought that "if the *mystery* of faith had not already been swept under the carpet for decades by an excessively rationalist Thomism, men like Loisy [and presumably Le Roy] would not have denied the use of reason within theology." Gilson was "so determined to make faith and mystery the hinge on which reason turns ... not because he rejected reason or philosophy, but because he felt that something was being forgotten when fideism was condemned during the modernist crisis, namely, the mystery of faith" (Murphy 2004, 3).

108 The second series of ten lectures focused on knowledge and morality. See Étienne Gilson 1937a. In his lectures, Gilson indicated several deficiencies in Malebranche's philosophy and cited Malebranche's thought as an example of a Christian philosophy gone awry: "A philosophy may invoke a revelation and be false, but if false it is not on account of the revelation, but because it is bad philosophy; the errors of Malebranche, deeply and genuinely Christian as he was, would be a sufficiently good example" (ibid., 406).

109 The final election of Gilson to the Collège de France as Professor of Medieval Philosophy took place on 17 January 1932. Due to a preliminary election held in the fall of 1931, Gilson knew that he would be appointed. "From 1932 to 1951 Paris was Gilson's focus and the Collège de France the seat of his intellectual activity" (Shook 1984, 208).

110 Louis Auguste Rougier (1889–1982), an academic who published more than forty works on the history of religion, philosophy, epistemology, linguistics, economy, and constitutional law, was a militant atheist who proposed a return to the comfortable system of ancient pagan mythology. Philosophically, Rougier was a logical empiricist. Although a full biography of Rougier is needed, he has the reputation of being not only a right-wing extremist but also a collaborator and anti-Semite. The latter charge is difficult to reconcile with the fact that two of Rougier's three wives were Jewish. See Marion 2004a.

of Malebranche is there to demonstrate the vanity of controversies.[111] Finally, the book you had the kindness to review is completely based on what it criticizes me for not having seen.[112] That can pass for a response, I hope, in the eyes of those interested in these questions. As for the others, that hardly matters either for them or for me.

The missing reference to *Sierp* refers to an additional note that I had written on the back of my last page which the printer did not see. It is not of great importance and I will add the text in the next volume.[113]

Rougier's lengthy (856 page) refutation of scholasticism (Rougier 1925) was reviewed by Gilson (1926b), Loisy (1925), and Guignebert (1927). Rougier borrowed so heavily from Gilson's writings that Fr. Gabriel Théry, O. P., one of the founders of the *Bulletin thomiste*, publicly reprimanded him. See Théry 1925 and Descoqs 1927.

Shook described Rougier as "a strange character, a sensationalist," "a man of great ambition and incredible devices." In 1921, a year after he published his doctoral theses as *La philosophie géometrique de Poincaré*, Rougier asked Gilson to help him become his successor in Strasbourg. Gilson did nothing. Later, Rougier became a possible candidate for the Collège de France, but his name did not stand. Like most successful professors, Gilson aspired to a chair in the Collège, not so much because of its prestige or the increased opportunities for personal research, but because a chair would accommodate his regular absences in Canada at the Pontifical Institute of Mediaeval Studies. Also, Gilson thought that he would have a better chance of securing a full chair in medieval philosophy at the Collège than at the Sorbonne where he was *professeur sans chaire*. See Shook 1984, 101–102, 104, 205–207, 348, and, on Théry, Gilson 1959.

111 The history of Malebranche's works is inseparable from the polemics they generated with individuals such as Simon Foucher, Dom Robert Desgabets, Louis de la Ville, François Lamy, Pierre-Sylvain Régis, and G.W. von Leibniz. Malebranche's furious dispute with Antoine Arnauld was one of the harshest and most acute in the history of philosophy. See Malebranche 1980, xiv–xx; Alquié 1977, 190–91.

112 See Louis Rougier 1931b. After examining and disagreeing with the main points of Gilson's interpretation of St. Thomas, Rougier concluded that "[l]a méthode de sympathie, qui se confond pour M. Gilson [and P. Théry] avec sa foi chrétienne, ne lui permet pas d'avouer que la philosophie de Thomas d'Aquin soit une philosophie incohérente, pas même que ce soit une philosophie éclectique" (ibid., 370–371). Rougier even found Gilson's humor to be "sinister" (ibid., 365).

113 Gilson 1932a, 2ed., 8

I hope the Sorbonne does not disappoint you too much and I am sure the students will be happy to have you. We will talk about this soon after my arrival. I return on December 21st. In the meantime, thank you again.

Your friend,

Ét. Gilson

É. Gilson and Jacques Thibaudeau, Montreal, 1927

27

L'Escale
La Panne
Friday, 3 August 1934

Dear friend,

An exceptional carelessness deprived me of the *Le Temps* last night. Consequently, it is today, arriving at La Panne, that I learned of your nomination.[114] One dares not congratulate you. What our friend Gabriel Marcel calls "the category of the wholly natural" comes fully into play. May this at least be an opportunity for your friends to express their affection for you and, for you to realize once more how much your brilliance is real.

The faithful servant of the Saints—Descartes playing the role of a blessed layman—gives importance to a nomination where the timpanist-soloist of the Opera fortunately drowns out the voice of the poet Henriette Charasson.[115] When we would read the lists of the newly honored, we would often say before the name of one notoriously mediocre, "And Gilson is not here!" There was disorder in that; from now on there will be a little less of the irrational in the world.

In the midst of all the testimonies of good will that you receive, allow me to call to mind all that your goodness and your work have brought me for twelve years already.

We share in the joy of your entire family,

---

114 The reference is to Gilson's nomination for the *Legion d'Honneur* which also was announced on the front page of the 5 August 1934 edition of *Le Temps*. Gilson received other honors in 1934: Docteur Honoris Causa de l'Université catholique de Milan and Associé étranger de la Pontifica Accademia Romana di S. Tommaso d'Aquino.

115 Henriette Charasson (1884–1972) was a French Christian poet, some of whose works were set to music. A member of the Catholic intelligentsia involved with L'Action Française, Charasson has been described as a Catholic of strong convictions, "très imprégnés d'un maurrassisme littéraire ou poétique" (Prévotat 1997, 178). In attempting a feeble joke, Gouhier, who had a passionate interest in the theater from the outset of his academic career, may be alluding to one of Charasson's works during this period (see Charasson 1934a–f). Gilson who devoted numerous books to individuals, many of whom were saints, is the "faithful servant of the Saints."

Henri Gouhier

I don't think that you were very upset by *Les âges de l'intelligence.*[116]

28

31 August 1934

Dear friend,

I had put aside your exquisite letter of congratulations so I could thank you for it at my leisure; then, I sent out card after card, and now you are leaving without our having seen one another.[117] Have a good trip to Prague; the city will console you with philosophers, I hope. I would really like you to find the time to write either a letter or articles on the problem of the private schools.[118] We need to pool our ideas and test

116 Brunschvicg 1934.

117 In March 1935 Gilson became a *Chevalier de la Légion d'Honneur.*

118 Gilson denounced the lack of qualified personnel to teach in private schools and the low level of those schools compared to state schools. See Gilson 1934d. A letter from the President of the Catholic Union of Reims published on 4 August 1934 reproached Gilson for underestimating the vision of the directors of private schools, the capacity of the instructors, and intelligence of the parents of students. Gilson replied: "Il s'agit de l'école chrétienne comme élément intégrant de l'ordre catholique français; or il y a bien des manières pour cet élément de ne pas se constituer . . . . La première est de laisser les choses dans l'état où elles sont; j'espère que personne n'y songe . . . ." (Prouvost 1991, 120). In his articles that appeared in *Sept* during 1934 and 1935 Gilson repeatedly addressed the topic of Catholic education and private schooling. See Gilson 1934a and Edie 1959, 35–38. The quality of education in France also concerned Gouhier. See, for example, Gouhier 1931b; 1933b; 1940; 1946, 1966. Gilson believed that "the mark of a good school was it being a happy school" (Gilson 1946). His own teaching exemplified this principle. A journalist characterized one of Gilson's lectures in 1946 at the Collège de France as follows: "J'ai rarement ri de si bon cœur, et d'un si franc éclat, qu'au cours de 'très haute graisse' de M. Étienne Gilson sur la connaissance métaphysique selon Duns Scot.... Gilson s'amuse parmi ses textes comme s'il plaidait contre son voisin de vigne à Vermenton (Yonne). Il joue à nous effrayer. Il se présente lui-même comme un téméraire qui avance plus qu'il ne peut prouver, qui commente son propre commentaire, qui fait des folies. Il va se retrouver le nez par terre. Il nous joue avec l'accent une farce paysanne..." (Guth 1946).

them against each other. Moreover, I have the impression that we are all pursuing Platonic dialogues in Pompeii, on the eve of the eruption.

Thank you for the *Rivista* and your excellent article.[119]

As for the named Teicherb (I believe it is a *female*), she must be an elegant woman. I must have insulted her without wanting to do so. Alas! I didn't know then what the sources were for the conclusion of the *De anima*, and I was dumb enough to say it....She doesn't know either, but today I do know (*Epistola de anima* = Alcher de Clairvaux),[120] and I am no more proud on account of it. It is incredible how history can make a fool of us; one should not allow her to do so. It is true that philosophy.... You know I am fond of Brunschvicg, who is goodness itself, and I don't take comfort in seeing what ideas can do to a man. As Delbos said to me about 1910 or 1912, when I was discussing philosophy with him: "Above all, Gilson, love your wife and your children."[121] Let me add to that two or three friends, of which you are one, and there is no one ahead of you.

Yours,

Étienne Gilson

29

The Institute of Mediaeval Studies
St Michael's College
University of Toronto
Toronto 5.
6 October 1934

My dear friend,

Your letter caught up with me in Toronto and brings with it a bit of French air. Prague must have been what all philosophical congresses

119 Gouhier 1934a.

120 Gilson made appropriate changes in his history of philosophy in the Middle Ages; see Gilson 1922, 2nd ed., 302–303.

121 Gilson held Professor Delbos in great esteem and considered him as "l'un des maîtres que j'ai plus aimé" (Gilson 1934a, 46).

are like; no disillusion is possible on that score.[122] Rougier has triumphed, as was inevitable; Brunschvicg has a terrible fear of him, but he is especially attached to him by the strongest of ties: Rougier thinks "correctly" and his deep hatreds, of electoral appeal, are exactly in synch with what Brunschvicg deeply loathes.[123] What I regret not having seen is Nuremberg[124]; my consolation is that an "*alter ego*" visited it. I believe what happened there had an importance, a planetary "significance" at any rate. A pure essence has been unveiled, after having been sought for so long, and it is finally admitted in public. Since the birth of Jesus Christ, nothing more important could happen than the rejection of Jesus Christ. That is what has been done. What surprises me is that our French adversaries of Hitler do not see that they are working for him in hoping to have man save man from slavery. They are the shameful

---

122 On 7 September 1934, Gouhier delivered a paper in Prague on "Positivisme et revolution"; see Gouhier 1936.

123 Rougier (Rougier 1936; see Marion 2004b) and Brunschvicg (Brunschvicg 1936) also delivered papers at the Philosophical Congress in Prague. Gilson may be referring to an occurrence at the Congress—perhaps to the reception that Rougier's paper received. Gilson (see notes 110 and 125), and perhaps Gouhier, disliked Rougier and feared any success that he might have. Brunschvicg's "fear" had a number of possible roots. Brunschvicg, totally unreceptive to the logical positivism that Rougier advocated would not like to have seen Rougier in an influential position in France. In 1930, when Professor Edmond Goblot (1858-1935) retired from the Sorbonne, Rougier considered himself the natural successor. Brunschvicg worked behind the scenes to ensure that Jean Wahl was chosen instead. Later, in a nasty polemical article, the resentful Rougier exposed *lacunae* in Brunschvicg's scholarship and accused him of falsification. Rougier is said to have privately threatened to expose more scandalous material and publish a book on the matter These threats, towards a deeply admirable man later hounded by the Nazis during the war did much damage to Rougier's reputation (Marion 2004a, 15). Rougier's "thinking correctly" refers to the paper he delivered at the Congress that vigorously defended democracy and criticized Hitler's Germany. As a Jew and a Republican, Brunschvicg undoubtedly despised Nazism. Gilson's comment on Rougier's "deep hatreds, of electoral appeal," refers to the style of Rougier's writings which had to strike a scholar of Gilson's stature as shallow and bombastic but quite "electoral."

124 See Gouhier 1934b.

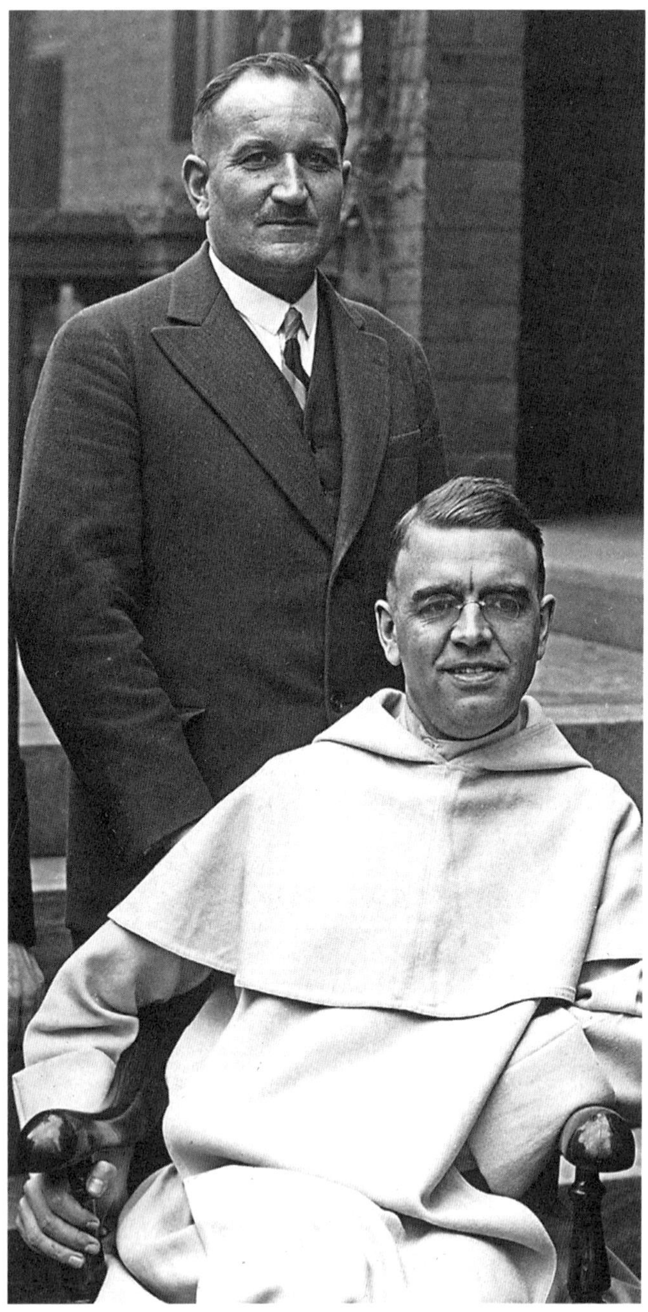

É. Gilson and M.-D. Chenu, Toronto, 1930

Hitlerians. But, most of all, if they don't believe that Hitler is grand—in his horror—they really are dangerous imbeciles.[125]

I received a letter concerning Philippe Devaux from the Rector of Liège. I already had ardently supported De Corte,[126] without knowing

125 During the discussion following Rougier's paper, Mr. Pfeiffer disagreed with Rougier's point that the divine origin of public power—which he took to be any "theocratic" system—is necessarily anti-democratic. According to Catholic moral doctrine, Pfeiffer pointed out, "Dieu, en créant l'homme de par sa nature comme un être social, donne à la nature humaine, entre autres principes de sociabilité, aussi ce principe que dans chaque communauté d'hommes il faut un certain ordre, donc une certaine direction, donc aussi un facteur dirigeant. Ce facteur dirigeant a la tâche de diriger la communauté vers le bien commun, vers le bien-être organisé et solidaire de chacun des membres de la dite communauté. Ce bien commun est aussi la condition de la légitimité morale de chaque pouvoir public. Ce facteur dirigeant, donc le détenteur du pouvoir public, peut selon la morale catholique être aussi bien le peuple tout entier, la totalité des habitants, qu'un groupe plus restreint, ou aussi une seule personne" (Rougier 1936, 600). For Gilson, the paper by Rougier, an atheist, served as an excellent example of an academic playing into Hitler's hands. Years later, in his "beautiful, frightening, penetrating prose-poem" (Shook 1984, 285), Gilson provided a more adequate treatment of this issue, i.e., of modern man losing reason and God and the ensuing futile attempt of man trying to save himself by establishing man as his own master, free to set up ideologies and values. See Gilson 1949.

126 The reference is to Henri Gouhier's old friends, Marcel De Corte (1905–1994) and Philippe Devaux (1902–1979). Both men had long and distinguished careers as professors at the University of Liège. See Gochet 1985 and De Corte 1975. Gilson cited and praised De Corte's work. See, for example, Gilson's preface to De Corte's *thèse d'agrégation de l'enseignement supérieur* (De Corte 1934) and his characterization of De Corte's treatment of Plotinus as "probably the deepest existing introduction to the method and spirit of the doctrine of Plotinus" (Gilson 1941, 57 n.10).

De Corte and Devaux very likely attended Gilson's lectures and came to know him when he was an exchange professor at the Université libre de Bruxelles in December 1923. The six lectures on "Descartes and Scholastic Metaphysics" that Gilson gave in Brussels, and later repeated in London, were incorporated into his *Études sur le rôle de la pensée médiévale* (Gilson 1930a, 141–255). De Corte and Devaux also may have met with Gilson and Gouhier in Paris. De Corte was a student at the École Normale Supérieure in 1930. Devaux studied in Paris in 1927 and 1928, and remained a research fellow until 1935. Both he and Gilson were at Harvard in 1929.

there was another candidate just as interesting. So, by return mail I am replying by saying all the good I think of Philippe Devaux and suggesting—which seems to me to be simple common sense—that only the nature of the tasks to be fulfilled can determine how to make the choice here. Then I say why each candidate seems to me to be competent, and I leave it to them to decide what kind of teaching they desire at present in their university: history and a systematic treatment of classical philosophy (Mr. de Corte), introduction to contemporary philosophy (Ph. Devaux). Both areas are necessary. The two candidates are about equal (one more set, the other more supple): based on their current organization and needs, it is for the university to say which of the two they wish to hire. Thank you for having informed me about the situation. You made it easier for me to be fair.

My wife and Bernard are again near Montreal, staying with friends where I myself had a marvelous week of fishing (ah! what beautiful catches in that Saint Lawrence) and hunting.[127] Have you ever spent three hours alone in a blind, in the middle of a stream four kilometers wide, clothed in rubber gear, seated *in* the water, in the company of fifteen wooden ducks, while two thousand meaty ducks are above you, out of range, with not one of them deigning to descend and offer itself up for a holocaust? Such is the "black duck," the shrewdest of all, the type that I had the bad luck to fall in with for five days. At least several waterfowl and gallinule testified to the fact that the bespectacled old man that I have become is still the "dead shot" that I was in my youth. God was I dirty going back! But I had the pleasure of having Father

---

Gilson became an Associate Member of the Royal Academy of Belgium in 1957. When Gilson went to Liège in November 1969 to receive an honorary degree he made the comment, "I have too many ex-pupils at Liège not to accept their invitation" (Shook 1984, 376).

127 In October of 1933, after Gilson, Thérèse, and their son, Bernard, spent a week at the Thibaudeau's summer home, they decided to return the following year. During the fall of 1934 the Thibaudeaus also hosted Jacques Maritain. See Michel 2002, 39. Gilson first met the Thibaudeaus in 1926. Both Alfred Thibaudeau and his wife, Eva, had fathers who had been Canadian senators. In addition to a home in Westmont in Montréal, the Thibaudeaus owned property, *La Pointe*, in Beauharnois on Lake St. Francis. Gilson came to know both places well. See Shook 1984, 213–214, 165, 177, 193, 213.

Chenu[128] eat my wild game—one of his peculiarities is never knowing what he is eating. Since it was a Friday, it couldn't get any better.

And *Sept?*[129] It is very far away. And France is too. Like you, I wish she would become another Spain; but, alas! we are an Empire—the second in the world—and our body is too large to allow us to become small by a natural regressive evolution. What must happen first is that they amputate, or we collapse: between largeness and smallness, disaster is for us an inevitable stage, if the time for being small has really come.

When you see our daughters tell them that Jacqueline's journal has arrived and interested me enormously. Also, tell Cécile to take her time and not worry about her exams. Tell both of them my health is good,

128 In 1930, Père Marie-Dominique Chenu (1895–1990), with support from Gilson and Father Théry, established the Institut Saint Thomas d'Aquin in Ottawa in 1930. It subsequently moved to the University of Montréal when the Dominicans became responsible for teaching philosophy there. It later became known as the Institut d'Études Médiévales. See Shook 1984, 193–194. Chenu became the regent of the Dominicum Studium at Saulchoir in 1932. A theologian with a strong contemplative bent who showed how St. Thomas invented the idea of theology, Chenu concentrated on an ascetic and spiritual reading of St. Thomas that vindicated human reason by arriving at a "perfect synthesis between the mysticism of the believer and the science of the theologian." Gilson, a layman, historian, and philosopher, covered much the same ground but from a different perspective. What Chenu saw from above as a theologian, Gilson saw from below as a philosopher. See Murphy 2004, 101, 128, 173–178, 269. Early in 1942, Chenu's booklet on the theological method of the École du Saulchoir was placed on the *Index*. Despite Gilson's many interventions with church authorities in Rome, this prevented Chenu from teaching. For Gilson's letters of consolation and advice, Chenu's replies, and a brief discussion of the themes dear to Gilson which appeared in Chenu's booklet, see Murphy 2005, 49–57. In his letter of 4 January 1947 to Pegis, Gilson remarked: "[Chenu] is just in the situation where Maritain and I would be, were we priests. God seems to be saving a few laymen to very definite purposes. Let this be off the record" (Shook 1984, 276 and 247–249, 258–259, 275).

129 In 1934, Gilson published a policy statement that he prepared for *Sept*, a popular journal of Catholic action founded by a Dominican of Juvisy, Marie-Vincent Bernadot. See Hourdin 1967. Its objective was to bring decision and unity into the ranks of French Catholics and to induce the French Republic to abandon its present educational policy of secularization. Gilson's policy statement served as the background for his collected articles on education that appeared in *Sept*. See Gilson 1934a.

but I would like to have one year of life as a savage with a fishing pole and a rifle in a wooden cabin. My wife and Bernard arrive in Toronto on Monday.

Warm regards to you three and the young ones,

Étienne Gilson

É. Gilson with the muskellunge he caught at La Point in Beaucharnois on Lake St. Francis, Quebec. For years, the mounted fish hung in Gilson's study at Vermenton.

30

4 July 1935

My dear friend,

I am in an awful rush getting ready to set sail with the Cook Agency, but I want to say goodbye to you and to yours before leaving. I am leaving behind no better friend than you, and how many as good? We embark tomorrow, Friday, but leave today for Le Havre. I think we will be happy to return to Paris in six months. I am taking the three volumes of Marie Noël[130] with me plus a few additional copies to distribute in America. I intend to lecture on her work several times, particularly in

130 The reference is to Marie Noël (Marie Rouget) (1883–1967) who had three volumes of poetry published in 1933. See Noël 1933a, b, c. Noël was recognized as one of the foremost poets of her time. She combined a profound religious sensibility with an intense feeling for the rustic beauty of her native Burgundy. Born in Auxerre, she lived there for the rest of her life publishing collections of poems at regular intervals. Her *Notes intimes* (Noël 1933d) contain moving meditations on her spiritual life in its everyday context. See Gouhier 1970. Gouhier's study of this poet is considered "indispensable for understanding Noël whose religious experience is inseparable from her work" (Sutton 1980 commenting on Gouhier 1971).

Gouhier explained why Noël's religious experience interested a philosopher: "*Le combat de Marie Noël,* ces mots désignent une expérience religieuse originale qui, en notre XXe siècle, représente un chapitre important de ce qu'un fidèle ami du poète, Henri Bremond, appelait l'Histoire littéraire du Sentiment religieux en France.

Expérience originale, donc vécue par une personnalité hors-série, de sorte qu'aucune explication n'est possible par réduction à un modèle connu. Comme 'le cas Péguy' comme 'le cas Bergson' dans une autre perspective, 'le cas Marie Noël' doit être pensé dans sa singularité radicale.

Expérience religieuse originale, entendons: elle est bien liée à une religion déterminée; il faut la voir là où elle est, dans l'univers théologique, mystique, liturgique, de l'Eglise catholique; mais son originalité ne tient pas à la vitalité exceptionnelle d'une foi dont la profondeur, l'intensité, la générosité animeraient d'un esprit nouveau les schèmes de la piété commune, plus ou moins figés en concepts et en formules dans la conscience du chrétien moyen. Dans 'le cas Marie Noël,' l'expérience vécue crée son propre schème en se pensant elle-même.

Car Marie Noël a pensé sa relation à Dieu .... Une extrême émotivité et une obstinée rigueur intellectuelle se joignent dans cette âme où l'expérience religieuse la plus pathétique inclut l'exigence d'un discours cohérent" (Gouhier 1971, 7–8).

the Alliances Françaises.[131] I know Auxerre well,[132] but by no means the author whom I never dared to go see. You will help me greatly if you can provide me some biographical information. My address until September 15th will be Ladeira da Gloria, No. 108, Rio de Janeiro, Brazil. Afterwards, and up to December, St Michael's College, Toronto (5), Ontario, Canada.[133]

If I had Marie Noël's address, I would have sent her a copy of my Saint Bernard. You might ask our friend Vrin to do it for me if you think it is a good idea.[134]

---

131 In November 1934, Gilson was designated *Membre du Conseil Supérieur de la Recherche Scientifique* (section eight: philosophical and social sciences). "This meant that he was to stand ready to participate in the Service des Œuvres Françaises à l'Etranger at the nod of several ministries, including National Education, Public Instruction, and External Affairs. Thus in early 1935 Gilson found himself committed to three special series of lectures to the Institut Français de Vienne, 13 to 17 May; to the Faculté Catholique de Salzbourg, 17 to 21 May; and, through the Brazilian embassy, to the planned Faculté des Lettres of the university in Rio de Janiero, late July to 19 September .... The foreign services were looking for lecturers who could draw a crowd, a bill Gilson obviously filled" (Shook 1984, 223–225).

132 Gilson had an extraordinary romantic attachment to Burgundy, especially to Auxerre the home of his mother's parents. See Shook 1984, 3, 397.

133 In 1935, Gilson agreed to deliver, in collaboration with George Brett, Dean of the University of Toronto's School of Graduate Studies, several lectures on Cartesian thought. Gilson presented four lectures on 5, 12, 19, and 20 November 1935 at University College in the University of Toronto. See Shook 1984, 226.

134 Gilson's work on Saint Bernard (Gilson 1934c) was based on his lectures given in 1933 at the Collège de France and at the University College of Wales (Aberystwith). Many years later, Thomas Merton (1915–1968) dedicated his own study of Saint Bernard to Gilson. See Merton 1954. In 1951, when Gilson's wife died, his son became ill, and Paris grew cold toward him, Merton recounted to Gilson a greater debt: "... I want at last to do what I should have done long ago-write you a line to assure you of my recognition of a spiritual debt to you which I too sketchily indicated in the pages of *The Seven Story Mountain* [Merton 1948, 189–194], and in a rather badly constructed section of the book at that. To you and to Jacques Maritain, among others, I owe the Catholic faith. That is to say I owe my life. This is no small debt. Can you feel as abandoned as you do when you are handing out to other people as great a gift as is the Kingdom of Heaven? But indeed it is the privilege of those who

Everything is ready for the 21 days at sea. There are, alas, one or two academics on the boat and, it is strange, the further I go the less I can bear them. This profession seems to me to be just as fatal to a man as to a woman. I regret leaving in full-blown controversy with the A. F.[135] They are childishly impudent types who treat their audience, as it should be treated, as idiots. The heart of the matter, which I would have insisted on had I stayed, seems to me to be their relationship with the Duc de Guise. The A.F. has not at all reacted to my rather clear allusion. On the other hand, now I receive free delivery of the *Royal Mail*. That is quite an interesting sign.[136]

---

bear such spiritual fruit to feel abandoned and miserable and alone, for poverty of spirit is the patrimony of the children of God in this world, and their pledge of glory in the world to come: 'for theirs is the Kingdom of Heaven'" (Shook 1984, 309).

135 Action Française (A. F.), the name of a political league and also its journal, "attempted during the first 4 decades of the 20th century to reestablish the monarchy in France .... Charles Maurras was the unquestioned head and the theorist of the movement .... Its influence was considerable, especially among Catholics. Although its principal directors were atheists, they believed that if French society was to prosper as it had in the past, it must return to both the political form and the religious practice of earlier times. The Church quickly became disturbed by the organization's influence over a section of the French clergy and faithful .... Because of the complaints of French bishops, the Holy Office prepared a prohibition of seven books by Maurras, and the periodical, but not the newspaper of the movement (Jan. 26, 1914). However, A. F.'s combat against anticlerical republicans and its struggle for a conservative type of Catholicism then in favor at the Vatican produced interventions in its favor at Rome. As a result, Pius X (1903–14) suspended publication of the decree. Benedict XV (1914–22) adopted the same attitude because of World War I. Pius XI (1922–39) received new complaints. ... A decree of the Holy Office (Dec. 29, 1926) published the text of the 1914 condemnation, and added to it, with the ratification of Pius XI, the newspaper *L'Action française*. ... The pontificate of Pius XII (1939–58) opened new perspectives. After long negotiations, the directive committee of A. F. sent a letter to the Pope expressing their sincerest sorrow for anything in their polemics and controversies that had been injurious and even unjust. The Holy See triumphed in the end, for Catholic youths ceased joining the movement." See Dansette 1967.

136 In December 1934, the Duke of Guise, pretender to the French throne, delegated the direction of royalist propaganda to his only son and heir, Henri, Comte de Paris. A new monthly, and eventually weekly, *Courrier Royal*, served as the organ

Theories aside, all this seems pretty pointless to me. The right-wingers hate one another while the leftists come together and unite. And we are certainly headed for a staggering blow. The deficit of some 12 billion will not be found under the hoof of the first horse that comes along; something will have to give for this to be set aright. In fact, I just snatched from the hands of a proletarian, a bourgeois who took off as fast as he could, pummeled by swings and hooks, pitifully screaming: "Defend me, defend me!" The proletarian was tough and I tried to appease him—this did not work because it was too late; but that scared

É. Gilson at Cluny, 1949 (A. Maurer)

---

of the House of France. The formal disassociation of the Duke of Guise from A.F. in November 1937 made its defeat more evident. See Weber 1962, 403–410.

Gilson emphasized that the Church respects the right of a people to choose the mode of government which seems best to them, be it a republican regime or

molly-coddle sniveling under the blows of that colossus gave me a somber idea of my "class." Is this an omen? We will have to see and perhaps there will be time for that in January.

Farewell, dear friend.

Yours sincerely,

Étienne Gilson

É. Gilson and his wife Thérèse at Cluny, 1949 (A.Maurer)

---

monarchy (Gilson 1935c). But Gilson wished to initiate the conversion of politics by conversion to a spiritual order. Christians have to *create* their own social order through their institutions. Gilson's articles for *Sept* in 1935 reflected the onset of his disillusion. Gilson had intended the journal to unite French Catholics, a prospect that began to seem less and less attainable. Malaise crept into Gilson's articles, most noticeably in Gilson 1935d, e, and f. "As Gilson grew less hopeful of mending rifts among French Catholics, he became more convinced that the church could not be committed to any particular party. This point runs through his last articles in *Sept* [Gilson 1935g, h, i]" (Shook 1984, 218 and Coutrot 1961). On 27 August 1937, by the order of Fr. Gillet, *Sept* ceased publication because of offending dominant Catholic opinion of the day and declaring that Franco should be condemned for waging a civil war in Spain. See Leprieur 1989, 16.

31

Randolph Hall
Cambridge, Mass.
U.S.A.
30 October 1936

My dear friend,

I am trying finally to reply to you, on a desk filled with a mess of letters which are all waiting for me to do the same for them, but most of which will remain in eternal oblivion. The idea of spending a delightful summer in Paris is just like you in every way so it must be good. In any case, since it will be worth a collection of Cartesian essays for us, which I am rejoicing over already, all your friends can only approve.[137]

H. Gouhier and Ferdinand Alquié at the Conference on Descartes, Royaumont Cultural Center, 1957

137 See Gouhier 1937, a "small, beautifully written collection of essays [that] may well prove to be the most influential work of the rich 1930s .... As a living, breathing portrait of Descartes, the book still stands alone" (Sebba 1964, 37no.169).

Thank you for your brief note. Labergerie[138] wanted one and I prefer that you do it. As for the Romanet project,[139] I declined the invitation, for the simple reason that, had I accepted all proposals of this kind, I would have already written four histories of medieval philosophy. I have no desire to recount what I know, and I am incapable of recounting what I do not know. The minor sin of my youth was doing everything that I could do; I am not going to do that any more these days. If you need someone for English philosophy, it seems to me you would find Keeling satisfactory.[140] He has written good things on Descartes, and

138 Gilson is referring to a request from a publishing house. See Maritain 1935.

139 The reference may be to a proposal from Louis Auguste Romanet (1880—1964), who came to Canada from France in 1903 as an employee of the fur trading company Revillon Frères. In 1916, Romanet joined the Hudson Bay Company and became a successful oil company inspector and an agent. Romanet also was interested in publishing; at one time, he operated a small used bookstore in Edmonton. A meeting with Lowell Thomas in Edmonton resulted in that author taking over the manuscripts on Romanet's autobiography and publishing them. See Thomas 1932. Like Gilson, Romanet fought in the Battle of Verdun. Romanet is buried in the Field of Honour, Edmonton Cemetery. See Pomohac 2004.

140 Stanley Victor Keeling (1894–1979), educated at Trinity College Cambridge (BA), University College Cambridge (BA), University College London (MA), and the Universities of Toulouse and Montpellier (*Doctorat ès Lettres*), taught at University College London. Upon his retirement in 1954, he went to live in Paris where he died.

Keeling never had the good fortune of hearing Gilson's lectures. Keeling considered the elucidation of Cartesianism in the philosophical milieu in which it developed to be "the special and magnificent contribution of that prince among Cartesian scholars, Professor Étienne Gilson of the Sorbonne" (Preface, Keeling 1934a). Gilson's reference to Keeling's writings on Descartes included two articles that appeared at the time of this letter. See Keeling 1934b and 1936.

Gilson wrote and thanked Keeling for his "exceedingly kind and accurate" review of *Études sur le rôle de la pensée médiévale* (Keeling 1933). Glad that Keeling saw the impossibility of Descartes's position of proving the real distinction of mind and body through the fact of sensation, Gilson added: "[B]y the way, it is because his [Descartes's] position was impossible that we are today enjoying the reading of other equally beautiful and impossible metaphysical constructions such as Malebranche's occasionalism, Spinoza's parallelism,

is always around in Paris somewhere. He is intelligent and, I believe, would agree to do it. The problem is finding out where Keeling is. He was at the University of London, but seems to have given up the joys of teaching. Moreover, he knows French.

Your question, how the Christian philosopher can have a dialogue with the non-Christian philosopher, is well beyond my own concerns and my capabilities.[141] I am not there yet. I am only at the point of asking myself how a philosopher today can have a dialogue with any other philosopher? Having observed over several years that such dialogues had become impossible and no longer exist, I stopped going to the Philosophical Society. But it is the same everywhere.[142] Today, one

---

Leibniz's pre-established harmony. Even error is not without metaphysical fecundity." See 7 January 1933 letter from Étienne Gilson to Keeling, Ms. Add 236, S. V. Keeling Papers.

141 As early as 1924, Gilson applied the notion of "Christian philosophy" to the philosophy of St. Bonaventure and, in 1929, used it to describe the thought of St. Augustine. In 1933 at Juivsy, two years after Gilson's famous debate with Émile Bréhier on the notion of Christian philosophy, some of the best French philosophers mounted an attack on the notion as a contradiction in terms and an illegitimate mixing of philosophy and theology. For a brief, but penetrating account of Gilson's understanding of Christian philosophy, to include references to key works on this notion, see Maurer's "Introduction" to Gilson 1993, ix–xxv. Gouhier, who contributed to the debate on Christian philosophy did not agree completely with either Gilson (Gouhier 1933–34) or Bréhier: "Pour revenir à Bréhier, ce dernier considérait que la science et la foi ne pouvaient aller de pair dans l'œuvre philosophique; pourtant le cas de Malebranche que j'ai personnellement étudié, posait une question insoluble pour Bréhier, car chez Malebranche l'intention religieuse et l'approche scientifique sont inséparables" (Gouhier 1988, 16).

142 Gilson's comments about the impossibility of dialogue between philosophers did not hold true of his relationship with Gouhier. Despite philosophical and methodological differences between the two, they enjoyed a fruitful and intimate dialogue of more than fifty years. Shook maintained that "Gouhier's attitudes both reflected and influenced Gilson's own" and cited two of Gouhier's works (*La philosophie et son histoire* and *L'histoire et sa philosophie*) as "vital to an understanding of Gilson" (Shook 1984, 171, 108; see also Letter 20). Bernard d'Espagnat agreed with Shook: "[S]on [Gouhier's] premier maître, Étienne Gilson, lequel, en dépit—ou à cause!—des différences de style de leurs recherches, fut toujours pour lui l'appui solide par excellence et l'homme, peut-être, avec qui il pratiqua avec le plus d'entrain l'échange d'idées"

of the Professors of Logic at Harvard, for whom I have great respect, explained to me that 2 rabbits + 2 rabbits ordinarily make 4 rabbits, but that, logically speaking, there could be 16 of them. This kind of logic is very fashionable here; unfortunately, they do not even adhere to it.[143]

(Espagnat 1997, 6). The precise nature and extent of the mutual influences between Gilson and Gouhier warrants further study.

If Gilson's comments on the impossibility of dialogue between two philosophers are to be taken at face value, one might agree with Gouhier's own early characterization of himself as a historian and characterize the dialogue as one not between philosophers. But such a solution is inadequate: Gilson and Gouhier were both historians and philosophers. Ferdinand Alquié attributed maximum philosophical flexibility to Gouhier by interpreting him as holding, but not professing, a philosophy of "openness" to all thoughts precisely because he saw them as attempts to conceptualize what remains inexpressible. See Alquié 1982, 19–22. And Gouhier characterized Gilson as having "un grand sens de l'*autre*, qui se manifestait par la liberté avec laquelle il disait directement son désaccord avec son interlocuteur, sans précautions rhétoriques, en même temps qu'il n'en voulait nullement aux autres de leur désaccord avec lui et ne leur attribuait aucune infériorité ou supériorité quelconque" (Belgioioso and Gouhier 2005, 116).

Ultimately, if one can pinpoint a basis for the long, profound dialogue between these two great thinkers, it resides not so much in the realm of the professional, academic, or theological, but rather in the respect Gilson and Gouhier shared for each other as friends. Early on, Gilson considered Gouhier as his "alter ego" (Letter 29); later, he spoke of him as being less like his student and more like a member of the family (Shook 1984, 108). Because they knew, trusted, and liked each other, real listening and learning could take place. Gouhier's final work testified to his fidelity to his teacher and great friend: "Mon premier livre d'histoire des idées—*La pensée religieuse de Descartes*, 1924—est dédicacé 'A Monsieur Étienne Gilson … .' Le dernier a aujourd'hui pour sujet l'œuvre et la pensée d'Étienne Gilson … . Je souhaite que ces trois essais donnent envie de lire Étienne Gilson" (Gouhier 1993a).

143 In 1936, the Philosophy Department at Harvard included several eminent logicians. Among them were Clarence I. Lewis (1883–1964) and Willard Van Orman Quine (1908–2000). According to Paul Weiss, who arrived at Harvard as a student in 1927, logicians dominated the Philosophy Department. Weiss recalled discussing with C. I. Lewis whether one plus one would ever not equal two. Weiss cited Gilson's teaching as having "inspired a passion for thoroughness." "All the rest at Harvard," said Weiss, "was so much hot air" (Weiss 1995, 8–10; see also Kennicott 2001).

I am not in Toronto this year, except for three, four-day visits.[144] I remained at Harvard after the festivities surrounding the 3rd Centenary to present the W. James Lectures on: *The Unity of Philosophical Experience*.[145] You will be horrified if you ever see them. I myself am because

---

At Harvard, Gilson was popular with his students and remained on excellent terms with the members of the Philosophy Department who repeatedly invited him to return to give lectures. Gilson fully appreciated what he referred to as the "Harvard atmosphere of intelligence, taste, and friendship" (Gilson's 10 November 1933 letter to Professor Ralph Barton Perry (unpublished)).

144 "From April through August 1936 Gilson's life was largely given over to preparing and revising his lectures for Harvard ... and in July [Gilson] wrote Phelan that 'I am finishing up the last of my Harvard lectures, and don't much like what I have done.'" Gilson arrived in Boston on 29 August 1936. On 2 September, he presented a lecture at Harvard on "Medieval Universalism and its Present Value" (Gilson 1937b). On 18 September, Gilson received an honorary degree from Harvard, and on 2 October he began his William James Lectures. In the fall of 1936, Gilson also commuted from Harvard to Toronto and lectured at the Institute and met with students on 10–14 October, 7–11 November, and 6–9 December. See Shook 1984, 226–231.

145 Prior to publication, Gilson's manuscript was read "and improved in some of its stylistic detail by Professor Ralph Barton Perry of Harvard, Reverend Gerald B. Phelan, President of the Institute, and by Daniel C. Walsh, a student of Gilson's in the early 1930s who was in 1936–7 teaching at Manhattanville College in New York. Gilson's English style preserved the clarity but not the richness and variety of his French. It was always, of course, remarkable and distinctive" (Shook's 30 June 1979 letter (unpublished) to Henri Gouhier, L.K. Shook Papers). In these lectures Gilson tried to demonstrate how Malebranche's thought exemplified "intelligible laws," flowing from the Cartesian experiment, that transcend history and belong to philosophy itself. The disastrous failure of Descartes's philosophy, and those like Malebranche who followed it, resulted from a false conception of abstraction that extended its mathematical usage into other domains.

Gilson's lectures contributed to another important set of lectures delivered four decades later. In 1973, Stanley Jaki first encountered Gilson's thought by reading *The Unity of Philosophical Experience* during a sixteen-hour flight from New York to Tokyo. Jaki's reading provided "the insight into the correlation between a realist metaphysics (which issues in a demonstration of the existence of God) and a truly creative method in science" (Jaki 1993, 46n.24) which Jaki developed in his Gifford Lectures, given in 1975 and 1976. See Jaki 1978. Jaki considers Gilson as "possibly the greatest Christian philosopher since Thomas Aquinas" (Jaki 2004, 27).

they resemble Farges and Barbedette.[146] Actually, I am appalled. It is the worse type of historical criticism, where all nuances are blurred into two or three rough ideas that dominate everything. In short, the evil that I detest I do, and with a stubbornness that astonishes me, but I cannot help it. It is a "Nicht anders können."[147] My consolation is to reread your two Malebranches, which fourteen students at Harvard, and sixteen in Toronto,[148] are now reading. One of them provided such intelligent praise of your books that I wished you could have heard it. He wondered how one could bring together such erudition with such a feeling for the life of the doctrines? I do too.[149]

The situation in France does not look good to you from up close; from afar, it is awful. What one sees from here clear as day, and which dominates everything, is the absolute, fixed, determined will that Germany has to unleash a new war. It is horrible and there is nothing one can do except to prepare oneself for what seems quite inevitable.[150] Are

---

146 The reference is to Albert Farges and Désire Barbedette, two Sulpicians whose compendium of scholastic philosophy in French and Latin had many editions. See Barbedette and Farges 1933 and Conlan 1967.

147 During the imperial *Diet of Worms* in 1521, when summoned to renounce or reaffirm his views, Luther is reputed to have stated: "Here I stand. I can do no other. God help me. Amen" (Bainton 1950, 142–144). In his important review of these lectures, Gouhier characterized Gilson's pursuit of the impersonal essence of various systems as attaining what is "of the most essentially personal." See Gouhier 1938c.

148 It is likely that Gilson also discussed Malebranche in a course at Harvard. In a 2 November 1935 letter to Ralph Barton Perry (unpublished, in Perry Correspondence), Gilson proposed giving a seminar on "Descartes and Malebranche." The Harvard College *Report* for 1936–1937 listed Gilson as having given a "Seminary in the History of Philosophy." See Harvard College 1936–1937, 99.

149 Equally laudatory appraisals of Gouhier's two theses can be found in Easton, Lennon, and Sebba 1992, 41–42, no. 98.

150 In March 1936, German troops marched into the Rhineland in defiance of the treaties of Versailles and Locarno. On 1 November 1936, Mussolini announced the anti-communist Axis with Germany urging Britain and France to join. On 25 November, Germany and Japan signed an agreement to protect world civilization from the Bolshevik menace. In August of the following year a new concentration camp was opened at Buchenwald, on 5 September the biggest-ever Nazi rally marked the opening of the Nazi congress in Nuremberg,

you announcing to me a minister Chautemps?[151] There, I am so lacking in political understanding and memory that I no longer even know who this is really about. I am always for the cabinet in power so long as blood does not flow. Right now, I am for those who try to avoid a civil war, and I will always be for them, whoever they might be.

I am glad they have lowered the retirement age and earnestly hope the laws are put into effect immediately, across the board, and without discrimination. That would create room at the top; there are too many young people who are marking time or have no positions. This is excellent.

Thank you again for your kind letter. With fond wishes to you and yours,

Étienne Gilson

and on 6 November Italy joined the anti-communist pact between Germany and Japan.

151 The reference is to Camille Chautemps, Minister of the Interior. See Gouhier 1930a. In May 1936, the PCF-Socialist-Radical "Front Populaire" won overwhelmingly in the parliamentary elections and the first "united front government" after the 7th Congress took power. The three United Front governments, two headed by Blum, the Socialist, and one by Chautemps, the Radical, lasted almost two years.

H. Gouhier, the Academician

31 Juillet 1925
Maison Jacques Baud
Morzine (H^te^ Savoie)

6, RUE DE PONTHIERRY
MELUN (S-ET-M)

Mon cher ami

Je comprends votre incertitude touchant le choix d'un poste ; il est certain que ce choix n'influencera en rien votre carrière dans l'enseignement supérieur, en tout cas pas de manière sensible ; vos préférences personnelles ne se prêtent guère à l'argumentation, et par conséquent je crois que vous seul pouvez en décider. Il me semble simplement que votre présence à Evreux serait une « utopie », et comme vos thèses seront très probablement imprimées à Poitiers (Société française d'imprimerie et de librairie, ex Oudin), il pourrait y avoir pour vous un gros intérêt à être sur place, afin d'aller vite. Ceci dit, vous seul pouvez prendre parti.

M. Brunschvicg, dont j'ai lu le rapport, ne m'a rien dit d'aussi précis qu'à vous, car je n'ai guère parlé avec lui qu'entre deux interrogations. Son impression, qui rejoint votre dessein primitif, me paraît *décisive* quant au plan de votre travail. En droit, il n'y a donc aucune hésitation possible, et c'est à la première solution qu'il faut revenir. Comment l'édition et la vente seront elles possibles, ce sont des points que l'on réglera après devis de l'imprimeur. Jusque là continuez à *condenser* le plus possible, vous y gagnerez à tous les points de vue. Bon courage, mon cher ami ; les miens se joignent à moi pour vous adresser nos meilleures amitiés.

Votre affectueusement dévoué

Et. Gilson

Copy of letter by É. Gilson.

le 20 février 1931

Cher Ami,

Vrin m'a dit mardi que vous étiez en Angleterre. Déjà! J'avais cru que c'était pour le printemps. Je sais que vous jouez là-bas une grosse partie — et pour vous et pour ce que vous aimez. J'ai compris que c'est la méditation de plusieurs années qui va prendre forme. Soyez sûr que ma pensée vous accompagne fidèlement, avec une confiance d'autant plus sûre que je sens derrière ces conférences quelque chose comme ce moi profond dont parle Bergson à la fin de l'Essai, prêt à s'achever dans un acte libre…

Ici nous vivons dans une affreuse tragédie, avec des craintes que l'on ne peut pas écrire.

Nous nous unissons pour vous dire notre affection

Henri Gouhier

Copy of letter by H. Gouhier.

APPENDIX I

GILSON'S STUDENT ESSAY ON MALEBRANCHE

Thoughtful and precise work. You know and provide a clear analysis of the most important texts.
Runs on a little in places.
Malebranche's role and the critique of certain subjects seem to me slightly exaggerated in explaining the intensity of the anti–scholastic polemic.
One rather strange mistake on the relationships of perfection.

MALEBRANCHE'S POLEMIC AGAINST ARISTOTLE AND SCHOLASTIC PHILOSOPHY

Satisfactory overall.

Étienne Gilson

Correction by V. Delbos[1]

[1] It is not uncommon to say that at the foundation of all philosophy there are two parts, each of which has its own role to play: "a destructive part" charged with the task of clearing the land and creating a clear site for a new theory as well as a "constructive part" responsible for the task of building a new edifice in place of the old one.[2] Even though the two

1 Professor Delbos's comments, found on the cover page and in the margins of Gilson's essay, appear in bold print within the text. Words Delbos underlined have been italicized. My comments in the text and footnotes are in brackets []. Paragraphs have been numbered for ease of reference. An earlier version of this essay and commentary appeared in Fafara 1989.

2 See Lucien Lévy–Bruhl 1899, 2. While discussing his professors at the Sorbonne, Gilson mentioned Professor Frédéric Rauh (1861–1909) who "announced that before undertaking to build (pars construens) one should first destroy (pars destruens)" (Gilson 1962, 28–29). For Gilson's brief bi-

parts are mutually dependent on each other, we know it is the founder of a new philosophy who has to fight hardest against the old biases so that his successors can follow a designated path. Cartesianism provides an interesting example of the reverse happening. Descartes, who, it seems, should have met entrenched resistance either from the principle of authority, methodologies, or earlier theories, was satisfied with briefly criticizing them and quickly moving on to construct his own structure. Malebranche, on the other hand, in elaborating a completely new theory based on a foundation similar to that of Descartes's, was not content with repeating the objections his teacher leveled against Aristotelianism, and so elaborated them that they ended up becoming almost an integral part of his own system. **One reason, no doubt, behind the tenacity of Malebranche's critiques of Aristotelianism is that he had more direct contact with the Peripatetics than did D[escartes].** In this essay we shall try to explain the nature of Malebranche's polemic against Aristotle and the scholastics, and why, contrary to all expectations, it developed as it did.

[2] For Malebranche, the principle of authority is the first superstition from which we must free ourselves if we desire to attain knowledge of the truth. One repeatedly hears: "This is true because the ancients say so." But it is just as absurd to believe that the book one writes will be the eternal code of truth as it is to believe the ancient authors were infallible masters of truth and not simply its guardians. How could anyone imagine that two thousand years after Aristotle, no one has found any error in his writings? Could Aristotle have discovered the whole truth all at once? One only has to look at the endless battles and controversies surrounding his doctrine to convince oneself that the truth, which is essentially an "indivisible unity," cannot be contained in it.

[3] Furthermore, can one philosophize just by unquestioningly accepting other people's ideas, ancient or not? Is not philosophy, above all, the work of reason, the highest human faculty that alone can pursue the search after truth? Consequently, while it is indisputable that it is instructive to read ancient authors to discuss their opinions, it also is indisputable that memorizing ready–made formulas and passing them on to others is a complete waste of one's own time and that of others **To go further would not, I believe, suit Malebranche very much.** One could say that even if the ancients posed and solved every single problem

bliographical note on Rauh, see Gilson, Langan, and Maurer 1966, 760 n.28. See also Canivez 1974, 476–78 and Horner 1997.

it would still be wrong to accept their arguments on authority, without discussion, for it is a mediocre philosophy that consists in cramming one's head full of other people's opinions.

[4] There are numerous other arguments which account for the blindness of those who defend the principle of authority: laziness of mind which refuses to reflect, hatred of abstract truths, and, above all, vanity where one studies less to learn than to gain a reputation as an intellectual and a widely read person. All this is what makes the philosophy of the schools less a science of reason than of memory in which "thinking" consists in recounting someone else's thoughts. Is it necessary to add to these arguments the "deference mingled with foolish curiosity that makes people admire what is furthest from us," what is oldest and most obscure. "We search for [ancient] medals although they are encrusted with rust, and we carefully guard the lantern and worm–eaten slipper of some ancient: their antiquity constitutes their price" (*Search*, 138–39).[3] But what! Why not more so than antiquity do we not have a legitimate claim here, more than Plato, Aristotle and Epicurus? Aristotle, Plato and Epicurus were men like us, of the same species as us. Moreover, "in our time the world is older by two thousand years, it has gained more experience, and should be more enlightened; and it is the age of the world and its experience that make for the discovery of truth" (*Search*, 139).

A clear and interesting thesis.

[5] Freed from the principle of authority we can look Aristotle and his successors in the eyes and judge them for ourselves. The first thing that strikes us in reading their writings is the lack of order in the arrangement of ideas, the near complete absence of method. For instance, Aristotle never asks if there is a particular progression he ought to follow in studying any question and if it is necessary to begin with the most simple to go on to the most complex. Nowadays, we know how one ought to seek the truth; Viète[4] and Descartes, who have transformed algebra and analysis, have taught us how to put order into our thoughts. We do not try to understand the theories of conical sections before having studied basic geometry. Aristotle sorely needs such lessons. For without

3 The reference, and each reference hereafter in parentheses, is to the English translation of the text cited as found in *The Search after Truth* (Malebranche 1980). See also p. 170, n.2.

4 For Viète (1540–1603), see Malebranche 1958–67, I:401, 520n.320; II:538n.38. See also Malebranche 1992, I:1461n.1 for page 310.

doubting for an instant that the human mind can immediately solve the most difficult problems, and before knowing the nature of matter or the composition of bodies, he looks for the reason why old men's hair turns white. By following such a method in research, it is hardly surprising he concludes that the reason why old men's hair turns white is the same that makes some horses have eyes of two different colors. The value of this kind of science is clear.

[6] In seeking the ultimate reason for this deplorable manner of proceeding it is easy to see that it consists in ignorance of a term which is at one and the same time the goal and the means of achieving that goal—the clear and distinct idea. Today no one is unaware that truth can lie only in that which is clearly and distinctly conceived. Aristotle took the opposite approach by beginning from what is most confused in the knowledge that we have from sensation. For him, deceptive and *imprecise* **This is a word which M. never uses** sensory data are the best starting point. Since "a general idea of being" is added to these data he continually falls into the ridiculous abstraction of faculties. In reality, the "clear, intimate, and necessary presence of God (i.e., the being without individual restriction, the infinite being, being in general) to the human mind acts upon it with greater force than the presence of all finite objects" (*Search*, 241). But, however great and vast it might be, this idea of being has become so familiar to us by our being accustomed to it—it touches us so lightly that "we almost believe ourselves not to see it." Little by little, we lose sight of its origin and we consider it as formed by the confused collection of particular beings even though those particular beings only appear to us within it. What follows from this? As soon as philosophers notice a new effect in the cosmos, since their minds are preoccupied with this general and abstract idea of being, they apply it at once to this new effect: "immediately they fancy a new entity to produce it. Fire heats things—therefore there is something i[n] fire that produces this effect, something different from the matter of which fire is composed" (*Search*, 242–43). This gives rise to the countless abstractions which so hinder the progress of physics—acts, powers, causes, effects, substantial forms, occult qualities, etc. When we carefully examine the definitions of these terms, we will find nothing but some confused sense data, plus the general and abstract idea of being. What kind of physics begins from such abstractions instead of clear and distinct ideas? Actually, it would be logic. **Good** [with a line drawn alongside the text from the last reference to the end of this sentence]

Ordinary philosophers certainly want to make Aristotle's physics explain the basis of things, but they do not see that they are explaining "nature through their general and abstract terms—as if nature were abstract" (*Search*, 243).

[7] All that can come from this ignorance of the logical order of demonstration and contempt for clear ideas is an incoherent jumble. And that really is the adjective which suits *scholastic* science which is nothing but its own logic. **Not very clear.** Originally, the logic of the schools was only a means of arriving at the truth; but, by a strange reversal of terms, it soon ended up becoming an end, and some came to believe that logic should be studied for its own sake. In order to establish this strange science some have not hesitated to accumulate all kinds of rules and precepts; ultimately, to reason soundly according to these rules they are obliged to pay so much attention to the procedures they use that it becomes impossible to think simultaneously about the objects they are studying. On the contrary, true method is nothing more than a discrete guide; it consists of only a small number of very intelligible and closely interdependent rules. Consequently, it is not for those who love only mysteries **Good** [with a line drawn alongside the previous six lines] and bizarre and extraordinary inventions. It demands only a desire for clarity and the attention necessary "for [always] preserving the evidence in the mind's perceptions, and for discovering the most hidden" (*Search*, 437).

[8] The clearest consequence of the method employed by the philosophers of the schools is that it leads to a sequence of absurdities in physics, and, over and beyond physics, to the worst errors in ethics and religion. From the above, we already can understand what Aristotle's own physics would be: a series of bizarre combinations carried out purely and simply with the abstract definitions of things. Appearances seem to teach us that if fire warms us, if color strikes our eyes, if phenomena generally appear to us, it is because these things contain something more or less like the impressions they make on us. We have seen how the belief in substantial forms is born and develops in us. **This could be clearer and more concise** [with a line drawn alongside the previous six lines]. An example will show us the consequences that can be had in physics by using these forms and attractive, retentive, concoctive, and expulsive faculties. We can look at how Aristotle solves the problem to which we have already alluded: why does the hair of old men become white? Philosophers who look into this matter using

Descartes's method are sufficiently aware that the universe is extension and movement—everything in it occurs mechanically, like clockwork. Thus, they should have looked into what makes up color, and what is the true nature of hair. But Aristotle operates otherwise; by regarding each quality of matter as an independent being his resolution of the problem consists only of logical definitions. White is composed of much heat and a little humidity; therefore, old men have more heat than humidity. Heat is "that which unites things of the same type." Humidity is "what is not easily contained within its own boundaries but is within external foreign boundaries."[5] Let us try to substitute the definition for the defined. Assuming that heat and humidity are what we said and that white is composed of much heat and a little humidity, we can say that old men's hair whitens because "what is not easily contained in its own boundaries, but within external foreign boundaries" overcomes "what unites things of the same nature."[6] We have to admit that one need not be too demanding to be satisfied with such solutions.

[9] Thank God that the explanations in the physics of Aristotle and his followers have no worse fault than being ridiculous! What is unfortunate is that over and above science they affect and seriously offend religion and morality.

[10] In reality God is constantly present to our mind; it is in Him that we understand and see all things. But ever since man was degraded by original sin our mind "constantly spreads itself externally; it forgets itself and Him who enlightens it." Ever since the fall of our first father, instead of seeking God in all things we recoil from Him with a kind of aversion. Man feels himself to be a sinner. This is why he dreads meeting the creator; "he prefers to imagine a blind nature or power that he can master" than to fear the presence of a just God "who knows all and does all" (*Search*, 657). **Well presented.**

[11] Substantial forms really are just a pretext which we use to persuade ourselves that God is not that close to us and he does not act directly within nature. The philosophers of the schools who so closely ally themselves with this doctrine ought to realize that by distancing God they diminish Him. To say that it is not God but the faculties and the substantial forms which make a body have this or that distinct

5 Malebranche 1997, 473.

6 Ibid., 477.

nature is to say that "God lacks intelligence, or that He cannot make all these remarkable things with extension alone" (*Search*, 230).

[12] Besides diminishing God, the philosophy of the schools has other serious consequences; if one pushes this philosophy to its extremes, it negates Him and leads to the most barbaric of all paganisms. We have seen that ever since original sin man distances himself from God by transferring a part of the divine power to material objects; this is what gives rise to the preference for the efficacy of secondary causes. Against all evidence that it is God who acts in everything and everywhere, and that wisdom dictates that we prefer the universal cause to particular causes, we concede that bodies really have their own power to act and that they do not cease to exercise it upon us. Hence, we attribute all the goods we have received from material objects to those objects themselves and not to God who is the one who really sent them to us. If God has placed the sun, the moon and the stars above us, if He has surrounded them with glory and power, if He conferred on them the power to fill us with the benefits which these stars send us, should we not honor them? **Good** [with a line drawn alongside the previous six lines] This is at the very origin of the idolatry which Cicero mentions: "if the Egyptians adored not only the sun, the moon, and the river Nile, whose overflow caused the fertility of their country, but also went so far as the vilest animals, it was because of some utility they derived from them" (*Search*, 684–85). Thus, logically the theory of substantial forms leads to idolatry and to paganism. If we can believe that the heart of the philosophers who profess this theory is still Christian, we at least have to admit that their mind is essentially pagan (*Search*, 446).

[13] The defenders of Aristotle's philosophy are very well aware of all the danger such a position presents, and generally they modify it somewhat: doubtlessly, they say, one would be speaking like a pagan if one were to admit the existence of independent divinities within the universe; and we do not maintain that position. But we do think that above the visible material world is a sort of general nature and world spirit which uses substantial forms only to diversify its action. Regardless of how these philosophers phrase it, they still fall into paganism for God alone is the universal cause and there is no need to "feign a certain *nature*, a *primum mobile*, a *universal soul*, or any such chimera of which we have no clear and distinct idea; this would be to reason like a pagan philosopher" (*Search*, 662). Can one claim that if there were no certain nature acting on its own volition, and if God does all things,

one would not be able to distinguish the natural from the supernatural? That is an extreme distinction to put into Aristotle's mouth. Those who show so much respect "for the opinions of this miserable and pitiful" philosopher ought to be able to realize that the "nature" of which they speak has become for many an idol worthy of receiving the honors due to the divinity and that they are taking us back to believing with the ancients that it is some nature or even "the sun and man that beget men" (*Search*, 668).

[14] One can readily believe that the direct consequence of doctrines which give a divine power to creatures is to turn man away from God and from the duties which one owes Him in order to bring man closer to matter and sensible things. This is how that dangerous philosophy creates a deep divide between the human soul and God; transplanting substantial forms into man himself, this philosophy will go so far as to say that the soul is the form of the body. **Good** [with a line drawn alongside the three previous lines] Thus the union which so intimately binds the soul to God is eliminated solely for the sake of preserving its unity with a body that we have never seen and whose existence we would even be ignorant of had God Himself not revealed it to us. Is it not surprising that "Christian philosophers, who ought to prefer the mind of God to the mind of man, Moses to Aristotle, and Saint Augustine to some worthless commentator of a pagan philosopher, should regard the soul more as the *form* of the body than as being made in the image and for the image of God" (*Search*, Introd. xxxiii)?

[15] And so man soon cuts himself off from God so as to turn towards his body and devote himself to the material things which surround him. The true philosophy actually teaches that all good and all *evil* **In what sense?** comes to us from God and that nothing real in the world exists or acts except by his will. Conversely, Aristotle who places the reason for effects in secondary causes as well as in the first cause warrants our attaching ourselves to objects. If we want to be happy, we should attach ourselves to that which gives us happiness. What then could be more reasonable than to attach ourselves to "sensible objects if they are the true causes of the happiness [we] find in their possession"? With such a philosophy one is not far from a justification of avarice, ambition, debauchery, and all the vices (*Search*, 682).

[16] Even though it does not present them in logical order, this brief exposition of the main criticisms that Malebranche raised against Aristotle's doctrine enables us to see that this certainly is not just an

academic debate, but a profound antagonism between two philosophies. It is not enough for Malebranche to present some objections to details and engage in a few skirmishes; he throws into the fray all the dialectical vigor, searing irony, and priestly indignation at his disposal. For him, it is truly a matter of setting *one altar against another*. **This expression may not be very appropriate here.** Now what we have to do is try and determine why Malebranche's polemic, which the works of Descartes should have rendered unnecessary, was so much more violent than that of Descartes's; in other words, to ask ourselves what made the "scholastic peril" more dangerous for Malebranche than for his predecessor.

[17] First of all, what is so striking in Malebranche's polemic is the kind of abhorrence he attaches at every moment to the principle of authority—*at least* **This is to be emphasized** in philosophical matters. Where Descartes had been satisfied with rather brief critiques Malebranche persists, returning repeatedly to this point, always with a biting and aggressive irony. It seems that there is never enough mockery for those philosophers for whom "Aristotle is what reason and clarity are to others" (*Search*, 151). One main reason which, to some extent perhaps, explains Malebranche's distaste for the principle of authority can be found in the overall spirit of the Oratorian order to which he belonged. In the 17th century, the independence of mind enjoyed at the Oratory was well known, and often contrasted with the Jesuit *esprit de corps* which Malebranche himself reproached for its doctrinal uniformity. Although this is pure supposition, one would undoubtedly be correct in thinking that the intellectual daring of a Richard Simon,[7] for instance, whose works were two centuries ahead of the most advanced modern Biblical exegesis, could not but have confirmed Malebranche's independent attitude and personal autonomy.

[18] But the real reason Malebranche attacks the principle of authority even more than Descartes does is that this principle, only ridiculous when being used in the name of Aristotle, became really dangerous now that it was being used in the name of Descartes himself. An entire school had effectively been created under the patronage of that great

7 For Simon, see Gouhier 1926b, 37–48, and Anon. 1990. Malebranche was a student of Simon who was regarded as the "father of Biblical criticism." Simon was ordained in 1710 and then took up residence in the Oratory in Paris. His *Histoire critique du Vieux Testament* (1678) provoked Catholic and Protestant criticism and led to his expulsion from the Oratory. Afterwards, he published several works under pseudonyms.

name. It was not just for La Fontaine that Descartes was "the mortal whom the ancients would have made a god."[8] The new school, as one might think, was not exempt from the failings of all schools: Descartes had become a sort of infallible oracle. The new school had its principles, its dogmas, and its orthodoxy, and, even though all this was not taken to the extreme, the school had become so *intransigent* **avoid this** that, to it, Malebranche seemed to be the worst of the heretics. Descartes only had to wage war against Aristotle, whose only merit was being a two thousand year old Greek. Malebranche devotes so much space to attacks against the principle of authority because he had to wage war against the recent glory of Descartes himself.
Is this really certain ???? [with a line drawn alongside the previous two lines]

[19] Moreover, the polemic against Aristotelianism was not to end with the last scholastic; it was necessary to pursue the substantial forms right down to their last entrenchments, deep within the heart of the new philosophy. By showing that, sometimes implicitly, sometimes explicitly, Malebranche considered Cartesianism to be a partial ratification of some of the most dangerous errors of the schools, we have doubtlessly explained the genuine fury he displayed against Aristotle's teachings.

[20] On what was for him the key issue of the theory of ideas, Malebranche broke very sharply with Descartes and his successors, Arnauld and Régis. If Descartes were ever tempted to retain the scholastic substantial forms in material bodies, what absolutely forbade him from doing so was the basis of his own system—the concept of a mechanistic physics. But wherever mechanism lost ground, wherever it became necessary to see something other than a rigorously predetermined combination of movements, substantial forms reappeared more powerful than ever. Descartes defined the soul as a thing whose entire essence is thinking. Ideas are nothing more than products of the thinking substance and the idea of God, the highest in dignity—the idea which has the most objective reality of all—is contained like all the others within the human understanding. Even when ideas require the assistance of a superior cause, it is still within the mind that they are produced. Little reflection is needed to show that this clearly is a remnant of Aristotelianism. One can rightfully be surprised that "the

8 "Descartes, ce mortel dont on eut fait un dieu/chez les païens ..." See "Discours à Mme de La Sablière" in La Fontaine 1991, I:384. Lévy-Bruhl (1899, 39) cited the same text.

Cartesians" who reject the terms "nature" and "faculty" for external objects find it acceptable to use them for the soul. They deny the philosophers of the schools the right to say fire burns, and immediately afterwards they themselves say that the soul thinks. For all intents and purposes, it would be much more acceptable to admit faculties for the body than for the soul. **That polemic against certain Cartesians is quite distinct from that which Malebranche ventured against scholasticism.** If one were to say instead that bodies are the principle of their own movement, "all my ideas would be overthrown. But I would rather agree to this than to say that the mind enlightens itself." (Search, 623). Like it or not, once one rejects substantial forms the conclusion is that minds, far from having the faculty of producing ideas, see them in intelligible extension which is in God. All truths and all relationships are contained in intelligible extension—relations of quantity from which flow theoretical truths and the whole of science; relationships of perfection from which flow practical truths and the whole of ethics. **Relations of perfection are not enclosed in intelligible extension** [with a line drawn alongside the previous two lines].[9] Beyond intelligible extension and containing it in itself, we see God directly, without the help of any idea; and, despite its being "incomprehensible" we contemplate His supreme intelligibility.

[21] Once we set aside the faculty of thinking that Descartes attributed to the human soul, are we finally freed from the subjection to Aristotelian philosophy? No. There still remains one last task to perform that bears not so much on the human soul but on material objects, for, Descartes, one has to admit, did not know how to extract from the fertile idea of a mechanistic physics all the truths it contained. After having denied the external world all the qualities one ordinarily attributes to it, except for extension and movement, he used his discovery to distinguish the soul from the body, placing thinking substance on one side, and extended substance on the other. In reality, the distinction established by Descartes remains completely superficial. The soul and the body really are distinct substances, but that does not prevent the direct action of one upon the other. For Descartes, the human body and soul are "intimately blended with one another."[10] This granted material objects at least a shadow or

9 The moral law is not seen in the Vision in God but discovered through the attraction towards the good experienced by the will. See Malebranche 1958–67, I:445–446 and Delbos 1924, 289–290.

10 *Meditations* Six; Descartes 1904, 7:80–81.

a reflection of that power that Aristotle bestowed on them with his theory of substantial forms. Descartes stripped extension of its qualities but retained its power to act on thought; in brief, under the influence of an old substratum of pagan thought, he admitted once again that, apart from God, an action can affect our human understanding. As a matter of fact, the distinction of soul and body may be stated much more forcefully than the way Descartes formulated it. Extension should be distinguished so clearly from thought that afterwards no relation whatsoever between these two substances could ever be implied. Not only is extension distinct from thought, but one also should say that the human mind has never seen a material object ever since God created the world. The mind can see only the ideas of things contained in intelligible extension, which alone can be participated in by the human understanding. One must divorce oneself from Aristotelianism completely and maintain that if objects do not have substantial forms in them that give them independence they also do not have the power of acting on us to any extent whatsoever; our mind knows nothing about things by any direct action they might have on it. When Descartes wished to prove the existence of the material world, he put forth only the strongest proof that reason alone could provide. Divine veracity does not suffice if it is only the revelation contained in Sacred Scripture that can compel us to believe that the external world exists.

[22] By no means do we pretend to claim that Malebranche systematically freed himself from the Aristotelianism that he found in other philosophers. We simply wished to explain the reason for the extraordinary amount of space in his work devoted to criticism, and, in particular, why such criticism is more important to him than it was for Descartes. The reason is that Malebranche's system is much further removed from the philosophy of the schools than even that of Descartes himself. **This is indeed possible** [with a line drawn alongside the previous two lines]. The fact that Malebranche, even unconsciously, rejected precisely that which Cartesian philosophy retained from Aristotelianism certainly seems to prove it.

[23] It would certainly be futile to defend Aristotle against Malebranche's attacks. What the French philosopher knew of the Greek philosopher was the dead part of his work: the physics. That makes it all the more necessary to say that little determination is needed to conclude that Malebranche's own explanations in physics are ridiculous. **Not to the same extent perhaps** [with a line drawn alongside the previous

two lines] That the occult faculty of corporeal attraction should have eliminated the clear and distinct idea of impulse is indeed a little like the apotheosis of an obscure idea. As for Aristotle's metaphysics, it is clear that Malebranche did not know it and viewed it only through the *absurd* **Excessive** disfigurements it took on within decadent scholasticism. Moreover, it is doubtful whether Malebranche would have regarded the Greek philosopher more kindly had he understood him better; he would have simply made him say fewer absurdities. Perhaps he also would have thought twice about writing the following sentence which is surprising to find in the works of such an irreconcilable adversary of Aristotle: "For only God is at once both motor and immobile" (*Search*, 678). Finally, he might have asked himself if Aristotle, confronted with his own theory, would not have been right to revise certain points of his mordant critique of the theory of ideas as: "using empty words and uttering poetical metaphors."[11]

COMMENTARY

BY RICHARD J. FAFARA

The Setting: Gilson's Studies at the Sorbonne. In July 1903, immediately after receiving his *Baccalauréat ès lettres* from the Sorbonne, Étienne Gilson's life took an unexpected turn. As a high school student mainly interested in religion and art, Gilson was exposed to philosophy, but he understood little and had no intention of pursuing it further. However, a year of military service in the infantry in 1903-1904 afforded him the opportunity to read and reread Descartes's *Méditations* and Léon Brunschvicg's, *Introduction à la vie de l'esprit*. Despite young Gilson's persistence in reading these authors, he came away unenlightened. What struck him was the "amazingly gratuitous arbitrariness" of these philosophers. The annoyance generated by reading and not understanding philosophy prompted Gilson to pursue it.[12]

In 1904, Gilson enrolled in the Faculty of Letters of the University of Paris. His professors included Victor Brochard, Victor Delbos, Gabriel Séailles, Victor Émile Egger, Émile Durkheim, André Lalande, Frédéric

11 See p. 180, n.8.

12 Gilson 1962, 17–18. See Shook 1984, 9–13.

Raugh, Lucien Lévy-Bruhl, and Marcel Mauss, Jules Lachelier and Émile Boutroux, who were semi-retired.[13] After attending three lectures by Lévy-Bruhl on Descartes, Gilson decided to write his doctoral thesis on Descartes and under Lévy-Bruhl. In 1905, Gilson received his *Diplôme de licencié ès lettres avec la mention philosophie*. The following year, under Lévy-Bruhl's direction, Gilson presented "Descartes et la scolastique" for the *Diplôme d'études supérieures de philosophie*. Awarded the *agrégation* in 1907, Gilson began teaching at various lycées and followed Lévy-Bruhl's advice to continue his research on Descartes and the scholastics.

We know from Father Shook's authoritative biography of Gilson that during 1904-1907, as an assignment for a course given by Victor Delbos, Gilson submitted an essay entitled "La polémique de Malebranche contre l'Aristote et la philosophie scolastique."[14] Whether by his own choice or Delbos's suggestion, the topic of Gilson's essay coincided nicely with his interest in Descartes and the scholastics. It provided the young Gilson the opportunity to determine how another great Cartesian viewed Aristotle and his scholastic followers and to specify how Malebranche's reaction to them compared to that of Descartes's.

Professor Delbos, a pupil of Ollé-Laprune and Boutroux, concentrated his work as a historian of philosophy on Spinoza and Kant; he taught at the Sorbonne from 1902 until his death in 1916. During this period, Delbos became interested in great French philosophers and in philosophers who admitted the importance of religious belief. As early as 1903 Delbos devoted a series of public lectures to Malebranche who met both criteria. From 1906 onward, Delbos undertook a concentrated study of Malebranche's thought to write a book on him for Bloud & Gay's collection, *La pensée chrétienne*.[15]

As a young student at the Sorbonne, Gilson's early work on Descartes takes on significance because of its formative role in his later research that revolutionized scholarship on Descartes and the Middle Ages. Much less well known and appreciated is Gilson's exposure during this same period to the thought of Nicolas Malebranche; this provided the basis for Gilson's considerable contribution in the field of Malebranche studies.

---

13 Ibid., 30, 37.

14 Shook 1984, 19

15 See Delbos 1924, vii-ix,

Gilson's Essay. Malebranche's repeated insistence that Aristotle's philosophy is barren, obscure, puerile, and even inimical to the Christian faith sets the context for Gilson's study.[16] Gilson's specific question in the essay is twofold: what is the nature of Malebranche's critique of Aristotle and his scholastic followers, and why does it differ from that of Descartes in terms of magnitude and intensity? Included in the question is the issue of determining why Descartes appears to be an anomaly in the history of philosophy. Usually, the development of new philosophical thought involves a critique and liberation from prejudices and mistakes of the past so as to establish room for a new philosophy. However, Gilson views Descartes as a counterinstance, as one who expends little time in criticizing prejudices and mistaken theories of the past and who engages in mere summary critique before elaborating on his own position [1].[17]

Most of Gilson's study, which is restricted exclusively to Malebranche's *Recherche de la vérité*, focuses on the main criticisms which Malebranche presents against Aristotle. Like Descartes, Malebranche stresses that authentic philosophy has little reliance on the notion of authority. Many are the reasons for uncritically accepting the ancients–laziness, dislike of abstract truths, respect for old things, and vanity associated with studying not to learn but to be considered a "savant." Philosophy built on such a foundation becomes, like the philosophy of the schools, a science of memory where thinking is not synonymous with reason but with parroting someone else's opinion. Malebranche not only questions the belief that the ancients discovered the truth, but he also considers the two thousand years of experience and enlightenment that separate us from the ancients as an asset in discovering the truth [2–4].

More substantive is Malebranche's charge regarding the lack of a philosophical method in Aristotle and his successors. Because of Descartes, we know that seeking the truth requires that one begin with simple problems and proceed to the more complex ones. Aristotle makes the fundamental methodological mistake of beginning with sensation, that which is most confused, and not with clear and distinct ideas. The confused given of the senses, coupled with the general idea of being, which

---

16 Malebranche 1958–67, I:58–61, 165–170, 289–303, 397–403, 418–421, 456–483; II:26–30, 300–320, 346–368.

17 References to specific paragraphs in Gilson's essay are indicated within brackets [ ].

is always present to the human mind, explains Aristotle's propensity to account for nature by general and abstract ideas such as substantial forms. Beginning with sensory experience of the material world, Aristotle and his followers explain knowledge by a theory of abstraction and invent an ontology based on the distinction between potency and act which multiplies imaginary entities like substantial forms, qualities, and faculties in a vain attempt to account for the world as it appears to the senses. The result is a physics that is nothing more than a tissue of absurdities built on logical definitions.[18]

Gilson proceeds to examine briefly Malebranche's view on the harmful effects of Aristotelian philosophy in metaphysics, ethics, anthropology, and epistemology. Whereas Descartes traces the tendency to accept sense experience as the source of knowledge to the habits of childhood, Malebranche locates its source in original sin, which disrupts the balance established by God between soul and body and changes the relationship between the two into a kind of dependence of the soul on the body.[19] From this disruption stem Malebranche's reasons for regarding Aristotelian and scholastic philosophy as fundamentally pagan and contrary to religion and morality.

Malebranche maintains that the human being is intimately united to God. As such, the soul's definition as thought better assures its true spirituality than the peripatetical thesis conceiving it as the "form" of the body, a complement to "matter," and not a substance really distinct from it. Because of original sin we easily mistake our present condition for its natural condition, focus on physical objects rather than on God in whom we see all things, and endow bodies with power instead of admitting a just, all–knowing God, the unique cause of all. According to true philosophy, not the philosophy of the pagans, every instance of causality, every "efficacity," has something of the divine because to act is to produce new being. Creation means producing something which did not yet exist.

Attributing powers such as substantial forms to nature itself and endowing nature with secondary causality, as Aristotle and the scholastics do, results in contradiction and sacrilege: it attributes divine power

18 Malebranche 1958–67, 1:165–170, 459–463; 2:300–308. For the classical treatment of this issue in Descartes, see Gilson 1930d.

19 Although Malebranche does not reject Descartes's explanation (*Principles* I, art.71; Descartes 1904, 9, pt.2, 58–59), he does subordinate it to his own view. See Malebranche 1958–67, I:69–77, 232–265.

to creatures, risks turning nature into an idol, and leads to paganism. Slightly modifying this position by denying the existence of independent divinities and speaking instead of a general nature or world soul that utilizes substantial forms only to diversify its action likewise results in paganism. If natures really act and God does everything, how do we distinguish the natural from the supernatural?

Although Malebranche's theory of occasional causes eliminates all secondary causality, it does not mean that there is no structure governing creation. Rather, God has established general laws so that His activity is regulated, constant, and uniform. He acts regularly as the occasion demands. Following Aristotle in regarding the soul as the substantial form of the body separates the soul from God and perverts ethics; if the soul is more united to the body than to God, then its body is the cause of the soul's beatitude and bodily pleasures are the supreme good [14–15].

The crux of Gilson's essay consists in explaining why Malebranche's reaction to Aristotle and his followers, which usually takes the form of biting and aggressive irony accompanying rejections of the principle of authority in matters philosophical, is so much more vitriolic than that of Descartes. After citing the independent spirit of thought within the Oratory exemplified by Richard Simon[20] as a possible contributory factor, Gilson locates the real reason behind Malebranche's vehemence in his intention to extend the critique to Descartes himself. According to Gilson, Malebranche's detection of a ratification of substantial forms within Descartes meant that the critique of substantial forms, the most dangerous error of the schools, now had to encompass the dogmatism and intransigence of the new orthodoxy found in the "school" of Descartes's followers. In reality, Malebranche's polemic against Aristotle does not end with the last scholastic; it continues with an attempt to eliminate substantial forms within Cartesianism itself [16–19].

Despite a philosophy of clear and distinct ideas which establishes a mechanistic physics based on extension and movement devoid of substantial forms and totally independent of mind, Descartes defines the human soul as a substance whose essence is "thinking" and employs

20 See note 7 above. Bossuet's funeral oration for P. Bourgoing praised the liberal spirit of the Oratory whose members had no other solemn vows except baptism and ordination to the priesthood, ". . .où une sainte liberté fait le saint engagement" (Delbos 1924, 4). Malebranche began his theological studies while Bourgoing was the superior general of the Oratory.

notions such as "nature" and "faculty" to the extent that ideas are "products" of this substance and contained in the mind. Although unwilling to say that fire burns, Cartesians, nevertheless, maintain that the soul thinks. A consistent rejection of substantial forms, Malebranche would argue, means breaking with Descartes on the nature of ideas, denying that the mind has the ability to produce ideas and maintaining that it sees all things in God [19–20].

Similarly, Malebranche considers Descartes's distinction between soul and body to be superficial. On the one hand, Descartes's account of the world in terms of extension and movement enables him to distinguish the soul from the body as two distinct substances; on the other, Descartes admits the interaction of these substances, and, at least in the case of man, allows that they be "intimately blended one with the other." For Malebranche, thought and extension are so distinct that there can be no rapport whatsoever between the two substances. His doctrine of occasionalism leaves no room for the pagan willingness of old to attribute power to act to mind or body. That power belongs to God alone. Hence, according to Malebranche, we know nothing about material objects by any direct action that they have on the mind because the mind does not see material objects themselves. What it does see is their ideas in God. Consequently, Malebranche denies the adequacy of Descartes's recourse to divine veracity to demonstrate the existence of the world. Only Sacred Scripture which reveals God's action can constrain us to believe that a world corresponding to our ideas exists. The extent of Malebranche's critique of Aristotle along with his rejection of Aristotelian remnants within Descartes appear to prove Malebranche's being further removed than Descartes from the philosophy of the schools [21–22].

Gilson concludes his essay with a series of brief comments. Defending Aristotle's thought to Malebranche would be pointless. Malebranche was familiar only with distorted versions of Aristotle's *Physics*, the dead part of the Aristotelian corpus. Nor did he know Aristotle's *Metaphysics* and viewed it only in a deformed state within a declining scholasticism. Gilson doubts that a better understanding of Aristotle would have resulted in Malebranche's being more sympathetic to Aristotle's philosophy although it might have caused revisions in his own on the nature of God and the nature of ideas.

Professor Delbos's Comments. Overall, Delbos was satisfied with the essay as an intelligent analysis of the key texts even though he suggests that Gilson might have exaggerated certain points in order to explain the intensity of Malebranche's polemic. Delbos does not furnish details on what might have been exaggerated, but his comments on particular points within Gilson's essay provide some clues. The strongest, clearest criticism centers on Gilson's misunderstanding of Malebranche's position on how relations of perfection are known [20]. Although viewed as a peculiar ("singulière") error by Delbos, this issue is only tangential to Gilson's main thesis. Three of Delbos's other comments deal with central issues in the essay.

First, Delbos cites Malebranche's having had more direct dealings with the peripatetics than Descartes as one reason for the intensity of the polemic itself [1]. Delbos may be referring either to Malebranche's personal dealings with the followers of Aristotle or the manner in which Malebranche conducted those dealings. The former allows for a long list of possibilities. According to his biographers, Malebranche's study of scholastic philosophy from 1654 to 1656 under the famous peripatetic Mr. Rouillard at the Collège de la Marche disappointed him and may have been the basis of his severe critique of scholastic verbalism.[21] Malebranche also found that the theology which he studied from 1656 to 1659 at the Sorbonne was infected with the same scholastic disease.[22]

---

21 See André 1886, 5–6 (also in Robinet 1961, 14): "A l'âge de seize ans <en 1654> sa santé étant un peu affermie, il alla commencer son cours dans le Collège de la Marche, sous M. Rouillard, fameux péripatéticien. Après quelques jours d'exercice, le jeune philosophe s'apperçut bientôt qu'on l'avoit trompé. Il ne trouva dans la philosophie ni rien de grand, ni presque rien de vrai: questions de mots, subtilitez frivoles, grossièretez pitoiables, equivoques perpétuelles, nul esprit, nul goût, nul christianisme .... il demandoit toujours à voir clair, ne voulant rien croire sans raison. Ce qui parut sans doute d'un fort mauvais augure aux sectateurs d'Aristote."

22 Ibid., 6–7 (Robinet 1961, 16): "La theologie n'étoit principalement en ce temps là q'un amas confus d'opinions humaines, de questions badines, de puérilitez, de chicanes, de raisonnemens à perte de vuë pour prouver des mysteres incompréhensibles; tout cela sans ordre, sans principes, sans liaison des véritez entre elles; barbarie dans le stile, fort peu de sens dans tout le reste. On n'y donnoit presque rien aux dogmes de la foi, au lieu qu'on s'arrêtoit volontiers à ces disputes vaines que S. Paul nous ordonne d'éviter comme des folies. L'abbé Malebranche. . . fut surpris, au delà de ce qu'on peut dire, de voir des gens graves traiter sérieusement des questions la plûpart si peu sensées. Accoutumé de bonne heure à réfléchir, voici ce qu'il trouvoit bizarre dans la méthode des Écoles. Dans la philosophie, qui est tout entière du ressort de la raison, on

In 1660, when he entered the Oratory, the thinking of Bérulle and St. Augustine permeated its intellectual climate allowing a "positive" theology based on the interpretation of scripture alongside scholastic theology. Both within and outside of the Oratory, a multitude of spiritual writers reproached the scholastics, in their punctilious method of questioning with its divisions and subdivisions, for having lost sight of the essential truths of philosophy and theology.[23]

Generally, Malebranche's dealings with the scholastics parallel those of Descartes, i.e., having scholastic professors as a student as well as a lifelong correspondence and differences with followers of Aristotle. The two differ in that Descartes's language *vis à vis* the scholastics is much more circumspect than that of Malebranche; Descartes tries as a "consummate borer from within" to engage in dialogue with his scholastic contemporaries hoping through using their conceptual apparatus to carry them with him.[24] Most likely, Delbos's comment meant to attribute the intensity of the polemic to Malebranche's manner in addressing the philosophical issues at stake. In this respect, Delbos is correct. In his disagreement with the peripatetics, Malebranche is much more candid than Descartes. Other aspects of Malebranche's personality, however, bear on this issue. Malebranche's extreme sensitivity coupled with his zeal to defend the truth despite a repugnance for engaging in quarrels also contributes significantly to the passion of his arguments.[25]

Secondly, Delbos interprets Malebranche's break with certain Cartesians over the nature of ideas and the soul's being able to think as distinct from his disagreement with the scholastics [20]. Delbos may be referring to Malebranche's working within a basically Cartesian metaphysics while attempting to correct Descartes and his followers such as Arnauld and Régis by elaborating his theory of seeing all things in God.[26] Or, perhaps, Delbos is referring to Malebranche's differences with the scholastics that do not center on psychological and epistemo-

vouloit qu'il se payât de l'autorité d'Aristote, et dans la théologie, qui doit être uniquement appuyée sur l'autorité divine, qu'il se payât de raisons, ou plutôt de raisonnemens qui, pour l'ordinaire, ne sont rien moins que raisonnables. Le voilà donc encore une fois degouté de l'école . . . ."

23 Gouhier 1926a, 9–10.

24 Grene 1991, 6–8.

25 Rodis–Lewis 1963, 20.

26 See Delbos 1924, 195 and Malbreil 1979.

logical differences.[27] However, in the *Recherche* Malebranche argues for his theory of mind and knowledge by eliminating the scholastic thesis as the first logical possibility and that which is the most common, i.e., the one which is held by the peripatetics.[28] Recent scholarship has argued that Malebranche's original conception of the Vision in God derives not from Cartesianism as illuminated by Augustinianism, as Malebranche tells us, but primarily from scholastic treatises on angelic knowledge.[29]

Finally, Delbos questions Gilson's central point that Malebranche, much more so than Descartes, attacks recourse to authority in philosophy because the attack in the *Recherche* includes not only the Aristotelians but also the new Cartesian school[30] tainted with remnants of Aristotelianism. Delbos's hesitation on this point in the essay designates it as one that he thought Gilson might have exaggerated. The tentativeness of Delbos's comment, i.e., double question marks following the comment [18], corresponds to the tentativeness of his comment on the cover page of the essay. Although cautiously expressed, Delbos suggests that Gilson failed to explain the subject of his essay. On this point, one can only agree with Delbos.

---

27 For Malebranche's dispute with Villemandy and L.F. Boursier, see Malebranche 1958– 67, 18:420–23 and 19:864 respectively.

28 Ibid., I:418. See Connell 1967, 162–163; Rodis–Lewis 1967, 123; and Rodis–Lewis 1963, 61.

29 Malebranche's account of the influences on his thought can be found in Malebranche 1958– 67, vol. 6-7:198–201. While acknowledging that "[f]ew writers have exceeded Malebranche in the bitterness of his contempt for the Scholastics," Desmond Connell (1967, 1–2 and 146–151) contended that a profound scholastic influence in the form of treatises on angelic knowledge may have contributed to Malebranche's original conception of the Vision in God. One of the principal reasons why this influence has been overlooked is that since Malebranche rejects decisively the scholastic teaching on human knowledge, no one thought of consulting the scholastic treatises on angels in which the link with Malebranche is to be found, i.e., how a purely immaterial spirit acquires its knowledge of the material world. Lennon (1980, 783) agreed: "Connell's main contention must be accepted." The debate on Malebranche's sources, however, is far from settled. See Connell 1974, 1978; and Malebranche 1992, I:1339 n.4 and 1465n.1.

30 Gouhier 1926a, 8–9.

Gilson does not establish psychologically or textually that Malebranche's dismissal of relying on authority is intentionally severe to ensure its implicit extension to Descartes's school. In criticizing such recourse as illegitimate, Malebranche follows Descartes's own methodological principle of insisting on evidence and reason.[31] Thus, Malebranche's attitude towards the scholastics can be interpreted legitimately as "a measure of the thoroughness of his Cartesianism."[32] Moreover, the texts criticizing a reliance on authority vary in tone depending on which audience Malebranche targets. His most scathing remarks target Aristotle and his followers, whereas comments on the same issue directed against Descartes and any uncritical followers are tempered due to Malebranche's conviction that, unlike scholasticism, Descartes's philosophy is fundamentally sound though not completely free of error.[33]

Gilson attributes the force and extent of the polemic within Malebranche's thought to its being further removed from the philosophy of the schools than that of Descartes; Delbos admits this as possible. Gilson emphasizes Malebranche's rejecting "even unconsciously" within Descartes precisely what is retained from Aristotle [22] but, unfortunately, he does not elaborate on this intriguing statement. At one point, Gilson alludes to the religious aspect of Malebranche's thought in the context of his profound antagonism to Aristotle ("it is truly a matter of setting one altar against another" [16]), but this suggestion also remains undeveloped. Delbos questions the appropriateness of Gilson's choice

---

31 *Principles*, IV, art. 207; Descartes 1904, 9:325.

32 Malebranche 1958–67, 1:449. See Connell 1967, 41. Even Malebranche's critique of Descartes always is based on the Cartesian method; see Malebranche 1958–67, 1:1350n.2 for page 15, and 1616n.1 for page 770.

33 "Descartes a découvert en trente années plus de vérités que tous les autres philosophes" (Malebranche 1958–67, 1:64). Although Malebranche accepts the new philosophy without reservation, he sees its defects: "M. Descartes était homme comme les autres, sujet à l'erreur et à l'illusion comme les autres." (Ibid., 1:412; see also 2:446–449). Malebranche advocates following the example of Descartes, a true savant, provided that one avoids becoming a blind follower of a sect: "Être Péripatéticien ou Platonicien, Gassendiste ou Cartésien, c'est là un défaut; car ce n'est pas assez craindre l'erreur que de se rendre à l'autorité des hommes qui y sont sujets" (ibid., 4:4). Malebranche's philosophical differences with Descartes may be timidly and cautiously expressed in his early works so as not to be accused of a rupture with Descartes. See Connell 1955, 550.

of language, but it is not clear whether he objects to the use of the term "altar" in a philosophical discussion, its applicability to Aristotle or to Malebranche, or both.

Gilson's essay has other limitations. It treats the polemic and related issues as found only in the *Recherche*, especially in *Eclaircissement XV* which deals with causality. Reliance in his essay on Bouillier's edition of the *Recherche*[34] precluded Gilson from treating the question of any development in Malebranche's thinking. However, the essay contains no indication that Gilson felt constrained by not considering anti–Aristotelianism within the rest of Malebranche's considerable corpus or the possible evolution of Malebranche's thought on this issue.[35] Also, Gilson briefly mentions Malebranche's inadequate understanding of Aristotle but never discusses why, despite an ability to read Greek, Malebranche makes no attempt in the *Recherche* to understand Aristotle's thought. Malebranche's view of history as a vain discipline is part of the reason he merely uses Aristotle to defend and justify his own position.[36] Furthermore, the essay does not adequately take into account the largely negative and critical function of the *Recherche* which explains why a critique of Aristotle and his followers is integral to it.

In the *Recherche*, Malebranche, determined to overthrow the foundations of pagan philosophy, explains the disorder that sin has caused in the world, and, by combating the prejudices and illusions of the senses, he shows us the true nature of experience.[37] Obviously, the last task is the most important since a pagan conception of nature cannot be overthrown until one has shown that the perceptions on which it is based are not truly natural to man. Nor can one show the disoriented

34 See Malebranche 1880.

35 See, for example, Malebranche 1958–67, 4:23, variants a–f of the *Conversations chrétiennes* where, over time, Malebranche's attack on Aristotle becomes much less aggressive.

36 See Adam 1967, 228, 239–242. "[L]e sens des attaques de Malebranche contre Aristote sera surtout de montrer ce qu'est sa propre pensée. Pour Malebranche, la pensée d'Aristote n'a pas un sens aristotélicien, mais un sens malebranchiste. Il l'utilise comme une sorte de repoussoir pour mieux manifester le mérite de sa pensée personnelle" (ibid., 241). Descartes had little use for wasting one's time studying the history of philosophy; this creates an interesting dilemma for his followers seeking truth in his works. See Gouhier 1980b, 40–42.

37 Malebranche 1958–67, I:10–11.

character of man's understanding until one, first of all, has shown the facts which demonstrate its malfunction. Malebranche's mission to destroy Aristotelianism necessitates integrating its critique into his work. Thus, Malebranche's critique of Aristotelianism is not, as Gilson claims, "almost an integral part of Malebranche's system,"[1], but absolutely essential to it.[38]

Criticism of Gilson's essay cannot be overly harsh; we know neither the nature of Delbos's assignment nor the level of effort expected by him. Father Shook emphasized the positive by noting that the penetrating criticism such as that which Delbos provided turned Gilson into a first rate scholar.[39]

Malebranche without Theology. Gilson's treatment of Malebranche derives, at least to some degree, from the general academic atmosphere at the Sorbonne and from Professor Delbos's approach to Malebranche and the history of philosophy. In writing about his professors at the Sorbonne between 1904 and 1907, Gilson stressed the extraordinary respect for freedom that inspired their teaching. "Our masters may well have told us *how*, in their opinion, we should think, but not one of them ever presumed to tell us *what* we should think."[40] Gilson also states that faith, be it Christian or Jewish, was absent from their public thinking. The wish to be religiously neutral meant that few among Gilson's professors felt free to teach "those truths that were to them highest and dearest." This led to a curious situation for philosophy itself.

To insure its religious "neutrality," Gilson's professors "restricted philosophy to those disciplines which, tending to establish themselves into so many separate sciences, broke away more and more completely from all metaphysics and even more from all religion." The history of philosophy did not especially stress what had interested the philosophers themselves, but rather what was considered important in its own right in philosophy. "Descartes announced positivism and Hume criticism; both were therefore important philosophers....Students were also introduced to a Malebranche without theology."[41] Gilson characterized Delbos

38 Gouhier 1926a, 8.

39 Shook 1984, 19.

40 Gilson 1962, 40.

41 Ibid., 35–39.

and his other professors as "pure Greek rationalists."[42] Despite rumors of Delbos being Catholic, "nothing in his teaching or in his writings would permit anyone to affirm it."[43] Moreover, Delbos, like Lachelier, Blondel, and so many other Catholic philosophers of the time, never "studied theology or felt any scruple about it." Delbos, according to Gilson," found in the later study of Malebranche his first introduction to theology properly so called."[44]

The attempt to be as objective as possible in presenting the history of philosophy, coupled with an extreme reserve and almost secretiveness concerning his personal life, may explain why Delbos's faith remained hidden from some students.[45] Perhaps this situation changed as Gilson progressed in his studies and career. We know that Gilson had a cor-

---

42 Ibid., 30.

43 Ibid., 35. Jacques Maritain had a similar experience: "Certains professeurs étaient croyants, mais rien ne paraissait de leur foi dans leurs enseignement. C'était le cas de Victor Delbos, éminent historien de la philosophie, esprit probe et profond, mais dont l'enseignement en grisaille laissait l'impression d'une méticuleuse prospection de belles ruines. C'est plus tard seulement que Jacques put entrevoir quelque chose des pensées intimes de Delbos, au cours d'une conversation . . . ." (Jacques and Raïssa Maritain 1993, 14:686).

44 Gilson 1962, 63–64.

45 "L'extrême modestie de l'homme—nous serions tentés d'écrire l'humilité du chrétien convaincu et éclairé qu'était Delbos—n'a guère permis qu'à ses intimes et à ses élèves d'entrevoir la doctrine personnelle de ce penseur qui volontairement différa d'exprimer son propre système, toujours prêt à s'effacer pour faire uniquement œuvre d'historien, satisfait du noble rôle d'interpréter, dans sa continuité, la tradition intellectuelle du genre humain" (Leclerc 1916, 657–8). For this aspect of Delbos's character, see Wehrlé 1932, 44 and 120. According to Wehrlé, "Il [Delbos] n'était pas seulement silencieux et violé; il était en quelque sorte secret . . . visiblement, il s'était fait une loi de garder pour lui et pour le Dieu qu'il n'a jamais cessé d'adorer le trésor jalousement dérobé aux regards de sa vie intérieure" (ibid., 13–14). ". . . Delbos fut le contraire d'un homme qui aime à paraître ou qui même simplement se prête à être regardé. Il resta caché jusqu'au bout. Il fut secret dans sa mort comme il avait été secret dans sa vie pour tout ce qu'il pouvait en dérober au regard des hommes" (ibid., 150–151). Maurice Blondel, a close friend and philosophical confidant of Delbos also discussed his personality; see Blondel 1966, 240, 243–245, 255, 264. In a letter to Blondel, Mr. Xavier Léon wrote, "[Delbos] c'était une espèce de saint, avec l'intelligence aussi pénétrante et le cœur aussi bon que le caractère était droit" (ibid., 269).

dial relationship with Delbos up until his death in 1916. Delbos first introduced Gilson to the thought of Maine de Biran, requested that he prepare materials for the *Bibliographie de philosophie*, and formally presented copies of Gilson's theses to the Institut de France. Afterwards, Delbos kept the young Gilson apprised of university openings, sent him books while he was a prisoner of war, and attended the same national and international philosophical conferences.[46]

In 1924, Delbos's study of Malebranche based on notes from his course given in 1910–1911 was published posthumously by his friend Joannès Wehrlé.[47] A summary of Delbos's 1903 lectures, comments on his lectures on Malebranche given at the École Normale Supérieure beginning in 1908, and the published study itself reflect a fundamental consistency in Delbos's approach to Malebranche's thought. Thus, there is good reason to believe that Delbos's study contains what Gilson heard in the form of lectures years earlier.[48] Regarded as "le livre décisif qui doit servir de guide,"[49] Delbos's work interprets Malebranche's thought as providing a metaphysical basis for a mathematical physics and as pushing, as far as possible, the agreement between religion and philosophy.[50] According to Delbos, Malebranche's thought was initially influenced by Descartes's separation of philosophy and theology; only afterwards does it evolve into a synthesis of elements borrowed from faith

46 See Shook 1984, 19, 47, 56, 58, 64, 80, 120, 125. Gilson frequently mentioned Delbos and cited his works. See, for example, Lefèvre 1925, 64 and Gilson 1953, 5 (trans. Maurer 1990, 40).

47 Delbos 1924, ix–xiv. Delbos, Wehrlé, and Blondel were classmates at the École Normale and remained close, lifelong friends. For Wehrlé's life, sarcedotal and academic career, and friendship with Delbos dating from student days at the École Normale Supérieure until Delbos's death, see Blondel 1939. Wehrlé's notes from Delbos's course in 1911–1912 served as the basis for two lectures on Malebranche that Delbos presented on 12 and 19 January 1916. Five months later, Delbos died and Blondel edited and published Delbos's entire set of lectures. See Delbos 1919. Wehrlé's important article on Malebranche (Wehrlé 1927) reflected the interpretations of Ollé-Laprune and Delbos—"qui restent à mes yeux les deux grands maîtres de l'exégèse malebranchiste" (Wehrlé 1928, 12).

48 See Constant 1904 and Hubert 1927, 271n.1.

49 See Gouhier 1938a, 170 and Wehrlé 1927, col.1804.

50 Delbos 1924, 339–340.

and drawn from philosophy.[51] Up until the end of his life, Delbos had serious reservations concerning the apologetical use of philosophy and denied the possibility of a conciliatory agreement between philosophy and theology.[52] He considered Maurice Blondel's philosophy of moral and religious action, which was heavily influenced by the thought of Ollé–Laprune, as the only possible solution to the question of the relationship between philosophy and theology.[53]

51 Ollé–Laprune (1870, 1:7) and Delbos (1924, 42 and 1919, 98) revived P. André's interpretation of Malebranche as above all a Cartesian in physics who completed the science of Descartes with the metaphysics of St. Augustine (André 1886, 14–15; Malebranche 1958–67, 17:51). According to Delbos (1924, 2), Ollé–Laprune's two volumes on Malebranche "restent la meilleure étude que nous ayons sur ce philosophe." More recently, André Robinet (1965, 11–12, 483–491) rehabilitated the thesis of Delbos. Both Hubert and Augusto Del Noce questioned "si le point de vue adopté par Delbos (recherche d'un fondement métaphysique à la science, pour faire apparaître le caractère critique de la philosophie Malebranchiste) n'y est pas un peu extrinsèque" (Hubert 1927, 283 and Rodis–Lewis 1963, 340n.2).

52 According to Wehrlé, "il ne semble pas non plus qu'il [Delbos] ait été favorable à l'établissement d'une philosophie qui pût conclure avec le catholicisme une sorte de concordat sur un plan d'objectivité conciliatrice. Comme il l'a déclaré lui–même, il trouvait fâcheuse 'appropriation de quelque philosophie, déjà constituée pour d'autres raisons, aux besoins apologétiques de la foi chrétienne'" [Delbos 1912, vii]. See also Wehrlé 1932, 125–126. Delbos emphasized this point by adding, "Presque toujours la philosophie religieuse s'est formée par artifice; constamment elle a cherché à vivre d'emprunts, d'utilisations; c'est pourquoi sans doute sa vitalité propre a été si peu vigoureuse et si peu féconde. Que ce soit le spiritualisme ordinaire, ou l'idéalisme, ou le criticisme, ou, comme cela est étrangement arrivé, le positivisme, ou toute autre doctrine existante qui fournisse à la foi en quête d'intelligence ses points d'appui rationnels: il apparaît toujours que l'âme de la religion vient se revêtir d'un corps étranger"(Delbos 1912, vii; Wehrlé 1932, 126). In commenting on Delbos's position, Sertillanges correctly pointed out that, "[à] ce compte, l'entreprise thomiste, aussi bien que celle de Malebranche ou de saint Augustin et de biens d'autres, serait d'avance condamnée" (Sertillanges 1941, 2:355).

53 Wehrlé 1932, 125–130. Gilson discussed both Blondel and Ollé–Laprune. See Gilson, Langan, and Maurer 1966, 358–362. Gilson noted that "Among the differences between Blondel and Ollé–Laprune was the former's initial ignorance of scholasticism (both philosophical and theological) which, however, he never ceased to attack, deride and charge with all sorts of philosophical and religious sins" (ibid., 795n.7.) In June 1962, Gilson confessed to

The religious neutrality of Gilson's professors that was based on the position that any philosophical doctrine submitting to some external authority was disqualified by that very fact[54] partially explains why years of further study would be required to provide Gilson with an understanding of theology. That understanding enabled him to situate Malebranche's philosophy in a new context and offered a more satisfactory account of Malebranche's anti-Aristotelianism and antischolasticism.

Gilson's Essay Revisited. During the 1920s, Gilson continued to build on his doctoral work on Descartes and confront Cartesian philosophy with medieval thought. Gilson produced classic studies of Descartes revolving around his elimination of substantial forms to explain the universe in terms of mathematical concepts and principles. This work allowed Gilson to revisit issues that he discussed in his essay for Delbos. In specifying the transformations of medieval philosophical notions and the resulting metaphysical impoverishment in Descartes's system, Gilson referred to Malebranche's occasionalism and vision in God as natural outgrowths of the elimination of forms, albeit within a philosophy radically different from Descartes's, which separates philosophy from faith.[55]

Gilson also modified the position he took in his student essay in explaining Descartes's being much less concerned than Malebranche to refute the scholastics. The matter was of little concern to Descartes, not because he was closer than Malebranche to the philosophy of the

---

Gouhier that Blondel's work "reste aussi illisible que jamais; sa position me paraît plus contradictoire que jamais," and then went on to say "je n'ai en tout cas aucun doute sur la haute qualité philosophique et religieuse de cette grande âme. Je voudrais être le quart du chrétien que fut Blondel. Ses erreurs mêmes (je pense à sa critique d'une scolastique dont il était ignorant) s'expliquent par le fait que sa génération—et celle de Delbos—était à son égard dans un état d'ignorance invincible. La mienne est arrivée juste à temps pour que l'étude de l'histoire lui permit d'en sortir, de s'en sortir et à travers combien d'embarras, de méprises, peut-être même de contradictions" (Prouvost 1994b, 472). See also Gouhier 1932b.

54 Gilson's comment regarding Blondel's experience within "the milieu of the École Normale Supérieure where every doctrine submitting to some external authority was disqualified by that very fact" also applied to Blondel's classmate, Victor Delbos. See Gilson, Langan, and Maurer 1966, 795n.9.

55 Gilson 1935b, 341–342.

schools, but because after the publication of the *Principles* Descartes was convinced that publishing his own physics would, *ipso facto,* clearly and absolutely destroy scholastic philosophy.[56]

Having discovered the necessity of understanding medieval doctrines in order to comprehend the true novelty of Cartesian philosophy, Gilson continued to study these doctrines themselves. This study of the medievals represented the decisive moment in his intellectual life. Initially, Gilson attempted to apply to the theologians of the Middle Ages the method of inquiry that Lévy–Bruhl and Delbos taught him to use in the study of modern philosophers. This approach did not succeed and, following the rule that one refrains from inventing in order to better understand, Gilson finally had to bow to the evidence that St. Thomas and St. Bonaventure did not philosophize like other philosophers because they were not philosophers but scholastic theologians[57].

In his work on St. Bonaventure, Gilson rejected the idea that Bonaventure and St. Thomas belonged to one and the same family of thinkers who attempted to construct a philosophy standing on its own feet and independent of faith. Gilson contrasted the philosophies of these two doctors opposing Bonaventurism to Thomism and presenting Bonaventure's philosophy as Augustinianism and Bonaventure himself as a thinker who philosophized from within the faith developing his thought from reflections on the truths revealed by Christ and the Church.

Inspired by his Franciscan vision of the world and supported by Augustinianism that the Franciscan theologians inherited from Alexander of Hales, Bonaventure's Christian philosophy was a conscious reaction

---

56 Ibid., 463–464: "'Mais aussi est–il vrai que j'ai entièrement perdu le dessein de réfuter cette Philosophie [scholastique]; car je vois qu'elle est si absolument et si clairement détruite, par le seul établissement de la mienne, qu'il n'est pas besoin d'autre réfutation.' À Mersenne, 22 décembre, 1641." Gilson added: "When the *Discourse on Method* appeared, it came too late on the scene to kill scholasticism. All the creative forces of contemporary thought had long turned away from it and had betaken themselves elsewhere. But it remains true that Descartes drew up the death certificate. To analyze the causes of death, to show what it was that prevented scholasticism from thinking and so from living, to define the rules of a method productive of new truths because opposed at every point to the old method, was to do much more than turn away from scholasticism. It amounted to suppressing it by supplanting it" (Gilson 1935a, 53; trans. Gilson 1990, 83–84).

57 Gilson 1962, 96.

against the heterodox Aristotelianism that had taken root at the Faculty of Arts in Paris. Bonaventure had not simply fallen short of the synthesis between Christianity and Aristotelianism which his contemporary Thomas Aquinas succeeded in bringing to completion; Bonaventure also envisioned the possibility of working out such a synthesis and deliberately rejected it. Although Bonaventure admired Aristotle as a man excelling in knowledge, nonetheless from a Christian point of view, he thought that the purely natural philosophy of Aristotle was mere folly. Bonaventure and Thomas are both Christian philosophers, but their Christian philosophies are essentially distinct.

In his third edition of *Le thomisme* (1927), Gilson began revising his earlier interpretations of St. Thomas's philosophy to show that it, too, had been developed from within the faith but on lines that were basically Aristotelian and that differed from those followed by St. Bonaventure and St. Augustine. For Gilson, St. Thomas is essentially a theologian who used philosophy but who was not a philosopher. Because Aquinas's theology "could not have been constituted as such unless it borrowed its techniques from an underlying philosophy having its own principles," Thomism, according to Gilson, had room "by the side of theology which should be nothing but theology, for a philosophy which should be nothing but philosophy." For this reason, St. Thomas is "the first and not the least of modern philosophers."[58] Because Thomism establishes itself on a different philosophical base in the 13th century, the Augustinians accused it not only of thereby breaking with St. Augustine, but also of breaking with the Christian tradition by returning to the pagan philosophy of Aristotle.

As an example of the difference between Thomism and Augustinianism, Gilson examines St. Thomas's critique of those who deny to secondary causality all efficacity in order to reserve to God the privilege of causality. For Aquinas, divine operation is necessary for the produc-

58 Gilson 1924b, ix and 53; Gilson 1921a, v and 76–124. Although satisfied that his conclusion remained correct, Gilson cautioned readers on specific points of his interpretation that could give the impression that Aquinas was a Christian rationalist. See Gilson 1932a, 432n.36 and Gilson 1930c, 53n.1. In concluding that St. Thomas wrote as a theologian and could not be reduced to a mere philosopher, Gilson may have been aided by his friend Jacques Maritain. See Shook 1986. For Gilson's discussion of his "odyssey" in discovering the true nature of scholastic and Thomistic theology see Gilson 1962, 97–105 and Gilson 1993, xiv–xviii.

tion of natural effects since secondary causes owe all their efficacy to the first cause which is God. But it is not superfluous that God, who can produce by Himself all the natural effects, should yet produce them by the intermediary of certain other causes. These intermediaries which He has willed are not necessary to God, but it is for their own sake that God has willed them. For Aquinas the existence of secondary causes is not evidence of a lack of power, but a tribute to the immensity of God's goodness. To adversaries like certain Augustinians viewing St. Thomas's thought from the outside, this doctrine seems to be a vindication of the rights of the creature against those of God, "an accusation all the more insidious as St. Thomas draws his inspiration ostensibly from Aristotle and seems to that extent to yield to the influence of pagan naturalism." For the same reason, the doctrine of illumination remains characteristic of the Augustinian tradition: it guarantees the maximum dependence of the intellect on God in knowing. From this point of view Malebranche's philosophy is "the absolute antithesis of Thomism." Malebranche never forgave Aquinas for inserting "natures" and "efficient causes" between natural effects and God.[59]

In his studies on Bonaventure and Aquinas, Gilson attempted for the first time to give precise and technical meaning to the expression, "Christian philosophy." The success of these studies increased Gilson's interest in St. Augustine, determined the way for a major part of his future work, and prepared the groundwork for an adequate treatment of Malebranche's antischolasticism.

As Gouhier masterfully argued, Malebranche was a Christian philosopher from the beginning of his career. Hence, Gouhier disagreed with Delbos's position that initially Malebranche separated the realms of faith and reason but gradually developed a reciprocal relationship between the two. If this were the case, one would have to speak not of an evolution but of a "conversion" on the part of Malebranche. Gouhier argued that Delbos's position cannot be established textually; moreover, it did not do justice to the Augustinianism, "faith in search of understanding," present as Malebranche's dominant concern from the outset. "Ce qui est premier dans l'ordre chronologique comme dans l'ordre de la dialectique, c'est l'union intime de la raison et de la foi, c'est l'idée d'une

59 Gilson 1924b, 197–198, 203n.21. Malebranche repeated the attempt of Al Ash'ari, a ninth century Mohammedan theologian, to reconcile a created world empty of all intrinsic efficacy with the Greek notion of natural and necessary laws; see Gilson 1922a, 347 and Gilson 1955, 184–185.

philosophie chrétienne où la raison éclairée par la foi part en quête du vrai bien."[60]

In true Augustinian fashion, Malebranche viewed the progress of atheism and attacks against Christianity as driven by the insufficiencies of scholasticism, especially Aristotle's physics, within religion. One need only recall that Luther declared war against Rome and Aristotle. Hence, Malebranche decided to separate doctrines of faith which had been arbitrarily and unfortunately linked to Aristotelianism and create a new philosophy.[61] Many attacked the faith when, in reality, their attack was against an infirm theology and propositions of Aristotelianism. For Gouhier and Gilson, Malebranche's *Recherche* was a work of Cartesian apologetics. The apologetic nature of Malebranche's philosophy was what accounted for his intense hatred of Aristotle as expressed in "a holy anger," "the explosion of a ... rancor ... of a violence of which Descartes never set the example."[62] Not surprisingly, Gilson attributed Gouhier's

---

60 Gouhier 1926b, 140–143 and Rome 1963, 319–322. Gouhier also dismissed Ollé–Laprune's and Vidgrain's attempts to explain the relation of faith and reason in Malebranche (Gouhier 1926b, 139; see Gilson 1928). So did others: "Delbos avait éprouvé une extrême difficulté à unir les divers témoignages de Malebranche, et avait supposé gratuitement une évolution dans la pensée du philosophe, alors que tout s'ordonne au contraire si l'on comprend que les ressources véritablement distinguées de la raison et de la foi sont mises au service de l'intelligence du 'fait chrétien'" (Forest 1928, 131). "Delbos malgré toute sa probité et son objectivité d'homme de science, lui [Gouhier] paraît, semble–t–il, encore trop loin des faits, trop sensible aussi peut–être au mystère et à la majesté des doctrines philosophiques, pour tout dire un peu timide et compassé. M. G.[ouhier] est plus direct, il a une hardiesse souple et vive, une gentille ironie, qui vont droit aux réalités, avec sympathie, mais avec bon sens précis, sans goût pour illusion" (Rolland–Gosselin 1926).

Using Gilson's work on St. Thomas, Gouhier (1926b, 161-162) arrived at the paradoxical conclusion that the Augustinian Malebranche conceived of theology as a Thomist. Others argued that Malebranche's notion of Christian philosophy "mêlait dogme surnaturel et spéculation métaphysique, sans distinguer suffisamment les compétences respectives. La notion d'une philosophie chrétienne, à prendre les choses en rigueur, s'en trouvait compromise, et tendait à perdre sa vraie signification" (Rolland 1938, 1–2, n.1).

61 Gouhier 1926a, 6–7; Malebranche 1958–67, 1:395

62 Gouhier 1926a, 10. The parallels between Gilson's student essay for Delbos and Gouhier's "Introduction" to his "great thesis" (1926a, 5–12) are striking. While agreeing with Gouhier's interpretation, Adam (1967, 242) is

successful interpretation of Malebranche to his understanding of Augustinianism, something Professor Delbos never possessed.[63]

Gilson developed his own interpretation of Malebranche as stemming from medieval roots, acting as a transitional figure in the history of philosophy, constructing a Christian philosophy within the Cartesian context, and dealing unsuccessfully with its inherent problems.[64] Gilson may not have agreed with Malebranche, but he always took him seriously as a first-rate thinker, treated Malebranche as a major figure in the history of philosophy, and used him extensively in works that philosophized on the data of the history of philosophy.[65]

---

less dramatic: "En critiquant les livres d'Aristote, Malebranche avait le souvenir d'un autre Livre. Et c'est pour faire de la philosophie au service de ce Livre qu'il a écrit les siens. Et ici, il n'y avait, d'aucune façon possible, place pour tout le monde à la fois." See also Gilson 1934b, 13.

63 "... l'étude consciencieuse de V. Delbos manquait de l'arrière-plan historique que la connaissance de l'augustinisme pouvait seule lui fournir... M.L. Brunschvicg observait récemment que l'heure des réparations dues allait enfin sonner pour Malebranche; le grand méditatif n'en recevra pas de plus brillante que les deux volumes consacrés par M. Gouhier à l'histoire de sa pensée" (Gilson 1928, 152). Robinet (1967, 333–334) elaborated Brunschvicg's point: "... il fallut les commémorations de 1916 et surtout de 1938 pour mettre au premier plan le souci des études malebranchistes. Vidgrain, Delbos, Bridet, firent beaucoup pour l'explication d'une philosophie considérée comme suspecte de théologie. Le mouvement profond de rénovation, de compréhension et d'exposition qui se dessinait prit sa forme définitive dans l'œuvre de M. Gouhier. En étendant l'enquête historique et en dégageant les traits réels de sa philosophie, M. Gouhier donnait à Malebranche l'autorité définitive et le droit de cité universitaire qu'on lui avait mesurés jusque-là. On pourra constater le regain d'intérêt pour les études malebranchistes qui suivit les publications de 1926."

64 See, for example, Gilson 1941, 88–98 and Gilson, Langan, and Maurer 1966, 89–107. The former has not received in France the attention it merits; see Jean-Luc Marion 1980, 34n.34. The latter is not cited in Easton, Lennon, and Sebba 1992.

65 See Gilson 1937a, 185–196, 210–218. In his 9 June 1966 letter to Gouhier, Gilson commented on the approach he took in *The Unity of Philosophical Experience*: "... [J]e crois à la possibilité d'une expérience sur les métaphysiques, où les doctrines servent seulement à vérifier in concreto la nécessité abstraite de certaines relations intelligibles. J'en ai parlé un jour, à Bruxelles je crois [see Gilson 1953], mais ce doit être une notion absurde car elle n'a soulevé aucun écho d'aucun côté. R.I.P" (Prouvost 1994b, 478).

APPENDIX 2

A PORTRAIT OF GILSON[1]

6 May 1935. From a conversation with Du Bos.[2] He admires in Gilson that simple common sense which does not require any simplifying. This is not the exact expression, but it is close. What is amazing about Gilson is the force with which he inflates common sense with intelligence. For most people that possess it, common sense is a deflated windbag of an anemic intelligence. Frequently—under the rubric of coarse common sense—we admire a kind of intellectual brutality which is plain laziness of the mind.* But with Gilson, the word *common* [*bon*] has regained the meaning of *right*.

* Or much less: the cult of Clement Vautel[3] represents common sense for the readers of the *Journal* [Gouhier's note].

---

1 My title for this excerpt from Henri Gouhier's personal notebook (unpublished).

2 Charles Du Bos (1882–1939) writer and French literary critic. Du Bos's works have been described as representing "une attitude parfaitement inactuelle, dans le meilleur sens du mot. Pour peu que nous nous plongions dans cette lecture, nous nous sentons enveloppés de calme et de recueillement. C'est l'atmosphère de la contemplation. Ce terme emprunté à la vie mystique. La critique européenne se tient ordinairement sur le plan de l'intelligence discursive. Finesse psychologique, intelligence nuancée, compréhension artistique très développée, telles sont les qualités fondamentales de cette critique, en particulier de la critique française, de Sainte-Beuve à Thibaudet. La critique de Charles Du Bos est d'une tout autre sorte. Elle a sa source, non pas dans l'intelligence analytique, mais dans une expérience intérieure d'espèce métaphysique, dans cet événement vécu que le chrétien nomme l'attouchement de la grâce, le mystique, l'illumination, l'artiste, la vision, le philosophe, l'intuition." See Curtius 1926.

3 Clément Vautel (1875–1954), a prominent novelist and journalist well known for his natal and antifeminist views, wrote for a number of French newspapers. From 1918 to 1940 his popular daily column, "Mon Film," in the *Journal* provided brief commentary on the news and gained a great following. Because of his political views Jean Lacouture (1990, II, 118) described Vautel as a "crétin conservateur."

Common sense, far from being an oversimplification of questions, is, on the contrary, what enables him spontaneously to show the real complexity of questions under their apparent simplicity.

I know few men who have fewer prejudices. He has an integrity that works with hair-trigger precision before every judgment: the reduction to the real is instantaneous. He will immediately see *what is beneath*. Never taken in by the sets, he begins by going into the wings.

There is a genius of common sense.

Gilson's works are perfectly objective. He is a historian. He never speaks about himself. On the objective plane, this historical serenity is the transposition of interior serenity onto the level of life. One senses that it is the same man who takes Bernard to the zoo and reconstructs the thought of Saint Thomas. There is an absolute equilibrium that manifests itself in each step this soul takes.

It is by such matters that he gives the impression of soul. Frequently, it is conveyed by frailness, even sickness—everything that is a diminishing of matter, or even a diminishing of the matter. Therein lies a sign of our degeneration. The soul is, above all, unity and health, equilibrium and dominion. Gilson cannot convey an impression of soul to aesthetes, to snobs of spirituality who only see the soul via the bodies of El Greco. It is true the soul is there, but not exclusively. Furthermore, we would understand nothing of El Greco[4] if all we took from him were these spiritualized forms of anemic bodies.

---

4 In his work, El Greco (1541–1614), a Greek/Spanish Mannerist painter, combined courtly elegance with religious fervor. Influenced by the dictates of the Counter Reformation in Toledo, Spain, El Greco intentionally elongated or distorted form to emphasize the spiritual quality of a figure or event so as to have an emotional effect on the viewer and impart a sense of piety. Penitence, as exemplified by the Catholic saints, was one of his common themes.

For Gouhier, Gilson "a été philosophe d'abord parce qu'il a toujours connu et aimé la vie dans sa plénitude. . . . [L]'activité de Gilson a toujours largement débordé la vaste culture du spécialiste." Maine de Biran's observation that "Il n'y a guère que les gens malsains qui se sentent exister" is complemented appropriately by Gouhier's point that "L'homme parfaitement sain se sent exister et la philosophie est comme une exigence de son unité. . . . La santé a sa profondeur lorsqu'elle est la santé lucide de saint Thomas, la santé exubérante de Rubens, la santé triomphante de Paul Claudel" (Gouhier 1980a, 162; Gouhier 1960, 45–47).

It is through this presence of soul, health, and equilibrium, that Gilson is related to Claudel.[5] If Claudel were as intelligent as Gilson, we would have a Catholic Goethe.

---

5 Paul Claudel (1868–1955) a French poet, playwright, essayist, and diplomat was a towering force in French literature. His works derive their lyrical inspiration, unity and scope, and prophetic tone from Claudel's faith in God. See Shook 1984, 178. "Claudel and Gilson had much in common. They were both exemplary Catholics who lived in the public eye, and both were active in the French cultural mission. Despite different interests they were both involved with literature. And in their respective modes of thought, both were realists."

THE FRENCH TEXTS

I

Strasbourg
7 novembre 1920

Monsieur,

Je vous remercie vivement de l'intéressant article que vous m'avez envoyé et de tout ce qu'il contient d'aimable à mon égard. Je n'ai jamais étudié d'aussi près que vous la question des rapports de la raison et de la foi chez Descartes; c'est donc plutôt à vous qu'il appartient de nous instruire et je ne prétends aucunement vous dire quels sont les défauts de votre travail, si toutefois il en a. Je ne veux donc vous dire, en dehors du plaisir réel que j'ai eu à vous lire, que les quelques scrupules qu'éveille dans ma pensé votre manière de traiter la question.

1. Vous cherchez à définir ce qu'a pu être la foi de Descartes. Êtes-vous sûr que ce problème soit susceptible d'une solution historique? Le P. Laberthonnière en fait une "foi sèche"; Espinas en fait une foi de chevalier errant, et ardente; vous croyez qu'elle est quelque chose de spontané et de connaturel à sa personnalité. II faudrait sans doute distinguer entre les époques, et sa foi peut avoir été tout cela successivement. En tout cas, les documents qui nous éclaireraient là-dessus me semblent extrêmement maigres; à moins, bien entendu, que vous n'en apportiez de nouveaux dans votre travail. Je ne doute pas de la foi de Descartes, mais j'ignore vraiment quelle nuance particulière elle présentait. Si je devais lui donner un épithète, pour sauver ma vie par exemple, je dirais que ce fut une sorte de *loyalisme*; je le dirais, et je le crois, mais je n'en sais rien.

2. On ne résout pas le problème en montrant que Descartes conçoit les rapports de la foi et de la raison comme les concevait saint Thomas. Descartes peut souscrire aux formules de saint Thomas ou même les reprendre, il n'en reste pas moins que le rapport *historique* entre ces deux éléments peut être fort différent dans les deux doctrines. Et je crois qu'il l'est. Chez les deux philosophes, il y a à la fois accord des deux éléments, et indépendance; mais en fait, la philosophie de saint Thomas me parait être née dans et pour sa religion; celle de Descartes me semble être née

de préoccupations autres que religieuses. Voyez quelle profonde différence avec Malebranche par exemple.

3. Je crois que vous avez tout à fait raison d'insister sur le caractère partial de l'histoire de la philosophie. Sur ce point je serai encore plus d'accord avec vous que sur le reste. Il faut espérer que les choses changeront.

Si vous me permettez un conseil, je vous engagerai à revoir l'histoire de la philosophie médiévale, afin de combler l'entre-deux entre Descartes et saint Thomas. Puis vous reviendrez à Descartes; et vous sentirez mieux alors combien il est éloigné du moyen-âge sur ce point, au moins du thomisme. Malebranche, au contraire, est à sa manière un scolastique.

Mais je crois que vous avez plus pressé à faire pour cette année. Croyez, en tout cas, que je serai toujours à votre entière disposition si vous croyez que je puisse vous être de quelque utilité.

Ét. Gilson.

2

Strasbourg
3, allée de la Robertsau
17 septembre 1921

Cher monsieur,

Permettez-moi de vous féliciter d'abord pour votre succès à l'agrégation—clef de votre vie intellectuelle—et pour la bonne idée que vous avez de mettre à profit l'année de travail qui vous reste à passer à Paris en amorçant vos thèses de doctorat.

Le sujet que vous me soumettez est certainement intéressant, mais il a pour vous deux inconvénients.

1. Il ne vous qualifiera pas pour un enseignement d'histoire de la philosophie, au moins pas *indiscutablement*. On vous qualifiera "Histoire des idées religieuses" et vous trouverez difficilement une chaire.

2. C'est un sujet sur lequel vous pouvez travailler longtemps sans aucune certitude d'aboutir; je ne suis pas sûr que les multiples recherches de détail que vous aurez à poursuivre sur les libertins vous conduisent à des trouvailles intéressantes, et, en ce qui concerne Descartes, il n'y aurait aucune raison de l'isoler d'un mouvement beaucoup plus vaste de renaissance catholique dans lequel il risquerait de se trouver un peu perdu.

Il va sans dire néanmoins que si vous teniez beaucoup au sujet vous pourriez essayer à vos risques et périls. Je vous conseillerais cependant plutôt de le tenir en réserve et de noter ce qui s'y rapportera dans vos études ultérieures sur la même époque. Si vous le voyez ainsi se dessiner, en faisant autre chose, rien ne vous empêchera de le reprendre plus tard sans avoir perdu un ou deux ans à des recherches aventureuses.

Quant à des sujets de travaux sur cette periode, et qui soient de vrais sujets, j'en vois, et beaucoup, et qui peuvent devenir très beaux. En voici quelques uns auxquels vous pourrez réfléchir.

1. *Histoire de l'averroisme latin du XIII au XVIIe siecle.*
La livre de Renan est à refaire en entier. Sujet très étendu; études fastidieuses par moments; mais vous conduira à des milieux italiens curieux et mal étudiés; aboutit au mouvement que vous vouliez analyser.

2. *Gassendi*.[1]
Entièrement à reprendre après le livre de P. F. Thomas qui n'est qu'un 'compte-rendu' des œuvres de Gassendi; le remettre dans son temps, faire l'histoire du développement de ses idées; montrer en lui l'homme de la Renaissance que Thomas n'a pas vu. Pourquoi G[assendi] qui, au XVIIe siècle était l'égal de Descartes a-t-il disparu. Gass[endi], et la physique corpusculaire (remarquez que Descartes et Gassendi sont deux témoins particuliers de ce mouvement)

Je vous signale en outre une rédaction manuscrite inédite d'une importante partie du *Syntagma philosophicum*, sans doute antérieure à celle qui a été imprimée. Thomas en connaissait l'existence et ne l'a pas utilisée! Elle est à la Bibliothèque municipale de Tours et la Bibliothèque de l'École en aurait sans doute communication. Bib. munic. de Tours, M^{ss} n$^{os.}$ 709–710.

3. *Correspondance de Mersenne.*
La publication en est urgente, mais il faudrait d'abord en faire une sorte d'inventaire analytique préparatoire à la publication. *Excellente thèse complémentaire*; vous situerait en plein cœur de l'époque que vous voulez étudier.

4. *Leibniz*.[2]
Leibniz *comme philosophe de la Renaissance* et étudié au point de vue de l'évolution et de la formation de sa pensée philosophique. Cherchez

1 Underlined twice in the original.

2 Underlined twice in the original.

dans la thèse de Blanchet le rapprochement avec Campanella; c'est la clef de Leibniz auquel nous ne comprenons plus rien faute de savoir que le XVIe siècle a duré au moins jusqu'au XVIIIe (excusez cette sottise, mais vous me comprendrez). Même les préoccupations religieuses de Leibniz, bien étudiées par J. Baruzi, datent du XVIe siècle.

5. *Malebranche: le dernier des grands scolastiques augustiniens.* Résurrection, dans le cas Malebranche, de la lutte engagée au XIIIe siècle entre thomisme aristotélicien et augustinisme traditionnel. Vous auriez là la clef de tous les cas de *modernisme*, jusqu'à l'abbé Bautain et au P. Laberthonnière inclusivement.

Je ne vous indique là, bien entendu, que des points de départ. À vous d'y réfléchir et de tailler dans chaque question le domaine qui vous conviendrait, en vous efforçant de travailler en profondeur plutôt qu'en étendue. Inutile d'ajouter que je serai toujours à votre disposition pour parler avec vous des questions quelles qu'elles soient, qui pourraient vous intéresser.

Croyez, je vous prie, à mon entier dévouement.

Ét. Gilson

3

Strasbourg
26 Septembre 1921

Cher monsieur,

Je crains d'avoir oublié, en vous écrivant, l'un des points de départ les plus intéressants qui soient pour étudier le début du XVIIe siècle. Je me suis souvent demandé quand et où commencait le mouvement augustinien qui passe par Descartes et s'épanouit chez Ambrosius Victor et Malebranche. Ce mouvement mériterait d'être étudié en lui-même; il passe par de grands hommes et je crois que certaines des questions que vous vous posiez y trouveraient leur réponse.

Veuillez croire, je vous prie, à mes sentiments tout dévoués.

Ét. Gilson

4

Strasbourg
27 septembre 1921

Cher monsieur,

Vous ne m'importunez aucunement, au contraire, et j'espère bien que nous aurons l'occasion de nous entretenir du sujet qui vous intéresse au cours de la prochaine année scolaire. Ma nomination ne se fera qu'à la fin du mois d'octobre, mais il paraît qu'elle se fera certainement; nous irons plus vite en parlant qu'en écrivant. En attendant voici ce que je pense exactement des questions que vous me posez.

1. Le livre de Blampignon est intelligent et c'est lui qui a fourni à Ollé-Laprune son point de départ.

2. Le livre d'Ollé-Laprune, vieilli par certains côtés, reste très remarquable, et je crois qu'il a vu le fonds de Malebranche. D'ailleurs, il existe, entre les mains de M. D. Roustan, je crois, un Malebranche inédit de Delbos qui complète certainement les deux volumes d'Ollé-Laprune. Le livre d'Henri Joly est absolument nul. Mais avec Ollé-Laprune et Delbos, c'en est assez pour que vous ne puissiez pas songer à donner une thèse sur Malebranche purement et simplement.

3. C'est donc bien de Malebranche comme cas privilégié de la renaissance augustinienne qu'il faudrait partir. Là encore vous avez devant vous Blampignon et Ollé-Laprune: ce dernier en particulier (tome I, Première partie, chap. 1) a signalé l'essentiel des antécédents augustiniens de Malebranche, mais son chapitre, très clairvoyant, ne donne que des indications et vous montrera très précisément dans quelles directions pourraient s'orienter les premières recherches. Surtout la faiblesse d'Ollé-Laprune est qu'il ignore le moyen-âge; il ne voit pas, malgré ses citations de saint Thomas, que Malebranche, en tant précisément qu'augustinien, est un antithomiste; c'est un scolastique de type augustinien, exactement comme saint Bonaventure. L'intérêt de Malebranche c'est que contrairement à Descartes, il ressuscite en plein XVIIème siècle l'augustinisme du XIIIe; c'est un épisode d'une lutte séculaire, et qui dure encore, entre deux orientations scolastiques différentes. Lorsque vous auriez étudié les augustiniens du XIIIe siècle vous serez surpris de voir à quel point Malebranche n'est que l'un d'eux et, à ce moment, vous pourrez *interpréter*, donner leur sens précis et historiquement démontrable, à tant de caractères de sa doctrine qui sont *connus*, mais *incompris*.

Exemples: Ollé-Laprune dit: c'est "une philosophie religieuse." C'est vrai, mais c'est vague. Exactement: c'est "la *Sagesse*[3] augustinienne," c'est-à-dire: la foi qui cherche l'intelligence. (Sur ce point Malebranche *copie* l'augustinien saint Anselme.)

La critique de l'aristotélisme par Malebranche est celle de tous les augustiniens pour qui aristotélisme = paganisme.

Vous trouverez beaucoup d'autres choses en cherchant dans cette direction. Ambrosius Victor doit être une source inépuisable de rapprochements. Mais pour situer exactement Malebranche dans l'histoire il faut déterminer le cours du mouvement augustinien, ses raisons d'être, si possible, et sa vraie signification. C'est la fausse idée d'une coupure entre le XVII siècle et le moyen-âge qui nous rend un homme comme Malebranche inintelligible, et je crois que l'histoire de la philosophie augustinienne en France au XVIIe siècle ou, tout au moins de la partie de ce mouvement qui conditionne immédiatement Malebranche, mériterait qu'on l'écrive.

C'est Mr. D. Roustan qui est chargé de l'édition de Malebranche. Son travail est très avancé mais je ne sais exactement où en est la question impression.

Veuillez croire, je vous prie, à mes sentiments dévoués.

Ét. Gilson

5

[Undated notes from Gilson attached to one of his letters to Gouhier sent during the early stages of his work on Malebranche]

A quoi je ferai observer:

1. que si la *philosophie* consiste en *métaphysique* Malebranche n'avait pas à l'apprendre de Descartes et il ne l'en apprendra jamais; car il tient la sienne de S. Augustin.

2. Malebranche *augustinien* est à l'état de repos, il ne philosophe pas pour son compte. Quand philosophera-t-il? Quand il aura trouvé la *physique* cartésienne de l'étendue et du mouvement.

3. L'ayant trouvée il devient philosophe car son équilibre intérieur est rompu; il le trouvera quand il aura complété la métaphysique d'Augustin par la physique de Descartes.

4. Il me paraît donc bien que c'est le strict mécanisme du *Traité de l'Homme* qui a dû déclencher son activité philosophique personnelle.

---

3 Underlined twice in the original.

5. Ceci posé, la préface en question est à mettre au premier plan parce qu'elle formule ce mécanisme avec une rigueur telle qu'elle invite à l'occasionalisme.

6

6, rue Ponthierry
Melun (S-et-M)
28 juillet 1922

Mon cher ami,

Je vous félicite bien cordialement de votre nomination à la Fondation Thiers, et d'autant plus que vous ne la devez qu'à vous-même. Si vos titres n'avaient été jugés suffisants, quels titres l'auraient été? Je suis heureux aussi que vous aperceviez les lignes directrices de votre thèse et dans la situation où vous allez vous trouver vous pourrez la pousser très activement; vous savez qu'à mon avis une thèse doit être achevée sans lenteur; ce n'est pas un "Lebenswerk." Quant à un Diplôme pour l'École Pratique des Hautes Études c'est aussi une excellente idée et je crois même qu'il peut y avoir intérêt à le faire; c'est un milieu qui n'est pas aussi vivant encore qu'il pourrait l'être, mais qui le deviendra, et j'ai pu constater dans bien des cas que c'était déjà une force plus considérable qu'on ne le suppose. J'ai fait inscrire pour l'une de mes deux conférences: *Descartes et la pensée religieuse de son temps*. Je l'ai fait avec l'espoir que vous seriez encore à Paris. Je vous serais reconnaissant de vouloir bien ouvrir cette série de conférences par trois ou quatre leçons (le terme étant impropre d'ailleurs) dans lesquelles vous nous exposeriez votre conception des rapports de la raison et de la foi chez Descartes d'après vos recherches antérieures. Inutile de fournir aucun effort nouveau sur la question; nous le tenterons ensemble après si vous le voulez bien. Je crois d'ailleurs que vous pourriez transformer votre travail de diplôme en un travail pour les Hautes Études, à moins bien entendu, que vous n'aperceviez un autre sujet. (Votre note dans la *Revue de métaphysique* était bien amusante; mais il est stupéfiant que personne ne se soit aperçu que Descartes était *conservateur*.) Je vous reparlerai de cela à la rentrée car je suis en préparation de voyage. En bon disciple de Descartes je vais fermer mes livres pendant cinq ou six semaines pour lire le livre du monde et pour me décrasser dans l'action. Je pars presque certainement le 12 août pour les régions affamées de la Russie; j'espère qu'en rentrant mon témoignage permettra de sauver quelques malheureux et, qui sait, quelques milliers peut-être. Je compte m'occuper surtout des enfants et des intellectuels; j'aime mieux cela que de m'ennuyer pendant un mois au bord de la mer.

Je vous remercie de m'avoir envoyé la liste d'agrégation; j'y ai vu beaucoup de noms avec plaisir et j'espère, que ceux-là resteront sur la liste définitive.

Croyez, mon cher ami, à mes sentiments tout dévoués.

Ét. Gilson

7

[carte postale]
21 Octobre 1922

Mon cher ami,

Nous reparlerons de cette question à la première occasion. Mon impression est cependant qu'il vaudra mieux éliminer la question historique, c.à.d. le II, 3 et vous en tenir à la reconstruction doctrinale dont vous m'indiquez les grandes lignes. Ce II, 3 serait en réalité une ou plusieurs autres thèses: il vous en restera largement assez avec une "Philosophie chrétienne de Malebranche" et votre thèse aura une parfaite unité. J'ai inscrit aux Hautes Études: *Descartes et la pensée religieuse de son temps*, titre vague et qui nous laissera toute liberté. Je ferai une conférence d'introduction et vous donnerai la parole pour trois ou quatre conférences comme vous voudrez; ensuite nous reprendrons la question ensemble.—Je crois décidément que vous devrez supprimer: *Les origines de la philosophie chrétienne*, sujet infini et passer de: *Foi et raison* à: *La gloire de Dieu*.

Bien cordialement à vous,

Ét. Gilson

8

[carte postale]
Revue d'histoire Franciscaine
17 avril 1924

Mon cher ami,

Votre livre est très beau, et comme il est bon je ne vois plus que le succès à lui souhaiter. Vous avez admirablement combiné vos comptes-rendus et vous feriez un excellent président du conseil. Pour l'Angleterre, faites envoyer un exemplaire au *Mind* et un autre au *Hibbert Journal*. Pour l'Italie, un exemplaire à la *Critica*, et un autre à la *Rivista di Filosofia neo-scolastica*. Puis, attendons. Ces deux pays sont d'ailleurs peu curieux, surtout l'Angleterre. Reposez vous et si la vision en Dieu vous résiste, assouplissez votre exposé; elle signifie peut-être *plusieurs* choses et remplit peut-être plusieurs fonctions. Je pars mercredi matin; à bientôt, en mai, et croyez à ma bonne amitié.

Ét. Gilson

9

23 mai 1924
[carte postale]
Revue d'histoire Franciscaine

Mon cher ami,

Je crois que vous agirez sagement en gardant l'an prochain tout votre temps pour votre thèse, à moins que de vous même vous ne désiriez faire un cours et n'y trouviez un profit. Mais il me semble que mieux vaut vous concentrer sur votre rédaction. Je chercherai une occasion de vous voir dès que j'aurai repris mon courant régulier, pour parler avec vous de tout cela; mais gardez vous libre.—Il va sans dire que je suis heureux de vous voir chercher la précision dans votre travail; danger senti est à demi conjuré. À bientôt et nos bonnes amitiés.

Ét. Gilson

Réflexion faite, si vous pouvez venir mardi prochain, 91 Blvd Port-Royal, à 20h 15, vous me trouverez certainement et même vous me rendrez probablement service.

10

[carte postale]
15 Juin 1924

Mon cher ami,

Je ne vois rien, absolument, à changer dans les pages que vous m'avez remises. Toute cette conclusion va très bien. La réunion où je déposerai votre thèse aura lieu mercredi prochain 20 juin, à 4 h ½; vous n'aurez donc qu'à vous trouver là vers cette heure-là; j'arriverai peut-être avec ¼ d'h de retard. Préparez une lettre à M le Président de l'École Prat [ique] des H[autes] É[tudes], sciences religieuses; demandant l'autorisation de faire un cours temporaire l'an prochain, en liaison avec mon enseignement et d'accord avec moi, et indiquant le sujet (le mot "religieux" y figurera, bien entendu).

M. McKeon a fait une *excellente* explication de Malebranche. Croyez à ma bonne amitié.

Ét. Gilson

11

28 juin 1924
Revue d'histoire franciscaine

Mon cher ami,

Toutes mes félicitations pour le beau et agréable succès que vous venez de remporter. J'en suis, faut-il vous le dire, fort satisfait, et je n'y vois qu'un commencement. Si vous avez quelques instants à perdre mardi vers quatre heures, vous pourrez me trouver au bureau de la librairie Vrin (succursale de la rue St. Jacques; ex-Mulot). J'aimerais arrêter avec vous les titres provisoires de vos thèses pour les annoncer au catalogue de la collection que l'on prépare; c'est le moment de les y insinuer, et j'ai même pris les devants, en proposant, sous toutes réserves:

1. *Biographie intellectuelle du P. Malebranche, de l'Oratoire.*
2. *La Philosophie de Malebranche et son inspiration religieuse.*

Nous en reparlerons, si vous avez le temps.

À bientôt, j'espère, et bien amicalement à vous.

Ét. Gilson.

12

6, Rue de Ponthierry
Melun (S-et-M)
9 octobre 1924

Mon cher ami,

Merci pour la peine que vous venez encore de prendre à cause de moi; voilà une amitié qui finit par vous coûter cher. J'ai précisément pris un abonnement (sans prime) à la *Vie Catholique,* car ce journal me semble correspondre à un besoin réel, et je ne lui reproche guère, jusqu'à présent, qu'un éditorial assez ferme, surtout pour un premier numéro. Je n'espérais pas être si vite présenté à ses lecteurs, ni surtout par vous.

Je vous signale, dans le feuilleton de P. Souday (*Temps,* 9 oct.–1924), le paragraphe suivant: "Mais je les remercie (scil. MM. Maritain et Massis) d'avoir carrément répudié Descartes; j'aime mieux ce franc anathème au fondateur de la philosophie moderne que les efforts de quelques autres pour travestir ce grand et libre esprit en homme bien pensant." *Es galt Ihnen!* comme disent les Boches. C'est pour vous. Nous allons donc mettre Paul Souday en observation et, au premier nom propre, il faudra l'exécuter. C'est dommage qu'il ne vous ait pas nommé; la matière était belle; mais il y reviendra.

Le Rabelais paraît vous avoir amusé. Tant mieux! Je doute fort de me voir participer à la suite de l'édition, car, même si l'on me le proposait, j'hésiterais à faire partie d'une équipe dont le capitaine est le Pierre Benoît de l'histoire des idées. Nous ne sommes pas des esprits libres, mon cher ami; rien à faire . . . . Nous travaillons trop pour que l'ignorance libératrice nous autorise à affirmer n'importe quoi.

À bientôt, et croyez à ma bonne amitié.

Ét. Gilson

P.S. Je viens de retrouver un étonnant humaniste franciscain du XIIIe siècle, auteur d'un *De virtutibus philosophorum* (!)[4] et qui cite les anciens aussi souvent que Montaigne. Je crains que mes préjugés catholiques ne soient cause de cette découverte, que j'aurais jugée improbable il y a huit jours. Ainsi vont les gens . . . .

---

4 Underlined twice in the original.

13

Dimanche, 26 octobre 1924

Mon cher ami,

Merci encore pour votre article si plein de sympathie, et plus encore pour votre réponse au sieur O. Habert. Seulement, je vous demande de me laisser la place car la mienne est partie aussi. Elle concorde avec la vôtre, sauf sur ce point (en quoi je suis d'ailleurs de votre avis) qu'il n'y a pas d'histoire catholique; c'est un point sur lequel vous pourrez revenir à l'occasion, car il en vaut la peine. Le plan de ma réponse est simple: 1. Je rétablis les textes, 2. Je dissocie mon *compte-rendu* de Delacroix des *livres* où je parle en mon nom. 3. Je déclare que je suis catholique. 4. Je déclare en outre que j'ignore de quelle chapelle il m'exclut, et je lui donne l'adresse de la mienne: *Saint François–Saint Dominique*, avec refus de supprimer l'un des deux noms.

Plus cela va, plus je suis sûr que la planète a le choix entre la religion et la sauvagerie, et que Dieu est dans le catholicisme. Mais s'il est bon d'être catholique pour éviter Guignebert, il importe autant d'éviter Habert. Le catholicisme est, par définition, l'exclusion de la secte. Ce que je regrette, et que ma réponse n'aura pas, c'est le mouvement de votre style. Le titre est le suivant: *Pour travailler tranquille*. Croyez à ma bonne amitié.

Ét. Gilson

14

6, rue de Ponthierry
Melun (S-et-M)
2 juin 1925

Mon cher ami,

J'ai remis votre manuscrit au secrétariat, avec mon rapport, et demandé pour vous le permis d'imprimer. Vous devez donc pouvoir en disposer dès à présent.

Voici mes impressions générales. La troisième partie est bonne (la vision en Dieu); je pense qu'en éliminant un certain nombre de pages qui ne sont que citations, pour condenser les idées en de brefs exposés, cela ira très bien. Les tableaux comparatifs avec Ambrosius Victor doivent être conservés mais reportés en Appendice (petits caractères), pour gagner de la place et ne pas couper le développement.

La deuxième partie contient un bon chapitre sur les rapports de Malebranche et Saint Augustin. Tous les autres sont plus ou moins mal venus, surtout au point de vue de la rédaction. C'est donc sur l'ensemble de *l'Union à Dieu par la volonté* que devrait porter votre effort; il faudrait essayer de repenser cela et d'obtenir une construction plus ferme, moins diffuse.

Je vous conseille d'en détacher le chapitre sur *la Morale* de Malebranche, très insuffisant, et d'en tirer, en le refondant, la matière de votre conclusion du tome II (*L'union à Dieu*). Vous y trouverez les idées de la vie intérieure comme resserrement de l'union avec Dieu; de la métaphysique comme orientation vers Dieu et détachement des corps; de l'efficace réservée à Dieu, lien de toute société spirituelle et fin de notre société comme il en est le principe; du caractère sacré (parce que divin) de l'efficace dont nous sommes les distributeurs et qui nous interdit toute conception simplement *profane* de la vie (VII *Entretiens*, 14. *Traité de Morale*, II, ch[apitre] 10 sv.).

Je pense enfin—en laissant ceci à votre appréciation—que votre thèse eût gagné beaucoup de relief à mettre en opposition très nette Malebranche et la scolastique thomiste. Il y a, un peu partout, et à l'état colloïdal, les éléments de cette opposition. C'est plus vigoureux chez Malebranche, qui a là dessus des chapitres pleins et terribles que vous n'avez pas: la scolastique est une idolâtrie. Il faudrait—me semble-t-il—condenser quelque part un bref tableau de sa critique de la scolastique. Je l'attendais à la philosophie du serpent; ce n'est pas parfaitement réussi.

Pour le plan auquel vous pensez actuellement, et qui tirerait deux thèses de votre manuscrit, je ne vois aucune objection à lui adresser.

Croyez à mon affectueux dévouement.

Ét. Gilson

P.S. Surtout, convainquez vous qu'une rédaction concise et une composition rigoureuse de vos développements vous fera gagner, non seulement de la place, mais même de la richesse quant au contenu des idées.

Marquez fortement les transitions qui articulent les paragraphes; *elles sont dans votre pensée*, formulez les.

15

Maison Jacques Band
Morzine (Hte Savoie)
31 juillet 1925

Mon cher ami,

Je comprends votre incertitude touchant le choix d'un poste; il est certain que ce choix n'influencera en rien votre carrière dans l'enseignement supérieur, en tout cas pas de manière sensible; vos préférences personnelles ne se prêtent guère á l'argumentation, et par conséquent je crois que vous seul pouvez en décider. Il me semble simplement que votre présence à Evreux serait une "utopie," et comme vos thèses seront très probablement imprimées à Poitiers (Société française d'imprimerie et de librairie, rue Oudin), il pourrait y avoir pour vous un gros intérêt à être sur place, afin d'aller vite. Ceci dit, vous seul pouvez prendre parti.

M. Brunschvicg, dont j'ai lu le rapport, ne m'a rien dit d'aussi précis qu'à vous, car je n'ai guère parlé avec lui qu'entre deux interrogations. Son impression, qui rejoint votre dessein primitif, me paraît *décisive*[5] quant au plan de votre travail. En droit, il n'y a donc aucune hésitation possible, et c'est à la première solution qu'il faut revenir. Comment l'édition et la vente seront elles possibles, ce sont des points que l'on réglera après devis de l'imprimeur. Jusque là continuez à *condenser* le plus possible, vous y gagnerez à tous les points de vue. Bon courage, mon cher ami; les miens se joignent à moi pour vous adresser nos meilleures amitiés.

Votre affectueusement dévoué,
Ét. Gilson

16

19 août 1925

Mon cher ami,

Je me trouve si loin de Malebranche en ce moment, que je craindrais de vous suggérer quelque sottise en vous conseillant. Au point où en est votre travail, vous ne pouvez attendre de bons avis que de vous même; achevez-le donc en vous inspirant de ce que l'on vous a dit; parmi les avis contradictoires que vous avez reçus, vous en trouverez toujours

5 Underlined twice in the original.

un qui vous conviendra. Je suis généralement en route de 7 heures du matin à 19 heures, et à des altitudes qui varient de 1.000 à 2.600 m.; j'ai le cerveau complètement vidé et je m'en félicite. Vous voyez que je serais en ce moment de très mauvais conseil. Bon courage, et croyez à mon affectueux dévouement.

Ét. Gilson

17

6, rue Ponthierry
Melun (S-et-M)
29 oct. 1925

Mon cher ami,

J'étais au courant de vos négociations avec l'éditeur; c'est cher, et ce sont pourtant les meilleures conditions que l'on pouvait espérer. Vous avez déjà réalisé un gain appréciable en diminuant votre manuscrit .... Je ferai mon possible pour que vous arriviez en temps voulu et je compte que nous réussirons. Votre manuscrit est déjà à Poitiers; je désire en suivre l'impression de près et vous prie de retourner toutes vos épreuves, corrigées, à la librairie J. Vrin où je les verrai. Ce détour peut, en réalité éviter bien des fausses manœuvres et gagner du temps. J'espère que tout ira bien, et même j'en suis sûr.

J'aimerais être aussi optimiste sur l'avenir immédiat de notre pays. Il y a des moments ou l'on se demande quels sont ses compatriotes, et combien sont ils.

Bien affectueusement à vous,
Ét. Gilson

18

Revue d'histoire franciscaine
28 novembre 1925

Mon cher ami.

Je serai heureux de vous voir Mercredi; mais venez à la fin de mon cours aux Hautes-Études, à 3h 15; nous aurons un moment avant mon cours de Faculté des Lettres, qui n'est qu'à 4 heures. Je viens de lire votre préface; c'est *très bon*; je suis très content; c'est du bon Gouhier.

Pour l'affaire Malebranche, vous êtes naturellement libre. De mon point de vue, c'est pour vous l'exploitation fatale, inévitable, sans compensation. À votre place, je n'aurais pas le temps.

À bientôt, et croyez à ma bonne amitié.

Étienne Gilson

19

6, rue de Ponthierry
Melun (S-et-M)
30 décembre 1925

Mon cher ami,

Il me paraît tout à fait impossible que la personne qui m'a si rapidement interviewé soit celle dont vous me parlez. Cette dame m'a formellement affirmé qu'elle n'habitait pas Paris et c'est même pourquoi elle n'a pu prendre avec moi aucun rendez-vous.

En ce qui concerne la thèse, inutile de m'envoyer désormais vos épreuves; vos corrections sont suffisantes, quoique non toujours parfaites (quelles corrections le sont ?). Méfiez-vous toutefois des renvois à votre tome I, dont vous n'avez pas les pages (p. 56, note 1). On va tirer votre tome II avant le tome I, et vous laisserez un blanc. Mieux vaudrait renvoyer aux chapitres, comme vous faites le plus souvent,

Les s qui vous gênent, et que vous indiquez comme d'un autre œil s , sont en réalité des s retournées. Il suffit de corriger ainsi s, et en marge /.*

Vous aurez en effet Laporte, si vous ne vous y opposez pas. Vos savez de quoi il vous parlera, et c'est vous qui aurez commencé la conversation.

Je serai content de vous voir lancer une série d'*Essais* et verrai avec plaisir votre projet. Mais D. Halévy est du meilleur conseil en ces matières. Merci de vos beaux vœux; transmettez les nôtres à vos parents, et gardez en d'abord une bonne part. Votre doctorat se passera très bien et vous ne devrez rien à personne; on dit à Melun: bel oiseau se fait de lui-même. C'est assez vrai, et vous le constaterez au cours de votre enseignement.

Excusez le décousu de ma lettre (je le sens), et ne croyez pas que, dans mon cœur, je vous expédie; mais je fournis en ce moment un travail tel,

* See copy of original letter on p. 51.

pour préparer mes cours, que je suis vraiment débordé. J'espère y voir plus clair d'ici deux ou trois mois.

Croyez à toute mon affection.

Ét. Gilson

20

6, rue de Ponthierry
Melun (S-et-M)
10 janvier 1926

Mon cher ami,

Je suis heureux que mon article ne vous ait pas été désagréable. J'ai pensé que le mieux serait de prendre publiquement votre livre au sérieux. En fait, j'ai l'impression que ces pages ont été beaucoup plus remarquées que je ne m'y attendais. Mon bon maître en est un peu surpris et j'ai essayé de lui expliquer que nous avions jadis commis un contre-sens; je ne crois pas l'avoir convaincu. Peut être est il à l'âge où l'on n'a plus commis de contre-sens; je le crois cependant homme à reconnaître notre erreur si ses occupations lui permettaient de reprendre la question.

Ne regrettez pas vos romans; vous passerez tout entier dans vos livres, quels qu'en soient les sujets.

Je crois qu'on vous présentera en 2e ligne (donc pour la forme) comme assistant de philosophie à la Sorbonne (emploi nouveau; 1 heure par semaine; dissertations à corriger; 3,000 frs.). Baruzi sera présenté en première ligne. Enfin, on a pensé à vous; c'est Lévy-Bruhl qui vous a mis sur le tapis et Lalande semble vous estimer grandement.

J'aurai des tirés à part et je vous les donnerai quasi tous, ou tous. Je mets généralement mes comptes-rendus dans le calorifère; c'est d'ailleurs un très mauvais combustible.

Aurez vous des épreuves pour L. Brunschvicg? Il est gentil et se tourmente d'écrire un livre anti-Gilsonien (*sic*). Je n'y peux rien, soupire-t-il. Je crois que vraiment cela le peine. Et moi, cela m'est si complètement égal! Ce que les autres pensent leur appartient si pleinement que je ne puis concevoir comment cela pourrait affecter ce que je pense.

Avez-vous lu le Maritain des *Chroniques*? C'est excellent et je crois que pour la première fois je suis totalement d'accord avec lui.

Bien amicalement à vous,

Ét. Gilson

21

6, rue de Ponthierry
Melun (S-et-M)
23 mars 1926

Mon cher ami,

J'ajoute cette lettre à celle que j'ai mise dans le paquet, pour vous dire que je viens de relire vos deux thèses en préparant les quelques questions sur lesquelles nous parlerons le 15 mai exactement comme nous avons l'habitude de le faire.

Votre première thèse est parfaite; vous y atteignez votre meilleur rendement et c'est un vrai plaisir de vous suivre. J'ajoute que l'équilibre général des deux thèses est maintenant excellent et que la rédaction de la deuxième est devenue tout à fait satisfaisante. Mon impression est donc extrêmement favorable et je suis assuré que tout se passera très bien; on pourra, sans l'ombre de peine, trouver de quoi vous féliciter chaleureusement sans avoir à vous flatter. Quant aux points de discussion, il serait superflu de vous dire qu'on en trouvera. Toutefois je ne vois pas en quoi je pourrai vous contredire ou vous reprocher des erreurs; je vous reprocherais de n'être pas allé assez à fond sur certains points si je ne songeais que votre plan était de mettre en évidence l'architectonique du système. Aussi nous pourrons parler sans avoir rien du tout à vous reprocher.

Quand reverrai-je pareille thèse . . . .

Reposez vous, mon cher ami, rappelez moi au bon souvenir de vos parents et croyez à mes sentiments d'affectueux dévouement.

Ét. Gilson

22

6, rue de Ponthierry
Melun (S-et-M)
21 mai 1926

Mon cher ami,

La "soirée Samuel" n'a aucune importance si la réclame s'en tient là, ou à peu près. Pour le reste, il importe que vous preniez la chose en main; si les croquis de Texcier, que j'ai vus dans la salle, peuvent être évités, cela n'en vaudra que mieux. Et s'il n'y avait ni croquis ni texte, ce serait parfait.

Tout s'est bien terminé. La scène que vous savez m'a été horriblement pénible; à deux heures du matin, la nuit suivante, j'ai du prendre un narcotique (exactement le Di-dial Ciba) pour échapper enfin à cette obsession. La dureté fondée sur l'erreur, et cette colère qui s'excite soi-même, avec des arguments qui reviennent comme des renvois de bile, et tout cela contre vous, m'a littéralement bouleversé. Bref, la vie continue, et le travail aussi; il reste cependant là dedans quelque chose que je ne comprends pas.

C'est moi qui dois rédiger le rapport sur votre soutenance.

Reposez-vous, mon cher ami, et remettez-vous doucement au travail dès que vous pourrez. Plus j'y pense, plus je crois qu'une fois Malebranche fini, le XIXè siècle vous sera un terrain favorable. Je ne vois qu'un concurrent à ce sujet: Voltaire et son temps. Pour aller au fond du mal et en tirer une anti-toxine, à base de sincérité.

Ma femme, qui communie dans nos sentiments et avec intensité, s'unit à moi pour vous adresser nos meilleures amitiés.

Ét. Gilson

23

6, rue Ponthierry
Melun (S-et-M)
17 janvier 1928

Mon cher ami,

Je me remets à ma correspondance, l'âme bourrelée de remords. Pour avoir laissé votre lettre trois jours sans réponse, il a fallu une sorte de maladie et, en effet, j'ai compris la preuve de l'existence de Dieu chez S. Augustin, ce qui m'a rendu insociable aux miens pendant tout ce temps. Le résultat, c'est que j'ai le cadre d'une sorte de S. Augustin, etc., etc. Mais passons aux affaires urgentes.

Si Morize doit aller vous chercher, il vaut mieux prendre le bateau qu'il vous indique. Vous ne serez d'ailleur nulle part mieux que sur celui-là, même en 2e et vous traverserez en 5 jours, 15 heures et quelques minutes. Donc prenez le; mais ne faites que verser des arrhes sur le prix du passage. Après votre mariage vous irez au Ministère des Affaires Étrangères voir Jean Marx, de ma part; il vous enverra, recommandé, à M. Hémard, qui vous fournira des réquisitions du Ministère à la C. G. T. (Comp[agnie] Gén[érale] Trans[Atlantique] !!!) et, lorsque vous retirerez votre billet, on vous déduira 30% sur le prix du passage. Ne les payez en aucun cas, vous ne les reverriez plus. Quant à Morize, il n'a rien à voir là dedans. C'est donc bien la C. G. T. qui fait la réduction sur réquisition des Affaires Etrangères. Les Aff. Etrangères prendront également vos deux passeports si vous les en chargez.

Donc, pour le moment, retenez une cabine à deux places, le plus au centre possible (j'entends: le plus loin possible de l'arrière), versez des arrhes et . . . mariez-vous. Le reste s'arrangera ensuite.

Je serais, moi aussi, bien heureux de vous voir, mais je ne vais jamais à Paris le lundi ni le jeudi qui sont la veille et le lendemain de mes cours. Ne vous dérangez aucunement pour venir; l'occasion se trouvera d'elle-même.

Autre chose. Mon ami l'abbé Baudin vous demande de vouloir bien accepter d'écrire le *Malebranche* dans la collection: *Les moralistes chrétiens*, où j'ai donné un *Saint Thomas* (Galbalda, éditeur). Pécuniairement, c'est intéressant, puisque l'auteur touche 10% sur le prix fort de 1,000 exemplaires payés d'avance à la mise en vente de chaque mille. La tâche ne vous sera pas très lourde, puisque c'est essentiellement un recueil de textes, mais M. l'abbé Baudin ne voit guère que vous qui puissiez relier ces textes par des liens métaphysiques authentiques, tels qu'ils existent chez Malebranche. Il s'agit de montrer la morale concrète de Malebranche tout en la faisant baigner dans son milieu métaphysique (quel style!). J'espère, de grand cœur, que vous voudrez bien accepter. Si vous croyez pouvoir le faire, veuillez répondre directement à M. l'abbé Baudin, Professeur à l'Université de Strasbourg, à la Toussaint, rue de la Toussaint, Strasbourg, Bas-Rhin.

À bientôt tant de même, j'espère, et, en attendant, croyez à mon amitié dévouée.

Ét. Gilson

24

The Institute of Mediaeval Studies
St. Michael's College
University of Toronto
Toronto 5, Ontario
Canada
10 novembre 1930

Mon cher ami,

Votre lettre m'a fait le plus grand plaisir, car les exilés éprouvent parfois que même lors qu'il n'a à se plaindre de rien l'homme n'est pas toujours heureux. Je prends note de votre nouvelle addresse lilloise; vous suivez une évolution normale et tout à fait en accord avec les saines traditions du lieu! Quant à votre "petit Comte" je comprends votre sentiment, car j'oublie mes livres aussitôt qu'ils sont nés. Je persiste à regretter l'introduction sur Saint-Simon; je crains que vous n'ayez imaginé que lorsqu'on a des intentions en écrivant, elles s'incorporent au texte. Mon expérience est qu'il ne passe dans notre texte qu'une petite partie de ce que nous pensons et que ce que nous n'écrivons pas du tout n'y passe pas du tout. Mais puisque le livre est né, il vivra sa vie sans vous ni moi et peut être même l'aimera-t-on pour ses défauts, s'il en a.

Rien de plus juste que ce que vous m'écrivez sur la coupure entre l'enseignement et la production; c'est vrai même lorsqu'on réussit à faire porter son enseignement sur l'objet même de son étude. Pourtant lorsqu'il faut choisir, je crois que l'on doit faire passer la production en premier lieu, parce que si l'on fait passer l'enseignement d'abord, on tue la production et abaisse le niveau de l'enseignement. Le cours d'un homme qui produit, même autre chose que ce qu'il enseigne, differe *toto genere* des cours du professeur qui n'est que professeur. C'est du moins ce qu'il m'en semble.

Je n'ai rien vu du tout des critiques du saint Augustin dont vous me parlez, mais je les trouverai sans doute chez Vrin. P. Archambault est un brave garcon qui croit que les livres des autres ne contiennent que ce qu'il en comprend et que la pensée des autres change ou évolue selon ce qu'il en comprend. Vous, au contraire, vous poussez vos amis en avant et voulez leur faire croire qu'ils ont en eux plus de richesses qu'ils ne croient. C'est plus encourageant. Vos deux volumes sur Descartes verront peut être le jour, mais je suis présentement loin d'eux, tout à mes

Gifford Lectures qui en sont à leur troisieme plan—mais c'est le bon. Les deux autres ont refusé de marcher et même de céder à la violence, au lieu que celui-là, jusqu'à présent, engendre ses propres chapitres avec la spontanéité d'un être vivant. Mais quelle histoire! Que ne va-t-on pas raconter! Brunschvicg et le P. Mandonnet vont s'unir pour m'anathématiser. À ce propos, savez vous comment le P. Mandonnet m'appelle? "une petite bête à bon Dieu" Ah! que n'en ai-je les ailes et la légèreté! Je perdrais volontiers la moitié de mes kilos pour m'approcher de ces jolies bêtes.

Je suis allé hier à Ann Arbor, Mich, où j'ai rencontré le jeune Schwob qui s'y trouve en qualité de Rockefeller-Foundation-traveling-fellow. C'est un beau titre. Nous avons parlé de vous et de Mme Gouhier, et vous auriez pu écouter. C'est un charmant garçon et ce Parisien en plein Michigan était pour moi la plus agréable des rencontres. Mon bon maître Lévy-Bruhl était passé par là huit jours plus tôt et je suis désolé de l'avoir manqué. Quant au P. Gillet, je l'ai vu à Ottawa, toujours simple, bon, intelligent, et malaxant la pâte dominicaine avec une admirable énergie. C'est le Foch des dominicains ; il prend les décisions avec une aisance résolue de vrai chef. Les O. P. des U. S. A. vont le sentir passer; comme entrée de jeu, il en déporte 40 à Rome, tout simplement, et va les installer à Sainte Sabine. Il crée un commissaire général pour l'Amérique centrale, réorganise partout les études, etc., etc. Tout cela en redingote et pardessus. C'est un vrai chef.

Vous savez que l'université n'a pas encore voulu de notre petite Cécile. On va essayer de l'occuper cette année et si cela ne marche pas, je ferai de mon mieux pour la décider à abandonner une entreprise où elle se ruine la santé sans résultat. Je crois que Jacqueline réussit assez bien, et même très bien. Quant à Bernard inutile de commencer à chanter ses louanges, je n'en finirais pas.

Une édition de Descartes sera bientôt nécessaire, en effet, et si vous voulez vous en occuper, je suis certain que ce sera bien fait. En ce qui concerne le *Common Place Book*, vous ferez bien de demander à votre collaborateur s'il connaît *Johnston*,[6] *The Development of Berkeley's Philosophy*? Ce livre attirera son attention sur le problème de l'ordre à suivre dans l'édition du texte; Fraser a tout dérangé et je crois que l'hypothèse de Johnston, proposée d'ailleurs par d'autres avant lui, est bonne. Tous vos autres projets me semblent intéressants et raisonnables; les programmes sont un poison, vous avez raison. L'université n'est qu'une boîte à

6 Underlined twice in the original.

examens, mais c'est ce qu'elle a toujours été depuis le XIIe siècle et le vrai travail se fera de plus en plus en dehors des universités.

Rappelez moi au bon souvenir de Mme Moyse, toutes mes amitiés à vos enfants et à leur mère; nous allons pouvoir nous voir désormais sans attendre le hasard des rencontres et je crois malgré tout, que Paris me sera commode. Je vous envois toutes mes amitiés et mes vœux les meilleurs pour le bon succès de vos entreprises, y compris le "gros Comte" que nous finirons bien par voir sortir.

Croyez moi bien votre,
Ét. Gilson

25

le 20 fevrier 1931

Cher ami,

Vrin m'a dit mardi que vous étiez en Angleterre déjà! J'avais cru que c'était pour le printemps. Je sais que vous jouez là-bas une grosse partie—et pour vous et pour ce que vous aimez. J'ai compris que c'est la méditation de plusieurs années qui va prendre forme. Soyez sûr que ma pensée vous accompagne fidèlement, avec une confiance d'autant plus sûre que je sens derrière ces conférences quelque chose comme ce moi profond dont parle Bergson à la fin de l'*Essai*, prêt à s'achever dans un acte libre . . . .

Ici nous vivons dans une affreuse tragédie, avec des craintes que l'on ne peut pas écrire.

Nous nous unissons pour vous dire notre affection.
Henri Gouhier

26

St. Michael's College
Toronto 5,
21 novembre 1931

Mon cher ami,

Je vous remercie de vos lettres, de la peine que vous avez prise pour mon livre et surtout de votre fidèle amitié. Je n'étais pas pressé de voir sortir mes *Gifford Lectures*; elles sont si schématiques que je ne les aime pas beaucoup. Chaque leçon devrait être un livre. Je veux espérer avec vous qu'elles feront cependant quelque bien. Je crois aussi qu'il est temps de construire quelque chose, car nous sommes dans le vide et c'est d'un enseignement positif que l'on a besoin. Avant de le donner, il fallait saisir l'essence des principes, car c'est la possession des vérités fondamentales qui donne à l'esprit sa liberté. Je n'en serai là qu'après la dernière de mes *Gifford Lectures*. Elles ouvrent des portes, il restera à entrer. Je suis actuellement aux prises avec l'épistémologie et la morale; je serais plus avancé si je n'avais été accablé de correspondance par les affaires du Collège de France, mais je pourrai bientôt rattraper le temps perdu.

Les choses se sont passées beaucoup mieux que je n'espérais et je crois que tout ira désormais sans difficultés. L. Rougier sera sans doute candidat, s'il ne l'est déjà. C'est même pourquoi, entre autres raisons, je préfère ne pas répondre à son article. En dépit de mon peu d'optimisme en matières temporelles, je ne puis croire qu'entre le plagiaire et le plagié, ce soit le plagiaire que l'on choisisse. Et puis l'exemple de Malebranche est là pour démontrer la vanité des controverses. Enfin, le livre que vous avez eu la gentillesse de revoir est tout entier fondé sur ce qu'il me reproche de ne pas avoir vu; cela peut passer pour une réponse, j'espère, aux yeux de ceux que ces questions intéressent. Quant aux autres, cela n'importe guère ni pour eux ni pour moi.

La référence de *Sierp* qui manque se réfère à une note additionnelle que j'avais écrite au dos de ma dernière feuille et que l'imprimerie n'a pas vue. C'est sans grande importance et j'ajouterai le texte dans le volume suivant.

J'espère que la Sorbonne ne vous déçoit pas trop et je suis sûr que les étudiants seront heureux de vous avoir. Nous en parlerons bientôt après mon arrivée, car je rentrerai le 21 décembre. En attendant, encore merci de tout cœur, et croyez à ma meilleure amitié.

Ét. Gilson

27

L'ESCALE
LA PANNE
vendredi, 3 août 1934

Cher ami,

Une négligeance exceptionnelle m'a privé du *Temps* hier soir. C'est donc aujourd'hui, en arrivant à la Panne, que j'ai appris votre promotion. On n'ose vous féliciter. Ce que notre ami Gabriel Marcel appelle "la catégorie du tout naturel" joue pleinement. Que ce soit au moins pour vos amis l'occasion de vous exprimer leur affection et pour vous celle de constater une fois de plus combien votre rayonnement est réel.

Le fidèle serviteur des saints—Descartes jouant le rôle de bienheureux laïc—donne du poids à une promotion où le timbalier—solo de l'Opéra couvre heureusement la voix du poète Henriette Charasson. Lorsque nous lisions les listes de nouveaux décorés, nous disions souvent devant le nom d'une médiocrité notoire "Et Gilson ne l'est pas!" Il y avait un désordre; il y aura désormais un peu moins d'irrationnel dans le monde.

Au milieu de tous les témoignages de sympathie que vous recevez, laissez-moi évoquer tout ce que votre bonté et votre œuvre m'ont apporté depuis douze ans déjà.

Nous nous unissons à la joie de toute votre famille.

Henri Gouhier

Je ne pense pas que *Les âges de l'intelligence* vous ait beaucoup ému.

28

31 août 1934

Cher ami,

J'avais mis de coté votre exquise lettre de félicitations pour vous en remercier à loisir, et puis, j'ai expédié cartes sur cartes, et voilà que vous partez sans que nous nous soyons revus. Bon voyage à Prague; la ville vous consolera des philosophes, j'espère. Je voudrais bien que vous trouviez le temps d'écrire soit une lettre, soit des articles, sur le problème de l'École libre. Nous avons besoin de mettre en commun nos idées et de les éprouver les unes au contact des autres. J'ai d'ailleurs l'impression que nous poursuivons tous des dialogues platoniciens dans Pompéi, à la veille de l'éruption.

Merci pour la *Rivista* et votre excellent article.

Quant à la dénommée Teicherb (Je crois que c'est *une*), ce doit être une femme exquise. J'ai du l'insulter sans le vouloir. Hélas! Je ne savais pas alors quelles sont les sources de la conclusion de *De anima*, et j'ai eu la sottise de le dire . . . . Elle ne le sait pas non plus, mais je le sais aujourd'hui (*Epistola de anima* = Alcher de Clairvaux), et je n'en suis pas plus fier pour cela. Ce que l'histoire peut nous rendre bêtes, c'est incroyable; il ne faut pas se laisser faire par elle. Il est vrai que la philosophie . . . . Vous savez que j'aime bien Brunschvicg, qui est la bonté même, et je ne console pas de voir ce que des idées peuvent faire d'un homme. Comme me disait Delbos vers 1910 ou 1912, quand je lui parlais philosophie: "Surtout Gilson, aimez bien votre femme et vos enfants." Ajoutons y deux ou trois amis, dont vous êtes, et il n'y a personne avant vous.

Bien vôtre,
Ét. Gilson

29

The Institute of Mediaeval Studies
St. Michael's College
University of Toronto
Toronto 5,
6 octobre 1934

Mon cher ami,

Votre lettre me rejoint à Toronto et m'apporte un peu d'air français. Prague doit avoir été ce que sont tous les congrès de philosophie; aucune désillusion n'est possible sur ce terrain. Rougier a triomphé, comme il était naturel; Brunschvicg en a une peur terrible, mais, surtout, il lui est attaché par le plus fort des liens: Rougier pense "juste" et ses haines gaillardes, d'allure électorale, rejoignent exactement les détestations intimes de Brunschvicg. Ce que je regrette de n'avoir pas vu, c'est Nuremberg; ma consolation, c'est qu'un "alter ego" y ait assisté. Je crois que ce qui s'est passé là avait une importance, en tout cas une "signification" planétaire. Une essence pure s'est dévoilée, après s'être si longtemps cherchée, et s'est enfin publiquement avouée. Depuis la naissance de

Jésus Christ, il ne pouvait plus se passer rien de vraiment important que le refus de Jésus Christ. Voilà qui est fait. Ce qui m'étonne, c'est que nos adversaires français de Hitler ne voient pas qu'ils travaillent pour lui en espérant sauver l'homme de l'esclavage par l'homme. Ce sont des hitlériens honteux. Mais surtout, s'ils ne croient pas que Hitler est grand—dans son horreur—ce sont de bien dangereux imbéciles.

J'ai reçu du Recteur de Liège une lettre au sujet de Philippe Devaux. J'avais déjà chaudement appuyé De Corte, sans savoir qu'il y avait un autre candidat aussi intéressant. Je réponds donc, par même courrier, en disant de Ph. Devaux tout le bien que je pense et en suggérant—ce qui me paraît le bon sens même—que la nature des fonctions à remplir peut seule ici décider du choix à faire. Je dis donc à quoi l'un et l'autre candidat me semble idoine, et je leur laisse le soin de décider quel genre d'enseignement ils désirent présentement dans leur Université: histoire et systématique de la philosophie classique (M. De Corte), initiation à la philosophie contemporaine (Ph. Devaux); les deux enseignements sont nécessaires; les deux candidats se valent (l'un plus ferme, l'autre plus souple): à l'Université de dire lequel des deux elle doit s'attacher le premier, étant donné sa composition actuelle et ses besoins. Je vous remercie de m'avoir éclairé sur la situation; vous m'avez rendu plus facile d'être juste.

Ma femme et Bernard sont encore près de Montréal, chez des amis où j'ai moi même passé une semaine merveilleuse à pêcher (ah! quelles belles prises dans ce Saint Laurent) et à chasser. Avez vous jamais passé trois heures seul sur un récif, au milieu d'un fleuve de quatre kilomètres de large, botté et vêtu de caoutchouc, assis *dans* l'eau, en compagnie de quinze canards en bois, pendant que deux mille canards en viande se trouvent au-dessus de vous, hors de portée, sans qu'un seul d'entre eux daigne descendre pour s'offrir en holocauste? Tel est le "canard noir," le plus malin de tous, sur les tribus duquel, pendant cinq jours, j'ai eu la déveine de tomber. Du moins, plusieurs, poules d'eau et gallinules me rendront ils ce témoignage, que le vieillard à lunettes que je suis devenu est encore le "dead shot" que je fus en mon jeune temps. Dieu que j'étais sale en rentrant! Mais j'ai eu le plaisir de faire manger de mon gibier au P. Chenu, dont une des caractéristiques est de ne jamais savoir ce qu'il mange. Comme c'était un vendredi, cela valait peut être mieux.

Et *Sept*? Il est bien loin. Et la France aussi. Je voudrais bien avec vous qu'elle devienne une Espagne; mais, hélas! nous sommes un Empire—le deuxième du monde—et notre corps est trop grand pour que nous puissions nous permettre de devenir petits par une évolution naturelle régressive. Il faut d'abord qu'on nous ampute, ou que nous nous écroulions: entre la grandeur et la petitesse, la catastrophe est pour nous un moment inévitable, si le moment d'être petits est vraiment venu.

Quand vous verrez nos filles dites leur que le journal de Jacqueline est bien arrivé et m'a prodigieusement intéressé. Dites aussi à Cecile de prendre son temps et de ne pas se faire de bile pour ses examens. À toutes deux, que ma santé est bonne, mais que je voudrais avoir un an de vie sauvage, avec une ligne et un fusil, dans une cabane de bois. Ma femme et Bernard arrivent lundi à Toronto. Mon affectueux souvenir pour vous trois et les jeunes.

Ét. Gilson

30

4 juillet 1935

Mon cher ami,

Je suis dans l'affreuse bousculade d'un départ d'Agence Cook, mais je veux vous dire au revoir, à vous et aux vôtres, avant de m'en aller. Je ne laisse pas de meilleur ami que vous derrière moi, et combien d'aussi bons? Nous nous embarquons demain vendredi, mais partons aujourd'hui pour Le Havre—Je crois que nous serons contents de retrouver Paris dans six mois. J'emporte avec moi les trois volumes de Marie Noël et quelques exemplaires en supplément pour les distribuer en Amérique. Je compte faire plusieurs fois une conférence sur son œuvre, dans les Alliances Françaises notamment. Je connais bien Auxerre, mais nullement l'auteur que je n'ai jamais osé aller voir. Si vous pouvez me donner quelques renseignements biographiques, vous me rendrez grand service. Mon adresse jusqu'au 15 Septembre sera Ladeira da Gloria, No 108, Rio de Janeiro, Bresil—Ensuite, et jusqu'en décembre, St. Michael's College, Toronto (5): Ont., Canada.

Si j'avais eu l'adresse de Marie Noël, je lui aurais envoyé un exemplaire de mon St. Bernard. Vous pourriez demander à notre ami Vrin de le faire de ma part si vous le jugez bon.

Tout est prêt pour les 21 jours de mer. Il y a, hélas, un ou deux universitaires sur le bateau et, c'est curieux, plus je vais moins je peux les supporter. Ce métier me semble aussi fatal à l'homme qu'à la femme. Je regrette de partir en pleine controverse avec l'A. F. Ce sont des types d'impudence enfantine, qui traitent leur public, comme il mérite d'ailleurs de l'être, en crétins. Le point névralgique, sur lequel j'aurais insisté si j'étais resté, me semble être leur relation au Duc de Guise. L'A. F. n'a aucunement réagi à mon allusion pourtant assez claire. Par contre—je reçois maintenant un service gratuit du *Courrier Royal*. C'est assez intéressant comme symptôme.

Théories à part, tout cela me semble assez vain. Les droites se détestent mutuellement tandis que les gauches se concentrent et s'unissent. Or nous allons certainement à un coup dur. Les quelques 12 milliards de déficit ne vont pas se trouver sous le fer du premier cheval venu et tout cela ne se règlera pas sans casse. Je viens justement d'arracher des bras d'un prolétaire un bourgeois qui se sauvait à toutes jambes et, bourré de swings et de crochets, hurlait lamentablement: "Mais défendez moi, défendez moi donc!" Le prolétaire était costaud et j'ai usé plutôt d'une conciliation qui ne fut efficace que parce qu'elle était tardive; mais cette moule apeurée pleurnichant sous les coups de ce colosse m'a donné une triste idée de ma "classe." Est-ce un présage? Il faudra voir et peut être sera-t-il encore temps en janvier.

Au revoir, cher ami, et croyez à ma très fidèle affection.

Ét. Gilson

31

Randolph Hall
Cambridge, Mass.
U.S.A.
30 octobre 1936

Mon cher ami,

J'essaye enfin de vous répondre, sur un bureau chargé d'une litière de lettres qui attendent que je fasse la même chose pour elles, mais dont la plupart resteront éternellement dans l'oubli. L'idée de passer à Paris un été délicieux vous ressemble de tout point, donc elle doit être bonne. En tout cas, puisqu'elle nous vaudra un recueil d'essais cartésiens, dont je me rejouis d'avance, tous vos amis ne pourront que l'approuver. Merci pour votre petite note. Labergerie en désirait une, et j'aime mieux que ce soit vous qui l'ayez faite. En ce qui concerne le projet Romanet, j'ai décliné l'invitation, pour la simple raison que, si j'avais accepté toutes les propositions de ce genre, j'aurais déjà écrit quatre histoires de la philosophie médiévale. Or je n'ai pas envie de raconter ce que j'en connais, et je suis incapable de raconter ce que j'en ignore. Mon petit péché de jeunesse était tout ce que je pouvais faire alors, et je n'en ferais plus autant aujourd'hui. Si vous avez besoin de quelqu'un pour la philosophie anglaise, il me semble que Keeling, qui a écrit de bonnes choses sur Descartes, et traîne toujours quelque part dans Paris, pourrait vous donner satisfaction. Il est intelligent et, je crois, accepterait de le faire. Le problème est de savoir où est Keeling. Il était à l'Université de Londres, mais semble avoir renoncé aux joies de l'enseignement. En outre, il sait le français.

Votre question: comment le philosophe chrétien peut-il avoir un dialogue avec le philosophe non chrétien, est bien au delà de mes préoccupations et des mes moyens. Je n'en suis pas là. J'en suis seulement à me demander comment aujourd'hui un philosophe peut avoir un dialogue avec n'importe quel autre philosophe? Après avoir constaté pendant plusieurs années que de tels dialogues sont devenus impossibles, qu'il n'y en a plus, j'ai cessé de mettre les pieds à la Société de Philosophie. Mais c'est partout la même chose. Aujourd'hui un des professeurs de Logique de Harvard, que j'estime beaucoup, m'expliquait que 2 lapins + 2 lapins font ordinairement 4 lapins, mais que, logiquement parlant, il pourrait y en avoir 16. Ce genre de logique est très à la mode ici; malheureusement, ils ne s'y tiennent même pas.

Je ne suis pas à Toronto cette année, sauf pour trois visites de 4 jours chaque. Je suis resté à Harvard, après les fêtes du 3e Centenaire de l'anniversaire, pour y faire les W. James Lectures, sujet: *The Unity of Philosophical Experience*. Vous serez horrifié si jamais vous voyez cela. Je le suis moi-même, car cela ressemble à du Farges et Barbedette. Je suis à vrai dire épouvanté. C'est le type de la pire historico-critique, où toutes les nuances sont noyées dans deux ou trois idées brutales qui dominent tout. Bref, le mal que je hais, je le fais, et avec une obstination qui m'étonne, mais je n'y peux rien. C'est un "Nicht anders können." Ma consolation, c'est de relire vos deux Malebranche, que 14 étudiants lisent à Harvard en ce moment, et 16 à Toronto. L'un d'eux me faisant ici même, la semaine dernière, un éloge si intelligent de vos livres, que j'aurais voulu que vous puissiez l'entendre. Il se demandait comment on peut joindre à une telle érudition un tel sentiment de la vie des doctrines? Moi aussi.

La situation de la France ne vous paraît pas belle de près; de loin, elle est affreuse. Ce que l'on voit d'ici clair comme le jour, et qui domine tout, c'est la volonté absolue, fixée, arrêtée, qu'a l'Allemagne, de déclencher une nouvelle guerre. C'est horrible; et il n'y a rien à faire qu'à se préparer à ce qui semble bien l'inévitable. Vous m'annoncez un ministère Chautemps? Là, je suis tellement dénué de sens et de mémoire politiques que je ne sais même plus de qui il s'agit au juste. Je suis toujours pour le cabinet au pouvoir tant que le sang ne coule pas. En ce moment, je suis pour ceux qui essaient d'éviter une guerre civile, et je serai toujours pour ceux-la, quels qu'ils soient.

Je suis heureux de penser qu'on a abaissé l'âge des retraites, et je souhaite vivement que les décrets soient appliqués tout de suite, en masse, et sans discernement. Cela ferait un appel d'air par le haut, et il y a trop de jeunes qui marquent le pas ou n'ont pas de positions. C'est excellent.

Merci encore pour votre bonne lettre et croyez, pour vous et pour les vôtres, à mon affectueux souvenir.

Ét. Gilson

APPENDIX I

Travail fait avec intelligence et exactitude. Les textes les plus importants sont connus et clairement analysés.
Un peu de longeur seulement, ça et là.
La part faite par Malebranche et la critique de certaines matières me parait quelque peu exagérée pour rendre compte de la vivacité de la polémique contre la scolastique.
Une erreur assez singulière sur les rapports de perfection.

LA POLÉMIQUE DE MALEBRANCHE CONTRE ARISTOTE ET LA PHILOSOPHIE SCOLASTIQUE

L'ensemble satisfaisant.

ÉTIENNE GILSON

Correction de V. Delbos

[1] C'est une banalité de dire que dans toute philosophie qui se fonde il y a deux parties dont chacune a son rôle propre: "pars destruens" chargeé de déblayer le terrain et de faire place nette pour la doctrine nouvelle,"pars construens" spécialement chargeé d'élever un édifice neuf à la place de l'ancien. Et, bien que ces deux parties soient étroitement corrélatives l'une de l'autre, on comprend que ce soit le fondateur même de la philosophie nouvelle qui doive lutter contre les vieux préjugés avec le plus d'ardeur, alors que ses successeurs n'auront qu'a suivre la route déjà indiquée. Mais le Cartésianisme nous offre un exemple très intéressant du contraire. Descartes qui devait, semble-t-il, rencontrer les résistances acharnées soit du principe d'autorité, soit des méthodes, soit des théories précédentes, Descartes se contente de les critiquer sommairement et se hâte de construire son édifice. Malebranche au contraire qui, tout en

élaborant une doctrine originale, la fondait sur des bases semblables à celles de Descartes, non content de reprendre les critiques que son maître avait adressés à l'Aristotélisme, les aggrave singulièrement et finit par en faire presque une partie intégrante de son système. **Une raison de cet acharnément dans les critiques de l'Aristotélisme c'est sans doute que M. plus que D. avait affaire directement à des péripatéticiens.** En quoi consista cette polémique de Malebranche contre Aristote et les scolastiques, et pourquoi contre toutes prévisions superficielles elle prit un tel développement, voilà ce que nous essayerons de montrer dans ce travail.

[2] Pour Malebranche, la première superstition dont il faut se libérer quand on désire parvenir à la connaissance de la vérité c'est celle du principe d'autorité. On entend répéter sans cesse: "Ceci est vrai parce que les anciens l'ont dit." Mais c'est une égale absurdité de croire que le livre qu'on écrit sera le code éternel de la vérité et de croire que les auteurs anciens sont des maîtres infaillibles et non de simples moniteurs. Comment peut-on s'imaginer que depuis deux mille ans qu'Aristote a écrit, on n'ait pu découvrir en lui quelqu'erreur? Aristote a donc trouvé d'un seul coup toute la vérité? Mais que l'on regarde au contraire les luttes et les disputes sans fin qui se sont élevées à propos de sa doctrine et l'on se convaincra que la vérité qui est essentiellement "un indivisible" ne saurait y être contenue.

[3] D'ailleurs est-ce faire œuvre de philosophie que d'accepter sans contrôle les idées des autres, fussent-ils anciens ou non? La philosophie n'est-elle pas avant tout l'œuvre de la raison qui, étant la faculté maîtresse de l'homme peut seule faire aboutir la recherche de la vérité? Par conséquent, qu'il soit instructif de lire les anciens pour discuter leurs opinions, c'est incontestable, mais il est également incontestable qu'emmagasiner dans sa mémoire des formules toutes faites et les transmettre telles quelles, c'est perdre complètement son temps et le faire perdre aux autres. **Encore de cela, Malebranche conviendrait peu, je crois.** On peut donc dire que même si les anciens avaient posé et résolu tous les problèmes on aurait encore tort d'admettre leurs raisons sans discussion et par autorité, car c'est une maigre philosophie que celle qui consiste à entasser dans son cerveau les opinions des autres.

[4] Nombreuses d'ailleurs sont les raisons qui expliquent l'aveuglement des partisans du principe d'autorité. La paresse d'un esprit qui refuse de méditer, la haine des vérités abstraites, la vanité surtout qui fait que l'on étudie moins pour apprendre que pour se faire une réputation de

savant et d'homme de grande lecture. Et c'est tout cela qui a fait de la philosophie de l'école une science de mémoire plus que de raison, dans la quelle "penser" consiste à raconter les pensées d'un autre. Faut-il ajouter à ces raisons le "respect mêlé d'une sotte curiosité qui fait qu'on admire davantage les choses les plus éloignées de nous" les plus vieilles et les plus obscures. "On recherche les médailles [anciennes[1]] quoique rongées de la rouille, et on garde avec grand soin la lanterne et la pantouffle de quelque ancien, quoique mangée [sic] de vers; leur antiquité fait leur prix" (*Recherche* I, 203; O.C., I, 282).[2] Mais quoi!: qu'est-ce donc que l'antiquité et ne là sommes nous pas à plus juste titre que Platon, Aristote et Epicure, puisqu'Aristote, Platon et Epicure étaient hommes comme nous, de même espèce que nous et de plus: "qu'au temps où nous sommes, le monde est plus âgé de deux mille ans, qu'il a plus d'expérience, qu'il doit être plus éclairé, et que c'est la vieillesse du monde et l'expérience qui font découvrir la vérité" (*Recherche* I, 203; O.C., I, 283).

Exposé clair et intéressant.

[5] Débarassés du principe d'autorité nous pouvons regarder Aristote en face et le juger, lui et ses successeurs, avec la liberté d'esprit qui convient. Or ce qui frappe tout d'abord quand on parcourt leurs écrits c'est le manque d'ordre dans les dispositions des idées, le défaut presque absolu de méthode. Jamais, par exemple, Aristote ne s'est demandé s'il n'y a pas une progression à suivre dans l'étude des problèmes et s'il ne faut pas commencer par les plus simples pour parvenir aux plus composés. De nos jours nous savons de quelle façon l'on doit chercher la vérité; Viète et Descartes, qui ont renouvelé l'algèbre et l'analyse, nous ont enseigné comment on conduit par ordre ses pensées. On n'essaye pas de comprendre les théories des sections coniques avant d'avoir étudié

1 Omitted in Gilson's transcription.

2 Gilson's references to Bouillier's edition of the *Recherche de la Vérité* (Malebranche 1880) remain in the body of the text as they appear in the original manuscript, i.e., title of the work referred to, followed by volume and page number in parentheses ( ). Bouillier's edition, based on the text of the sixth (1712) edition of the *Recherche* does not contain many of the changes Malebranche made to the earlier editions of this work. See Malebranche 1992, 1321–1323. Immediately following Gilson's references, I have added corresponding references to the critical edition of the *Recherche* as found in Malebranche 1958–67 (referred to as "O.C."). Discrepancies in orthography and punctuation between the critical edition and Bouillier's edition of the *Recherche* are minor.

la géométrie ordinaire; et ce sont là des leçons dont Aristote aurait eu grand besoin. Car sans douter un instant que l'esprit humain ne soit capable de résoudre d'emblée les problèmes les plus difficiles, avant de savoir quoique ce soit de la nature de la matière ou de la composition des corps, il cherche la raison pour laquelle les cheveux des vieillards deviennent blancs. On ne s'étonnera pas qu'un tel ordre dans ses recherches le conduise à écrire que c'est la même raison qui fait blanchir les cheveux des vieillards et qui fait que chez certains chevaux les deux yeux sont de différentes couleurs. On voit aisément la valeur d'une telle science.

[6] En cherchant la raison dernière d'une aussi déplorable façon de procéder il est facile de voir qu'elle consiste dans l'ignorance d'un terme qui est à la fois le but à atteindre et le moyen à employer: l'idée claire et distincte. Personne n'ignore aujourd'hui qu'il n'y a de vérité que dans ce que l'on conçoit clairement et distinctement. Aristote au contraire part de ce qu'il y a de plus confus dans les connaissances que nous avons de la sensation. Les données trompeuses et *imprécises* **Voilà un mot que M. n'employait point** de nos sens sont pour lui le meilleur des points de départ et comme "l'idée générale de l'être" s'y ajoute-t-il tombe sans cesse dans la ridicule abstraction des facultés. En effet la "présence claire, intime, nécessaire de Dieu, je veux dire de l'être, sans restriction particulière, de l'être infini, de l'être en géneral, à l'esprit de l'homme, agit sur lui plus fortement que la présence de tous les objets finis" (*Recherche* I, 341; O.C., I, 456). Mais cette idée de l'être, si grande et si vaste qu'elle soit, nous est précisément devenue si familière par l'habitude que nous en avons, elle nous touche si peu que "nous croyons quasi ne la point voir"; peu à peu nous perdons de vue son origine et nous nous la figurons comme formée par l'assemblage confus des êtres particuliers alors que ces êtres particuliers ne nous apparaissent qu'en elle. Que s'ensuit-il? Dès que les philosophes aperçoivent dans l'univers un effet nouveau, comme ils ont l'esprit préoccupé de cette idée générale et abstraite de l'être, ils l'appliquent immédiatement à ce nouvel effet, "ils imaginent aussitôt une entité nouvelle pour le produire. Le feu échauffe; il y a donc dans le feu quelque entité qui produit cet effet, laquelle est différente de la matière dont le feu est composé" (*Recherche* I, 342; O.C., I, 458). De là naissent ces innombrables quantités d'abstractions qui retardent tant les progrès de la physique, les actes, les puissances, causes, effets, formes substantielles, qualités occultes, etc. Que l'on examine soigneusement les définitions de ces termes, on n'y trouvera pas autre

chose que quelques données confuses des sens, plus l'idée abstraite et générale de l'être. Que sera donc une physique qui, au lieu d'idées claires et distinctes prendra de telles abstractions pour point de départ? Elle sera en réalité une logique. **B**[3] [with a line drawn alongside the text from the last reference to the end of this sentence] Et en effet les philosophes ordinaires veulent absoluement que la physique d'Aristote explique le fond des choses, mais ils ne voient pas qu'ils expliquent "la nature pour leurs idées générales et abstraites, comme si la nature était abstraite" (*Recherche* I, 343; O.C., I, 459).

[7] De cette ignorance de l'ordre logique des démonstrations et de ce mépris des idées claires un informe fatras pouvait seul résulter. Et c'est bien en effet la qualification qui convient à la science *scolastique* qui n'est autre chose que sa logique. **Pas très clair** La logique de l'école ne devait être primitivement qu'un moyen de parvenir à la vérité; mais, par un étrange renversement des termes, elle en est bientôt arrivée à se prendre elle-même pour fin, et l'on pourrait croire que la logique doit être étudiée pour elle-même. En vue de constituer cette science étrange on n'a pas hesité à accumuler les règles et les préceptes de tous genres, et finalement, pour raisonner juste selon ces règles, on est obligé de prêter une telle attention aux procédés qu'on emploie qu'il est impossible de songer dans le même temps aux objets que l'on étudie. La vrai méthode au contraire n'est qu'un guide discret; elle ne se compose que d'un petit nombre de règles très intélligibles et étroitement dépendantes les unes des autres. Elle n'est donc pas faite pour ceux qui n'aiment que les mystères **B** [with a line drawn alongside the previous six lines] et les inventions bizarres et extraordinaires; elle ne demande que le goût de la clarté et l'attention nécessaire "pour conserver [toujours[4]] l'évidence dans les perceptions de l'esprit et pour découvrir les vérités les plus cachées" (*Recherche* II, 47; O.C., III, 296).

[8] Le plus clair des résultats de la méthode employée par les philosophes de l'école est d'aboutir en matière de physique à un tissu d'absurdités, et, par delà la physique, aux pires erreurs morales et religieuses. On a pu déjà se rendre compte par ce qui précède de ce que pouvait être la physique d'Aristote: une suite de combinaisons bizarres effectuées avec des définitions purement abstraites des choses. Les apparences en effet

3 I have assumed that Professor Delbos used the capital letter "B" as shorthand for "bien."

4 Omitted in Gilson's transcription.

semblent nous enseigner que si le feu nous échauffe, si la couleur frappe nos yeux, si d'une manière générale les phénomènes nous apparaissent c'est qu'ils renferment quelque chose de plus ou moins semblable aux impressions qu'ils font sur nous. Nous avons vu comment la croyance aux formes substantielles prenait naissance et se développait en nous. **Ceci pourrait être plus net et plus bref** [with a line drawn alongside the previous six lines] Un exemple nous montrera les conséquences que peut avoir en physique l'emploi de ces formes et facultés attractrices, rétentrices, concotrices, expultrices, etc. Nous pouvons chercher comment Aristote résout le problème auquel nous avons déjà fait allusion: pourquoi les cheveux des vieillards deviennent-ils blancs? Les philosophes qui cherchent à connaître la matière en se servant de la méthode de Descartes savent assez que l'univers est étendue et mouvement et que tout se fait en lui mécaniquement et ainsi qu'en une horloge. Ils auraient donc cherché en quoi consiste exactement la couleur et quelle est la nature vraie des cheveux. Mais pour Aristote il en va tout autrement et la résolution du problème ne défend que de définitions logiques, chaque qualité de la matière étant considérée comme un être indépendant. Le blanc est composé de beaucoup de chaud et de peu d'humide, donc il y a chez les vieillards plus de chaud que d'humide. Or le chaud c'est "ce qui assemble les choses de même nature." L'humide c'est "ce qui ne se contient pas facilement dans ses propre bornes mais dans des bornes étrangères." Essayons donc de mettre la définition à la place du défini. Etant donné que le chaud et l'humide sont ce que nous avons dit et que le blanc se compose de beaucoup de chaud et d'un peu d'humide, on pourra dire que les cheveux des vieillards blanchissent à cause que "ce qui ne se contient pas facilement dans ses propres bornes mais dans des bornes étrangères" surmonte "ce qui assemble les choses de même nature." Avouons qu'il ne faut pas être fort exigeant pour se juger satisfait par de telles solutions.

[9] Mais plus à Dieu que les explications physiques d'Aristote et de ses sectateurs n'eussent d'autre défaut que celui d'être ridicules! Le malheur est que par delà la science elles atteignent et offensent gravement la religion et la morale.

[10] Dieu en effet est incessamment présent à notre esprit; c'est en lui que nous comprenons et voyons toutes choses. Mais depuis que l'homme s'est dégradé par le péché originel notre esprit "se répand incessamment au dehors et s'oublie soi-même et celui qui l'éclaire." C'est depuis la chute de notre premier père qu'au lieu de chercher Dieu en

toutes choses nous ne le rencontrons plus qu'avec une sorte d'horreur. L'homme se sent pécheur et c'est pourquoi il appréhende la rencontre du créateur, et "il aime mieux imaginer dans les corps qui l'environnent une puissance ou une nature aveugle avec laquelle il puisse se familiariser" que d'avoir à craindre la présence d'un Dieu juste "qui connaît tout et qui fait tout" (*Recherche* II, 436–7; O.C., III, 204). **Bien exposé**

[11] Les formes substantielles en effet, ne sont qu'un prétexte dont nous usons pour nous persuader que Dieu n'est pas si proche de nous et qu'il n'agit pas directement dans la nature. Mais les philosophes de l'école qui s'attachent particulièrement à cette doctrine devraient songer qu'en éloignant Dieu ils l'amoindrissent. Car, dire que ce n'est pas Dieu, mais les facultés et les formes substantielles qui font que les corps ont telle et telle nature distincte c'est dire que "Dieu manque d'intelligence, ou qu'il ne puisse pas faire ces choses admirables avec l'étendue toute seule" (*Recherche* I, 327; O.C., I, 438).

[12] La philosophie de l'école, d'ailleurs, a des conséquences autrement graves qu'amoindrir Dieu; si on la pousse jusqu'à ses extrêmes conséquences, elle le supprime et nous conduit au plus barbare des paganismes. En effet, nous avons vu que depuis le péché originel l'homme pour s'éloigner de Dieu transmet aux objets matériels une partie de la puissance divine et que de là naît le préjugé de l'efficace des causes secondes. Alors que de toute évidence c'est Dieu qui agit en tout et partout, alors que la sagesse commande de préférer la cause universelle aux causes particulières, on admet que les corps ont véritablement un pouvoir d'agir qui leur est propre et qu'ils ne cessent de l'exercer sur nous. Dès lors, tout ce que nous aurons reçu de biens des objets matériels sera rapporté à ces objets eux-mêmes et non à Dieu qui nous les aura réellement envoyés. Si Dieu a placé le soleil, la lune et les étoiles dans un lieu élevé, s'il les a environnés de gloire et de puissance, s'il leur a conféré le pouvoir de nous combler des bienfaits que ces astres nous envoient, n'est-ce pas pour que nous les honorions? **B** [with a line drawn alongside the previous six lines] Or c'est là l'origine même de l'idolâtrie puisqu'au dire de Cicéron: "si les Égyptiens ont adoré non seulement le soleil, la lune, et le fleuve du Nil, dont le débordement cause la fertilité de leur pays, mais encore jusqu'aux plus vils des animaux, c'est [au rapport de Ciceron[5]] à cause de quelque utilité qu'ils en recevaient" (*Recherche* II, 477; O.C., III, 249). Ainsi, en rigueur logique, la théorie des formes substantielles conduit à l'idolâtrie et au paganisme. Et si l'on peut croire

5 Omitted in Gilson's transcription.

que le coeur des philosophes qui la professent est encore chrétien, au moins faut-il avouer que le fond de leur esprit est païen (*Recherche* II, 59; O.C., II, 310).

[13] D'ailleurs les partisans de la philosophie d'Aristote sentent bien tout le danger que présente une semblable position, et ils la modifient généralement quelque peu: sans doute, disent-ils, ce serait parler en païen que d'admettre ainsi dans l'univers l'existence de divinités indépendantes; aussi ne le prétendons nous pas. Mais nous pensons qu'au dessus du monde matériel que nous voyons se trouve une sorte de nature générale et d'âme du monde qui n'utilise les formes substantielles que pour diversifier son action. Cependant, quoiqu'ils disent ces philosophes, c'est encore là retomber dans le paganisme car Dieu seul est cause universelle et il ne faut point "feindre une certaine nature, un premier mobile, une âme universelle, ou quelque semblable chimère dont on n'a point d'idée claire et distincte. Ce serait raisonner en philosophe païen" (*Recherche* II, 444; O.C., III, 213–214). Prétendra-t'on que s'il n'y a pas une certaine nature qui agit de son côté et que si Dieu fait toutes choses on ne pourra pas distinguer le naturel du surnaturel? Mais c'est là une distinction extravagante à placer dans la bouche d'Aristote et ceux qui montrent tant de respect "pour les opinions de ce misérable et pitoyable" philosophe devraient songer que la "nature" dont ils parlent devient pour bien des hommes une idole digne de recevoir les honneurs dus à la divinité et qu'ils nous ramenènt à croire avec les anciens que c'est quelque nature ou même "le soleil et l'homme qui engendrent les hommes" (*Recherche* II, 453; O.C., III, 223–224).

[14] On croira sans peine que des doctrines qui donnent à des créatures une puissance divine aient eue pour résultat immédiat de détourner l'homme de Dieu et des devoirs qu'il lui doit pour le rapprocher de la matière et des choses sensibles. C'est ainsi que cette dangereuse philosophie sépare profondément l'âme humaine de Dieu; car, transportant dans l'homme lui-même les formes substantielles elle va jusqu'à dire que l'âme est la forme du corps. B [with a line drawn alongside the three previous lines] Ainsi nous voyons supprimée l'union si intime qui relie l'âme à Dieu pour ne conserver que son union avec un corps que nous n'avons jamais vu, dont nous ignorerions jusqu'à l'existence si Dieu lui même ne nous l'avait révélée. N'y a-t-il pas lieu de s'étonner que "des philosophes chrétiens, qui doivent préférer l'esprit de Dieu à l'esprit humain, Moïse à Aristote, Saint Augustin à quelque misérable commentateur d'un philosophe païen, regardent plutôt l'âme comme

la *forme* du corps que comme faite à l'image et pour l'image de Dieu" (*Recherche* I, 1; O.C., I, 9–10).

[15] Ainsi l'homme en arrive bientôt à se détacher de Dieu pour se tourner vers son corps et s'attacher aux choses matérielles qui l'entourent. La véritable philosophie nous enseigne en effet que tout bien et tout *mal* **En quel sens?** nous viennent de Dieu et que rien de réel dans le monde n'existe et n'agit que par sa volonté. Aristote au contraire qui place la raison des effets dans les causes secondes aussi bien que dans la cause première nous autorise à nous attacher aux objets. Car si nous voulons être heureux, nous devrons nous attacher à ce qui doit nous donner le bonheur. Quoi donc de plus juste que de nous attacher "aux objets sensibles s'ils sont les véritables causes du bonheur que nous trouvons[6] dans leur jouissance"? D'une telle philosophie à la justification de l'avarice, de l'ambition, de la débauche et de tous les vices on se rend compte qu'il n'y a pas loin (*Recherche* II, 475; O.C., III, 247).

[16] Cet exposé sommaire des principales critiques que Malebranche a opposées à la doctrine d'Aristote—sans d'ailleurs les présenter selon un ordre rigoureux—fait, assez voir sans doute qu'il ne s'agit pas ici d'une simple querelle d'école mais d'un antagonisme profond entre deux philosophies. Malebranche ne se contente pas de présenter des objections de détail et de livrer quelques escarmouches, il s'engage à fond, avec tout ce dont il dispose de vigueur dialectique, d'ironie cinglante et souvent d'indignation sacerdotale. Il s'agit vraiment pour lui d'élever *autel contre autel*. **L'expression c'est peut être pas très juste ici.** Il nous reste maintenant à chercher pourquoi la polémique de Malebranche que les travaux de Descartes auraient du avoir tendue inutile fut beaucoup plus violente que ne l'avait été celle de Descartes lui-même; en d'autres termes à nous demander en quoi le "péril scolastique" n'était plus redoutable pour Malebranche que pour son prédécesseur.

[17] Ce qu'il y a d'abord de très frappant dans la polémique de Malebranche, c'est l'espèce d'horreur qu'à tout instant il affiche pour le principe d'autorité—*au moins* **Ceci est à souligner** en matière de philosophie. Là où Descartes s'était contenté de critiques assez sommaires Malebranche insiste, revient à plusieurs reprises et toujours avec une ironie agressive et mordante. On croirait qu'il n'aura jamais assez de railleries pour ces philosophes chez qui "Aristote [lui[7]] est ce que la

6 Gilson modified the original text which is in the first person singular.

7 Omitted in Gilson's transcription.

raison et l'évidence sont aux autres" (*Recherche* I, 219; O.C., I, 302). Une première raison qui expliquerait peut-être, dans une certaine mesure, le peu de goût de Malebranche pour le principe d'autorité pourrait être cherchée dans l'esprit général de l'ordre de l'Oratoire dont il faisait partie. L'indépendance d'esprit dont on jouissait à l'Oratoire était très connue au XVIIe siècle et on l'opposait souvent à l'esprit de corps des Jésuites aux quels Malebranche lui-même reprochait leur unité de doctrine. Bien que ce ne soit là une pure supposition on est sans doute en droit de penser que la hardiesse d'esprit d'un Richard Simon par exemple, dont les travaux devançoivent de deux siècles les résultats les plus avancés de l'exégèse biblique moderne, n'a pas été sans affermir Malebranche dans son attitude d'indépendence et d'autonomie personelle.

[18] Mais la véritable raison pour laquelle Malebranche plus encore que Descartes attaque le principe d'autorité, c'est que ce principe, simplement ridicule quand il parlait au nom d'Aristote, était devenu très redoutable maintenant qu'il parlait au nom de Descartes lui-même. Toute une école en effet s'était fondée sous le patronage de ce grand nom et ce n'était pas pour La Fontaine seulement que Descartes était "ce mortel dont on eut fait un dieu, chez les anciens." L'école nouvelle, on peut le penser, n'était pas exempte des défauts de toutes les écoles: Descartes était devenue une sorte d'oracle infaillible, elle avait ses principes, ses dogmes, son orthodoxie, et, bien que tout cela ne fut pas poussé au dernier degré, elle était devenue assez *intransigeante* **à éviter** pour que Malebranche lui apparut comme le pire des hérétiques. Ce qui fait donc que les attaques contre le principe d'autorité tiennent tant de place chez Malebranche c'est que là où Descartes n'avait eu à lutter que contre Aristote, Grec âgé de plus de deux mille ans et n'ayant que ce mérite, Malebranche avait eu à lutter contre la jeune gloire de Descartes lui-même. **Est-ce bien sur??** [with a line drawn alongside the previous two lines]

[19] D'ailleurs la polémique contre l'Aristotélisme ne devait pas s'arrêter au dernier scolastique; il fallait poursuivre les formes substantielles jusque dans leurs extrêmes retranchements, au sein même de la philosophie nouvelle. En montrant que Malebranche a considéré le Cartésianisme, tantôt explicitement tantôt implicitement, comme une consécration partielle de quelques unes des erreurs les plus dangereuses de l'école, nous aurons sans doute donné la raison de l'acharnement véritable dont il a fait preuve contre les doctrines d'Aristote.

[20] Malebranche en effet s'était séparé très nettement de Descartes et des ses successeurs, Arnauld et Régis, sur le point capital pour lui de

la théorie des idées. Si Descartes n'avait pas été tenté de maintenir dans les corps étendus les formes substantielles de la scolastique c'est que la conception du mécanisme physique qui était à la base de son système le lui interdisait absolument. Mais là où le mécanisme perdait ses droits, là où il était nécessaire de voir autre chose que des combinaisons de mouvements rigoureusement déterminés, les formes substantielles réapparaissaient aussi puissantes que jamais. C'est ainsi que Descartes définit l'âme: une chose dont toute l'essence n'est que de penser. Les idées sont donc de simples produits de la substance pensante, et la plus élevée en dignité, celle qui de toutes possède le plus de réalité objective, l'idée de Dieu, est renfermée comme toutes les autres dans l'entendement humain. Même quand les idées nécessitent le concours d'une cause supérieure, c'est encore dans l'esprit qu'elles sont produites. Mais un peu de réflexion suffit à faire voir que c'est là un reste évident de l'Aristotélisme. Il est permis de s'étonner que "messieurs les Cartésiens" qui rejettent les termes de nature et de faculté pour les objets extérieurs trouvent bon de les employer à propos de l'âme. On refuse aux philosophes de l'école le droit de dire que: le feu brûle, et l'on affirme soi-même immédiatement après que: l'âme pense. Mais à tout prendre, il serait beaucoup plus acceptable de reconnaître des facultés au corps qu'à l'âme. **Cette polémique contre certains cartésiens est très distincte de cela que M avait risqué contre le scolastique.** Que l'on dise plutôt que les corps sont le principe de leur mouvement, "cela renverse toutes mes idées, mais j'en conviendrai plutôt que de dire que l'esprit s'éclaire lui-même" (*Recherche*, II, 387; O.C., III, 145). Pour gré ou mal gré, si l'on rejette les formes substantielles il faudra finir par admettre que les esprits loin d'avoir la faculté de produire les idées, voient ces dernières dans l'étendue intelligible qui est en Dieu. Dans l'étendue intelligible sont renfermés toutes les vérités et tous les rapports; rapports de quantité, dont découlent les vérités théoriques et toute la science; rapports de perfection, dont découlent les vérités pratiques et toute la morale. **Ce n'est pas dans l'étendue intelligible que sont renfermés les rapports de perfection** [with a line drawn alongside the previous two lines]. Au dessus de l'étendue intelligible et la renfermant en soi, nous voyons Dieu directement, sans le secours d'aucune idée, et nous contemplons quoiqu'elle soit "incompréhensible" sa suprême intelligibilité.

[21] Une fois l'écartée la faculté de penser que Descartes confère à l'âme de l'homme, nous sommes nous enfin libérés complètement de la sujétion de la philosophie Aristotélicienne? Non et il reste encore

un dernier effort à faire qui doit porter, non plus sur l'âme humaine, mais sur les objets matériels, car, il faut bien l'avouer, Descartes n'a pas su tirer de l'idée féconde du mécanisme physique tout ce qu'elle contenait de vérités. Après avoir refusé au monde extérieur toutes les qualités qu'on lui prête d'ordinaire, sauf l'étendue et le mouvement, il se sert de sa découverte pour distinguer l'âme du corps, la substance pensante étante mise d'un côté, la substance étendue de l'autre. Mais en réalité la distinction établie par Descartes est toute superficielle; l'âme et le corps sont bien des substances distinctes mais cela ne les empêche pas d'agir directement l'une sur l'autre. Le corps et l'âme de l'homme sont pour Descartes "intimement mêlés l'un à l'autre." C'est donc que l'on a laissé aux objets matériels au moins une ombre et comme un reflet de cette puissance que par sa théorie des formes substantielles Aristote leur accordait. On a dépouillé l'étendue de ses qualités, mais on lui a conservé la faculté d'agir sur la pensée; en un mot on a encore, sous l'influence d'un vieux fond d'esprit païen, admis qu'en dehors de Dieu une action pouvait s'exercer sur notre entendement humain. La distinction de l'âme et du corps soit en effet se poser avec bien plus de force que Descartes ne l'a fait: il faut si bien distinguer l'étendue de la pensée que jamais plus dans la suite un rapport quelconque ne puisse être supposé entre ces deux substances. Non seulement l'étendue est distincte de la pensée mais on doit dire que jamais l'esprit humain n'a vu d'objet matériel depuis que Dieu a crée le monde; l'esprit ne peut voir que les idées des choses renfermées dans l'étendue intelligible qui seule est participable de l'entendement humain. Il faut donc se séparer de l'Aristotélisme jusqu'au bout et dire que si les objets n'ont pas en eux de formes substantielles qui leur donnent l'indépendence ils n'ont pas non plus le pouvoir d'agir sur nous à quelque degré que ce soit: notre esprit ne connaît rien des choses par une action directe qu'elles auraient sur lui et lorsque Descartes a voulu prouver l'existence du monde extérieur, il n'a exposé que la preuve la plus forte que la raison toute seule en peut donner. La véracité divine ne suffit pas s'il n'y a que la révélation des Saintes Ecritures qui puisse nous contraindre à croire que le monde extérieur existe.

[22] Nous ne prétendons nullement d'ailleurs que Malebranche se soit libéré systématiquement de ce qu'il rencontrait d'Aristotélisme chez les autres philosophes. Nous voulions simplement expliquer la raison de l'extraordinaire étendue que la partie critique occupe dans son œuvre, et spécialement, pourquoi cette critique a plus d'importance chez lui

que chez Descartes. La raison est que le système de Malebranche est beaucoup plus éloigné de la philosophie de l'Ecole que ne l'était celui de Descartes lui-même. **C'est possible en effet** [with a line drawn alongside the previous two lines] Et le fait que Malebranche, même inconsciemment, a rejeté de la philosophie Cartésienne précisément ce qu'elle avait conservé d'Aristotélicien semble bien le prouver.

[23] Il serait certainement puéril de défendre Aristote contre les attaques de Malebranche. Ce que le philosophe Français connaît du philosophe Grec c'est la partie morte de l'œuvre: la physique. Tant au plus faut-il dire qu'un peu de bonne volonté suffirait pour faire juger ridicules à leur tour bien des explications de la physique de Malebranche. **Pas peut être au même degré.** [with a line drawn alongside the previous two lines] Et c'est bien un peu l'apothéose de l'idée obscure que la faculté occulte de l'attraction des corps ait éliminé l'idée claire et distincte de l'impulse. Pour ce qui est la métaphysique d'Aristote, il est évident que Malebranche ne la connaît pas et ne la voit qu'à travers les déformations *absurdes* **Excessif** que la scolastique à son déclin lui avait fait subir. Il est douteux d'ailleurs qu'en connaissant mieux le philosophe Grec il eut adopté des sentiments plus doux à son égard; il lui aurait simplement fait dire un peu moins d'absurdités. Peut être aussi aurait-il hésité à écrire cette formule surprenante chez un adversaire irréconciliable d'Aristote: "Il n'y a que Dieu qui soit véritablement immobile et moteur tout ensemble" (*Recherche*, II, 469; O.C., III, 240). Peut être enfin se serait-il demandé, si en face de sa propre théorie, Aristote n'aurait pas été en droit de rééditer pour certains points sa critique mordante de la théorie des idées: τουτ' ἐστι κενολογεῖν ἐστι καὶ μεταφορὰς λέγειν ποιητικὰς.[8]

8 Aristotle, *Metaphysics*, Book 1(= Alpha) 9, 991a21–22, and XIII (=Mu) 5, 1079b27 (Aristotle 1936, 1:68, 2:202) where he stated that to assert the existence of the Platonic Forms or Ideas and say other things participate in them, "is to use empty words and to utter poetical metaphors." Gilson's transcription differs slightly from the original. At the outset of the phrase, Gilson added a demonstrative and repositions ἐστι. The original is κενολογεῖν ἐστι καὶ μεταφορὰς λέγειν ποιητικὰς.

APPENDIX 2[9]

6 mai 1935. Conversation Du Bos. Il admire en Gilson ce simple bon sens qui n'a pas besoin de se simplifier. Ce n'et pas la formule exacte, mais c'est à peu près le sens. En effet, ce qui est étonnant chez Gilson, c'est la force par laquelle il gonfle d'intelligence le bon sens. Le bon sens est chez la plupart des gens à qui on l'attribue, une baudruche dégonflée, de l'intelligence anémiée. Ou encore—sous le nom de rude bon sens—on célèbre une espèce de brutalité intellectuelle qui est simple paresse d'esprit.* Chez Gilson le mot *bon* a repris la signification de *droit*. Le bon sens, loin d'être une simpliste des questions, est au contraire ce qui lui permet de montrer spontanément la complexité réel des questions sous leur apparente simplicité.

Je connais peu d'hommes qui aient moins de préjugés. Il y a chez lui une probité qui fonctionne avec la précision d'un déclic devant tout jugement: la réduction au réel est instantanée. Il va immédiatement voir *ce qui est dessous*. Jamais dupe du décor, il commence par aller dans les coulisses.

Il y a un génie du bon sens.

Une œuvre comme celle de Gilson est parfaitement objective. Il est historien. Il ne parle jamais de lui. Mais, sur le plan objectif, cette sérénité historique est la transposition de la sérénité intérieure sur le plan de la vie. On sent que c'est le même homme qui conduit Bernard au zoo et qui reconstruit la pensée de St. Thomas. Il y a un équilibre souverain qui s'exprime dans chaque démarche de cette âme.

C'est par là qu'il donne l'impression d'âme. Souvent celle est donnée par la fragilité, la maladie même, tout ce qui est diminution de matière ou même diminution de la matière. Il y a là un signe de notre dégénérescence. L'âme est d'abord unité et santé, équilibre et domination. Gilson ne peut pas donner l'impression de l'âme aux esthètes, aux snobs de la spiritualité qui ne voient l'âme qu'à travers les corps à la Greco. Il est vrai qu'elle est là, mais pas exclusivement là. D'ailleurs ce serait ne rien comprendre à Greco que de prendre ces formes spiritualisées des corps anémiés.

* ou beaucoup moins: le culte de Clement Vautel représentant du bon sense pour lec lecterus du *Journal*.

---

9 An excerpt from Henri Gouhier's personal notebook (unpublished).

C'est par cette présence de l'âme, santé et équilibre que Gilson est parent de Claudel. Si Claudel était aussi intelligent que Gilson, nous aurions un Goethe catholique.

BIBLIOGRAPHY

Archival Materials

Gilson Papers. Étienne Gilson Archives. John M. Kelly Library of St. Michael's College. University of Toronto.

Gouhier Papers. Département des Manuscrits. Bibliothèque Nationale de France. Paris.

S. V. Keeling Papers. University College Archives. London.

Maritain Papers. Cercle d'études Jacques et Raïssa Maritain. Kolbsheim. France.

Richard McKeon Papers. Special Collections Research Center. The University of Chicago Library.

Perry Correspondence. Ralph Barton Perry: Letters from, to and about Well-Known People A-J. Harvard University Archives.

Rockefeller Archive Center. New York.

L. K. Shook Papers. John M. Kelly Library of St. Michael's College. University of Toronto.

Books and Articles

Adam, Michel. 1967. Malebranche et Aristote. *Bulletin de l'association Guillaume Budé* 2:227–42.

Alden, Douglas W. and Richard A. Brooks., eds. 1980. Vol. 6. *The twentieth century*. 3 vols. In Cabeen, D.C., gen. ed. 1947–1994. *A Critical Bibliography of French Literature*. 6 vols. New York: Syracuse University Press.

Alquié, Ferdinand. 1974. *Le Cartésianisme de Malebranche*. Paris: J. Vrin.

———. 1977. *Malebranche et le rationalisme chrétien*. Paris: Éditions Seghers.

———. 1982. Philosophie et histoire de la philosophie chez Henri Gouhier. *Nouvelles de la république des lettres* 2:7–23.

André, Yves Marie. 1886. *La Vie du R.P. Malebranche, Prêtre de l'Oratoire avec l'histoire de ses ouvrages*. Paris: Poussielgue Frères.

Anon. 1990. Simon, Richard. In Grégory 1990, 27:3232–33.

Anon., ed. 1936. *Actes du huitième congrès international de philosophie à Prague, 2–7 septembre 1934*. Prague: Comité d'organisation du Congrès; Liechtenstein: Kraus Reprint, 1968.

———, ed. 1937. *Independence, Convergence and Borrowing in Institutions, Thought and Art: Harvard Tercentenary Conference of Arts and Sciences*. Cambridge: Harvard University Press.

———, ed. 1953. *Actes du XIe Congrès international de philosophie, Brussels, August 20–26, 1953*. Amsterdam: North-Holland Pub. Co.

Archambault, Paul. 1926. Review of Gilson1925a. *Nouvelle Journée* 5:209–12.

———. 1928. *Vers un réalisme intégral, l'œuvre philosophique de Maurice Blondel.* Supplément. Paris: Bloud & Gay.

———. 1931. *Plaidoyer pour l'inquiétude*. Paris: Spes.

Aristotle, 1936. *The Metaphysics*. 2 vols. English translation by Hugh Tredennick. London: W. Heinemann; Cambridge: Harvard University Press.

Armogathe, Jean-Robert, Michel Autrand, and Jean Deprun. 1995. Hommage à Henri Gouhier. *Bulletin de la société française de philosophie* 89.

Bainton, Roland H. 1950. *Here I Stand: A Life of Martin Luther*. New York: Penguin.

Balz, Georg Adam. 1951. *Cartesian Studies*. New York: Columbia University Press.

———. 1952. *Descartes and the Modern Mind*. New Haven: Yale University Press.

Barbedette, Désire and Albert Farges. 1933. *Cours de philosophie scolastique, d'après la pensée d'Aristote et de S. Thomas mise au courant de la science moderne et dirigée contre le Kantisme et le modernisme*. 2 vols. Paris: Berche et Pagis.

Baruzi, Jean. 1907. *Leibniz et l'organisation religieuse de la terre d'après des documents inédits*. Paris: F. Alcan.

———. 1924. *Saint Jean de la Croix et l'expérience mystique*. Paris: F. Alcan.

Baudin, Émile. 1922. Review of Gilson 1922a. *Revue des sciences religieuses* 11:509–512.

———. 1923. Review of Gilson 1921a. *Revue des sciences religieuses* 3:233–255.

Belaval, Yvon., ed. 1974. *Histoire de la Philosophie*. Encyclopédie de la Pléiade. 3 Vols. Paris: Éditions Gallimard.

Belgioioso, Giulia and Marie-Louise Gouhier, eds. 2005. *Henri Gouhier se souvient … Ou comment on devient historien des idées*. Paris: Vrin.

Benoît, Pierre. 1924. Letter. In Souday 1924.

Bergson, Henri. 1959. *Essai sur les donnés immédiates de la conscience. Œuvres*. Textes annotés par André Robinet. Introd. par Henri Gouhier. Paris: Presses Universitaires de France.

Berkeley, George. 1930. *Berkeley's Commonplace Book*. Ed. with introd., notes, and index by G. A. Johnston. London: Faber and Faber.

———. 1901. *The Works of George Berkeley*. 4 vols. Ed. A.C. Fraser. Oxford: Clarendon.

———. 1948–1957. *The Works of George Berkeley, Bishop of Cloyne*. 9 vols. Eds. A. A. Luce and T. E. Jessop. London and New York: Thomas Nelson & Sons.

Blampignon, Abbé Émile-Antoine. 1861–62. *Étude sur Malebranche, d'après des documents manuscrits, suivie d'une correspondance inédite*. Paris: Douniol, 1861; Durand, 1862.

Blanchet, André. 1975. Henri Bremond, 1865-1904. Paris: Aubier-Montaigne.

Blanchet, Léon. 1920. *Campanella*. Paris. Reprinted New York: Burt Franklin 1964.

Blondel, Maurice. 1939. L'abbé Joannès Wehrlé. *Bulletin trimestriel des anciens élèves de Saint Sulpice*. Reprinted in de Lubac 1969, 13–20.

———. 1966. *Dialogue avec les philosophes: Descartes, Spinoza, Malebranche, Pascal, Saint Augustin*. Paris: Aubier-Montaigne.

Boyer de Sainte-Suzanne, Raymond de. 1968. *Alfred Loisy: Entre la foi et l'incroyance*. Paris: Éditions du Centurion.

Bréhier, Émile. 1926–1932 *Histoire de la philosophie*. 2 vols. issued in seven parts. Paris: F. Alcan.

Bremond, Henri. 1916–33. *Histoire littéraire du sentiment religieux en France: depuis la fin des guerres de religion jusqu'à nos jours*. Paris: Bloud et Gay.

Brezik, Victor B., ed. 1981. *One Hundred Years of Thomism: Aeterni Patris and Afterwards, A Symposium*. Houston: Center for Thomistic Studies.

Brightman, Edgar Sheffield., ed. 1927. *Proceedings of the Sixth International Congress of Philosophy, Harvard, 13–17 September 1926*. New York: Green and Company.

Brunschvicg, Léon. 1926. Les conditions d'existence de l'enseignement supérieur de la philosophie. *Bulletin de la société française de philosophie* 26:1–28. Gilson's remarks: 24–25.

———. 1927. *Le progrès de la conscience dans la philosophie occidentale*. Paris: F. Alcan.

———. 1928 La querelle de l'athéisme. *Bulletin de la société française de philosophie* 28:49–55. Gilson's remarks, 56–61, 66–69.

———. 1934. *Les ages de l'intelligence*. Paris: F. Alcan.

———. 1936. Religion et philosophie. In Anon. 1936, 375–387

Canivez, André. 1974. Aspects de la Philosophie Française. In Belaval 1974, 3:425–79.

Chappell, Vere., ed. 1992. *Essays in Early Modern Philosophers from Descartes and Hobbes to Newton and Leibniz*. 12 vols. New York & London: Garland.

Charasson, Henriette. 1934a. *En chemin de fer, pièce en un acte*. Paris: Gabriel Enault.

———. 1934b. *Madame est sans bonne, farce en un acte*. Paris: Gabriel Enault.

———. 1934c. *Les Réalités invisibles, pièce en un acte*. Paris: Gabriel Enault.

———. 1934d. *Une robe de soie, pièce en un acte*. Paris: Gabriel Enault.

———. 1934e. *Le Saut du diable, comédie en trois actes.* Paris: Gabriel Enault.
———. 1934f. *Séparation, pièce en un acte.* Paris: Gabriel Enault.
Chenaux, Philippe. 1997. La seconde vague thomiste. In Colin 1997, 139–67.
Chenu, M.-D. 1980. L'interprète de saint Thomas d'Aquin. In Couratier 1980, 43–48.
Coffey, R.M. 1967. Gillet, Martin Stanislas. In Mc Donald 1967, 6:490.
Colin, Pierre and Étienne Fouilloux., dirs. 1997. *Intellectuels Chrétiens et esprit des années vingt: Actes du colloque Institut Catholique de Paris 23–24 septembre 1993.* Paris: Les Éditions du Cerf.
Conlan, M.S. 1967. Farges, Albert. In Mc Donald 1967, 5:837.
Connell, Desmond. 1955. La passivité de l'entendement selon Malebranche, *Revue philosophique de Louvain* 53:542–65.
———. 1967. *The Vision in God: Malebranche's Scholastic Sources.* Louvain: Nauwelaerts and Paris: Beatrice-Nauwelaerts.
———. 1974. Malebranche et la scolastique. *Les études philosophiques* 4:449–63.
———. 1978. Cureau de La Chambre, source de Malebranche. *Recherches sur le 17e siècle* 158–72.
Constant, Léonard. 1904. Malebranche: Cours de M. Victor Delbos (janvier-mai 1903). *Revue de philosophie* (janvier) 93–99.
Couratier, Monique., ed. 1980. *Étienne Gilson et nous: La philosophie et son histoire.* Paris: J. Vrin.
Coutrot, Aline. 1961. *Un courant de la pensée catholique: L'hebdomadaire Sept.* Préface by René Rémond. Paris: Les Éditions du Cerf. Republished as *Sept, un journal, un combat: mars 1934–août 1937.* Paris: Éditions Cana, 1982.
Cremer, Théodore. 1912. *Le problème religieux dans la philosophie de l'action [de] M. Maurice Blondel et le P. Laberthonnière.* Préface de M. Victor Delbos. Paris: F. Alcan.
Curtius, Ernst-Robert. 1926. Charles du Bos. *Chronique des lettres françaises* 23–24 (sep–déc) 785–86, Encyclopédie de l'agora: http://agora.qc.ca/mot.nsf/Dossiers/Charles_Du_Bos (3 February 2006).
Damico, Helen, et al., eds. 1995–2000. *Medieval Scholarship: Biographical Studies on the Formation of a Discipline.* 3 vols. New York and London: Garland Publishing, Inc.
Dansette, A. 1967. Action Française. In Mc Donald 1967, 1:97–98.
Cremer, Théodore. 1912. *Le problème religieux dans la philosophie de l'action [de] M. Maurice Blondel et le P. Laberthonnière.* Paris: F. Alcan.
De Corte. Marcel. 1934. *La doctrine de l'intelligence chez Aristote.* Paris: J. Vrin.

De Corte, Madame Marcel. 1975. Marcel De Corte: Bibliographie: 1928–juin 1975. *Itinéraires* 196 (sep–oct) 117–33.

de Gandillac, Maurice. 1998. *Le siècle traversé: Souvenirs de neuf décennies*. Paris: Albin Michel.

de Lubac, Henri, ed. 1969. *Blondel-Wehrlé Correspondance*. Paris: Aubier-Montaigne.

———. 1986. *Lettres de M. Étienne Gilson adressées au Père Henri de Lubac et commentées par celui-ci*. Paris: Les Éditions du Cerf.

Delbos, Victor. 1912. Préface. In Cremer 1912.

———. 1919. *La philosophie française*. Paris: Plon.

———. 1924. *Étude de la philosophie de Malebranche*. Edited and introduction by J. Wehrlé. Paris: Bloud et Gay.

Delorme, S. and G. Bastide, eds. 1967. *Malebranche: L'homme et l'œuvre (Journées Malebranche de juin 1965)*. Paris: J. Vrin.

Denomy, Alex, ed. 1959. *Mélanges offerts à Étienne Gilson*. Toronto: Pontifical Institute of Mediaeval Studies and Paris: J. Vrin.

Descartes, René. 1904. *Oeuvres de Descartes*, 11 vols. Ed. C. Adam and P. Tannery. Paris: Les Éditions du Cerf., 2d edition Paris: C.N.R.S./J. Vrin, 1974–1986.

———. 1930. *Regulae ad directionem ingenii*, ed. Henri Gouhier. Paris: J. Vrin.

Descoqs, Pedro. 1927. Thomisme et scolastique à propos de M. Rougier. *Archives de philosophie* 5.

Martin Dimnik et al., eds. 1989. *Jubilee 1989: Pontifical Institute of Mediaeval Studies Foundation 1929–Papal Charter 1939*. Winnipeg: Jostens.

Doering, Bernard. 1983. *Jacques Martitain and the French Catholic Intellectuals*. Notre Dame: University of Notre Dame Press.

Donneaud, Henry., ed. 1994. Correspondance Étienne Gilson–Michel Labourdette. *Revue Thomiste* 94 (3) (juillet–septembre) 479–529.

Dronke, Peter., ed. 1998. *Etienne Gilson's Letters to Bruno Nardi*. Sismel: Edizioni del Galluzzo.

Easton, Patricia, Thomas M. Lennon, and Gregor Sebba. 1992. *Bibliographia Malebranchiana: A Critical Guide to the Malebranche Literature into 1989*. Carbondale and Edwardsville: Southern Illinois University Press.

École Pratique. 1923. *Annuaire de l'école pratique des hautes études, Section des sciences religieuses, 1923–1924*. Melun: Imprimerie Administrative.

———. 1924. *Annuaire de l'école pratique des hautes études, Section des sciences religieuses, 1924–1925*. Melun: Imprimerie Administrative.

———. 1925. *Annuaire de l'école pratique des hautes études, Section des sciences religieuses, 1925–1926*. Melun: Imprimerie Administrative.

Edie, Callistus James. 1959. The Writings of Étienne Gilson Chronologically Arranged. In Denomy 1959, 15–58.

Espagnat, Bernard d'. 1997. *Notice sur la vie et travaux de Henri Gouhier (1898–1994): séance du mardi 2 décembre 1997*. Paris: Institut de France.

Espinas, Alfred. 1925. *Études sur l'histoire de la philosophie de l'action; Descartes et la morale*, 2 vols. Paris: Bossard.

Fafara, Richard J. 1978. The Implicit Efficacity of the Idea in *Recherché de la vérité*. *The Modern Schoolman* 55:147–64. Reprinted in Chappell 1992, 11, *Nicolas Malebranche*, 95-112.

———.1989. Étienne Gilson's Early Study of Nicolas Malebranche. *The Modern Schoolman* 5:169–218.

———. 2003. Gilson and Gouhier: Approaches to Malebranche. In Redpath 2003, 107–55.

Febvre, Lucien Paul Victor. 1942. *Le problème de l'incroyance au XVIe siècle: la religion de Rabelais*. Paris : A. Michel.

La Fontaine, Jean de. 1991. *Oeuvres complètes*. 2 vols. Ed. Pierre Collinet. Paris: Éditions Gallimard (Pléiade).

Forest, A. 1928. Autour de la notion de philosophie chrétienne. *La vie intellectuelle*. (oct) 122–33.

Fumet, Stanislas. 1978. *Histoire de Dieu dans ma vie: Souvenirs choisis*. Paris: Fayard.

Garric, Robert. 1926. Henri Gouhier. *Revue des jeunes* 10 (10–25 juin) 544–49.

Gilson, Étienne. 1912. *Index scolastico-Cartésien, petite thèse pour le doctorat présentée à la Faculté des Lettres de l'Université de Paris*. Paris: F. Alcan, published definitively in 1913.

———. 1913. *La liberté chez Descartes et la théologie, grande thèse pour le doctorat présentée à la Faculté des Lettres de l'Université de Paris*. Paris: F. Alcan. Nouvelle ed. J. Vrin, 1982.

———. 1914. La doctrine cartésienne de la liberté et la théologie. *Bulletin de la société française de philosophie* 14:207–58.

———. 1919a. Review of Loisy 1919a. *Revue philosophique de la France et de l'étranger* 88 (juillet–décembre) 129–31.

———. 1919b. Review of Loisy 1919b. *Revue philosophique de la France et de l'étranger* 88:131.

———. 1921a. *Études de philosophie médiévale*. Strasbourg: Commission des Publications, de la Faculté des Lettres, Palais de l'Université.

———. 1921b. La signification historique du thomisme, *Études de philosophie médiévale*. In Gilson 1921a, 76–124.

———. 1921c. Review of Blanchet 1920. *Revue philosophique de la France et de l'étranger* 91:297–302.

———. 1922a. *La philosophie au moyen âge*. 2 vols. Paris: Payot. Reprod. 1 vol. 1925, 1930. 2d ed. revue et augmentée, 1944.

———. 1922b. La religion et la foi. *Revue de métaphysique et de morale* 29:359–71.

———. 1923a. A report on the course: Descartes et la pensée religieuse de son temps. In École Pratique 1923, 56–57.

———. 1924a. *La philosophie de saint Bonaventure*. Paris: J. Vrin.

———. 1924b. *The Philosophy of St. Thomas Aquinas*. Tr. Edward Bullough, ed. G.A. Elrington. Cambridge: Heffer. Translated from the text of the 3d prior to its publication.

———. 1924c. Pour travailler tranquille. *La vie catholique* (1 novembre) 2.

———. 1924d. Rabelais franciscain. *Revue d'histoire franciscaine* 1:257–87. Reprinted in Gilson 1932b, 197–241.

———. 1924e. Projet d'un commentaire historique du Discours de la Méthode. *Bulletin de la société française de la philosophie* 24:135–50. MM. Lalande, Robin, Weber, Laberthonnière, Beaulavon, and Rodrigues took part in the discussion. Gilson's remarks, 135–38, 140–50

———. 1924f. A report on Gouhier's series of lectures under Gilson's direction on: La vision en Dieu chez Malebranche et ses sources théologiques. In École Pratique 1924, 64–65.

———. 1925a. *Saint Thomas d'Aquin* (Collection: Les moralistes chrétiens, textes et commentaires). Paris: Gabalda.

———. 1925b. À propos de Rabelais franciscain. *Revue d'histoire franciscaine* 2:113.

———. 1925c. La pensée religieuse de Descartes. *Revue métaphysique et de morale* 32:519–37. Reprinted as Appendix 3 in Gilson 1930, 281–98.

———. 1925d A report on the course: Commentaire littéral de l'*Itinerarium mentis in Deum*. In École Pratique 1925, 54–55.

———. 1925e A report on the course: Recherches sur les origines de la réforme thomiste. In École Pratique 1925, 52–54.

———. 1926a. Pourquoi saint Thomas a critiqué saint Augustin. *Archives d'histoire doctrinale et littéraire du moyen âge* 1:5–127.

———. 1926b. Review of Rougier 1925. *Revue d'histoire franciscaine* 3:313–18.

———. 1927. Le rôle de la philosophie dans l'histoire de la civilisation. In Brightman, Edgar Sheffield 1927, 529–35. Reprinted in *Revue de métaphysique et de morale* 34:169–76.

———. 1928. Review of Gouhier's theses (Gouhier 1926a and b). *Revue philosophique de la France et de l'étranger* 106:152.

———. 1929a. *Introduction à l'étude de saint Augustin*. Paris: J. Vrin. 2d rev. et aug. 1943.

———. 1929b. Mediaevalism in Toronto. *Commonweal* 9 (1 May) 738–40.

———. 1930a. *Études sur le rôle de la pensée médiévale dans la formation du système cartésien*. Paris: J. Vrin.

———. 1930b. De la critique des formes substantielles au doute méthodologique. In Gilson 1930a, 141–68.
———. 1930c. L'idée de philosophie chrétienne chez saint Augustin et chez saint Thomas d'Aquin. *La vie intellectuelle* 8:46–62.
———. 1930d. Physique et métaphysique dans le système cartésien. In Gilson 1930a, 173–83.
———. 1931a. La notion de philosophie chrétienne. *Bulletin de la société française de philosophie* 31:37–93.
———. 1931b. Sur un 'Auguste Comte'. *La vie intellectuelle* 12:246–47.
———. 1932a. *L'esprit de la philosophie médiévale*. 2 vols. Paris: J. Vrin. 2d rev. 1944.
———. 1932b. *Les idées et les lettres*. Paris: J. Vrin.
———. 1933. Autour de la philosophie chrétienne, la spécificité de l'ordre philosophique. *La vie intellectuelle* 21:404–424. Reprinted as chapter 3 of Gilson 1935b. Eng. trans. Gilson 1990, 81–108.
———. 1934a. *Pour un ordre catholique*. Paris: Desclée de Brouwer.
———. 1934b. *The Spirit of Medieval Philosophy*. Trans. by A. H. C. Downes. New York: Charles Scribner's Sons.
———. 1934c. *La théologie mystique de Saint Bernard*. Paris: J. Vrin.
———. 1934d. Le culte de l'incompétence. *Sept*. 21 (21 juillet) 2.
———. 1934e. Sur quelques difficultés de l'illumination augustinienne. *Revue Néoscolastique de Philosophie* 36 (février), 321–31. This number of the review was published in *Hommage à M. le Professeur M. de Wulf*.
———. 1935a. *Le réalisme méthodique* (Collection: Cours et documents de philosophie). Paris: Tequi. English trans., Gilson 1990.
———, ed., introd., and notes. 1935b. *René Descartes, Discours de la méthode*. Paris: J. Vrin.
———. 1935c. En marge de l'Action Française. *Sept* 71 (5 juillet) 4.
———. 1935d. Par delà de Sillon et l'Action Française. *Sept* 69 (21 juin) 4.
———. 1935e. Action politique et action catholique. *Sept* 70 (28 juin) 4.
———. 1935f. En marge de l'Action Française. *Sept* 71 (5 juillet) 4.
———. 1935g. Les catholiques et l'action sociale. *Sept* 75 (2 août) 4.
———. 1935h. Qui est mammon. *Sept* 76 (9 août) 4.
———. 1935i. Action catholique et action politique. *Sept* 77 (16 août) 3.
———. 1935j. Review of Laberthonnière 1935. *La vie intellectuelle* 34:302–05.
———. 1937a. *The Unity of Philosophical Experience* (The William James Lectures given at Harvard University in the first half of the academic year 1936–37). New York: Charles Scribner's Sons.
———. 1937b. Medieval Universalism and its Present Value. In Anon. 1937, 194–215. Reprinted in Pegis 1949, 966–83.

———. 1938. *Reason and Revelation in the Middle Ages* (The Richards Lectures at the University of Virginia 1937). New York: Charles Scribner's Sons.

———. 1939. Mon ami Lévy-Bruhl, philosophe, sociologue, analyste des mentalités. *Les nouvelles littéraires* (18 mars) 1.

———. 1941. *God and Philosophy*. New Haven: Yale University Press.

———. 1946. Exportations intellectuelles. *Le Monde*, 5 juillet, 3.

———. 1948. *L'Etre et l'essence*. Paris: J. Vrin.

———. 1949. The Terrors of the Year Two Thousand. Toronto: St. Michael's College. Reprinted with an introduction by Armand A. Maurer, in *Logos* 3:1 (Winter 2000) 20–36. French translation: Les terreurs de l'an deux mille. Ecclesia 2 (1950) 9–19).

———. 1953. Remarques sur l'expérience en métaphysique. In Anon. 1937, 4:5–10. English trans. and study in Maurer 1990, 40–47.

———. 1955. *History of Christian Philosophy in the Middle Ages*. New York: Random House.

———. 1957. Where is Christendom? In Pegis 1957, 342–46.

———. 1959. In Memoriam: R. P. Gabriel Théry, O.P. (1891–1959). *Archives d'histoire doctrinale et littéraire du moyen âge* 26:7–10.

———. 1962. *The Philosopher and Theology*. Trans. Cécile Gilson. New York: Random House.

——— and Thomas Langan. 1963. *Modern Philosophy: Descartes to Kant*. New York: Random House.

———. 1965. *The Arts of the Beautiful*. New York: Charles Scribner's Sons.

———, and Thomas Langan, and Armand A. Maurer. 1966. *Recent philosophy: Hegel to the Present*. New York: Random House.

———. 1968. On Behalf of the Handmaid. In Shook 1968, 236–49.

———. 1969. 8 November letter to Richard Fafara (unpublished). Gilson Archives.

———. 1979. *L'athéisme difficile*. Ed. and pref. by Henri Gouhier. Paris: J. Vrin.

———. 1990. *Methodical Realism*. Trans. Philip Trower, introd. by Stanley L. Jaki. Front Royal: Christendom Press.

———. 1993. *Christian Philosophy*. Trans. and introd. by Armand Maurer. Toronto: Pontifical Institute of Mediaeval Studies.

———. 2003. Gilson and Gouhier : Approaches to Malebranche. In Redpath 2003, 107-55.

Gochet, Paul 1985. Notice sur Philippe Devaux. *Annuaire de l'académie royale de Belgique* 151:153–74.

Gouhier, Henri. 1920. Les rapports de la raison et de la foi selon Descartes. *Revue des jeunes* 4 (10 octobre) 17–29.

———. 1922. Descartes à la Convention et aux Cinq-Cents. *Revue de métaphysique et de morale* 29 (avril) 243–51.

———. 1922b. Intellectualisme et christianisme. *Revue des jeunes* 3 (10 septembre) 493–505.

———. 1924a. *Descartes et la pensée religieuse de son temps*. Paris: J. Vrin. 2d ed. 1972.

———. 1924b. Point de départ de M. Barrès. *Revue des jeunes* 1 (25 janvier and 10 février) 48–63, 126–45, 278–89.

———. 1926a. *La philosophie de Malebranche et son expérience religieuse* [Histoire philosophique du sentiment religieux en France, Tome 1]. Paris: J. Vrin. 2d ed., augm. J. Vrin 1948.

———. 1926b. *La vocation de Malebranche*. Paris: J. Vrin.

———. 1926c. Les livres nouveaux de la philosophie. *Livres et revues, Bulletin mensuel de bibliographie critique* 1 (12 janvier) 1–13.

———. 1927. Review of Brunschvicg 1927. *Les nouvelles littéraires* no. 264 (10 décembre) 10.

———. 1928. Review of Archambault 1928. *Les nouvelles littéraires* no. 290 (5 mai) 8.

———. 1929. *Malebranche* (Collection: Les moralistes chrétiens, textes et commentaires). Paris: Gabalda.

———. 1930a. M. Chautemps se lave les mains. *La tribune de l'Aube. Journal républicain quotidien* 30 (20 février).

———. 1930b. Review of Gilson 1929a . *Les nouvelles littéraires* no.372 (30 novembre) 11.

———. 1931a. *La vie d'Auguste Comte*. Paris: Éditions Gallimard.

———. 1931b. Les projets de réforme de l'enseignement devant la conscience catholique. *La nouvelle revue des jeunes* 2 (15 juin) 599–614.

———. 1932a. Introduction à la théorie thomiste de la connaissance. *Revue des cours et conférences*, 28 février, 15 et 30 mars, 15 avril, 15 mai.

———. 1932b. Review of Archambault 1931. *Les nouvelles littéraires* no.499 (7 mai) 7.

———. 1933–34. Digression sur la philosophie, à propos de la philosophie chrétienne. *Recherches philosophiques* 3:211–36. Reprinted in Gouhier 1947, 7–45.

———. 1933–41. *La jeunesse d'Auguste Comte et la formation du positivisme*. 3 vols. Paris: J. Vrin: 1. Sous le signe de la liberté, 1933; 2. Saint-Simon jusqu'à la Restauration, 1936; 3. Auguste Comte et Saint-Simon, 1941.

———. 1933b. Le problème du baccalauréat. *L'Europe nouvelle* 16 (no.814) (16 septembre) 888–89.

———. 1934a. L'itinéraire ontologique de Descartes. *Revista di filosofia neoscolastica* (mai) 259–276. Reprinted in Gouhier 1937, 107–41.

———. 1934b. Dans Nuremberg en fête. *La vie intellectuelle* 6 (1934) 31–1: 171–173.

———. 1935–36. Review of Laberthonnière 1935. *Recherches philosophiques* 5:525–29.

———. 1936. Positivisme et révolution. In Anon. 1936, 656–65.

———. 1937. *Essais sur Descartes*. Paris: J. Vrin. 2d ed, 1949. 3d ed. as *Descartes: Essais sur le Discours de la méthode, la métaphysique et la morale*, 1973.

———. 1938a. Introduction bibliographique à l'œuvre et à la pensée de Malebranche. *Revue internationale de philosophie* 1:161–74.

———. 1938b. Une nouvelle édition des œuvres de Malebranche. *Revue internationale de philosophie* 1:175–77.

———. 1938c. Review of Gilson 1937a. *La vie intellectuelle* 56 (25 juin) 404–12. Reprinted as appendix 2 in Gouhier 1947, 127–34.

———. 1940. Vers l'université nouvelle. *Revue des deux mondes* (août) 225–34.

———. 1944. *La philosophie et son histoire*. Paris: J. Vrin. 2d. 1948.

———. 1945. Témoignage de M. Henri Gouhier [pour L. Brunschvicg]. *Les études philosophiques* 20:19.

———. 1946. Le métier d'étudiant. *Voix universitaire* (1 mars) 1.

———. 1952. *L'histoire et sa philosophie*. Paris: J. Vrin.

———. 1960. Étienne Gilson ou la vitalité de l'esprit. *Ecclésia*, (mai) 45–49.

———. 1966. L'Université à la recherché d'elle-même. *La Table ronde* no. 227 (1966) 7–13.

———. 1968. Préface. In Boyer de Sainte-Suzanne 1968.

———. 1970. L'expérience religieuse de Marie Noël. *Cahiers Marie Noël* 2:22–31.

———. 1971. *Le combat de Marie Noël*. Paris: Stock.

———. 1975. Préface. In Blanchet 1975.

———. 1978a. *Cartésianisme et augustinisme au XVIIe siècle*. Paris: J. Vrin.

———. 1978b. Pour une histoire historique de la philosophie. In Mercier and Svilar 1978, 4:135–54.

———. 1980a. *Études sur l'histoire des idées en France depuis le XVIIe siècle*. Paris: J. Vrin.

———. 1980b. Les Deux 'XVIIe Siècle'. In Henri Gouhier 1980a, 35–48.

———. 1988. Propos sur l'inspiration en philosophie. In Parys 1988, 15–17.

———. 1993a. *Étienne Gilson, Trois essais: Bergson, la philosophie chrétienne, l'art*. Paris: J. Vrin.

———. 1993b. Étienne Gilson et la notion de philosophie chrétienne. In Gouhier 1993a, 40–58.

———. 1998. Itinéraire: Henri Gouhier, Histoire personnelle de la philosophie, Entretien avec Henri Gouhier. *Revue autrement* 102:9–15.
Grégory, Claude., ed. 1990. *Encyclopaedia Universalis, Thesaurus-Index.* 32 vols. Paris: Encyclopaedia Universalis France.
Grene, Marjorie. 1991. *Descartes among the Scholastics, The Aquinas Lecture 1991.* Milwaukee: Marquette University Press.
Guignebert, Charles. 1907. *Modernisme et tradition catholique en France.* Paris: Collection de la Grande Revue.
———. 1910. *L'évolution des dogmes.* Paris: Flammarion.
———. 1927. *Le christianisme médiéval et moderne.* Paris: Flammarion.
———. 1927. Review of Rougier 1925. *Scientia* 1–4.
———. 1933. Jésus. Paris: La Renaissance du livre.
———. 1935. *Le monde juif vers le temps de Jésus.* Paris: Albin Michel.
———. 1943. *Le Christ.* Paris: Albin Michel.
Guth, Paul. 1946. Rencontre avec Gilson. *Le Littéraire* (28 déc.) 1.
Habert, H. O. 1924. Note à propos d'études médiévales. *La vie catholique* (25 octobre) 9–10.
Hahn, Lewis Edwin, ed. 1995. *The Philosophy of Paul Weiss.* Chicago: Open Court.
Harvard College 1926–1927. *Report of the President of Harvard College and Reports of Departments: Faculty of Arts and Sciences.* Cambridge: Harvard University.
———. 1936–1937. *Report of the President of Harvard College and Reports of Departments: Faculty of Arts and Sciences.* Cambridge: Harvard University.
Herrera, R.A., and James Lehrberger, and M.E. Bradford., eds. 1993. *Saints, Sovereigns, and Scholars: Studies in Honor of Frederick D. Wilhelmsen.* New York: P. Lang.
Horner, Richard. 1997. A Pragmatist in Paris: Frederic Rauh's Task of Dissolution. *Journal of the History of Ideas* 58:289-308.
Hourdin, G. 1967. Bernadot, Marie Vincent. In McDonald 1967, 2, 332–33.
Hubert, R. 1927. Revue critique de quelques ouvrages récents relatifs à la philosophie de Malebranche. *Revue d'histoire de la philosophie* 1:269–93.
Jaki, Stanley L. 1978. *The Road of Science and the Ways to God.* Edinburgh: Scottish Academic Press.
———. 1986. *Lord Gifford and His Lectures: A Centenary Retrospect.* Macon: Mercer University Press.
———. 1993. Gilson and Science. In Herrera, and Lehrberger, and Bradford 1993, 31– 47.
———. 2004. *Science and Religion: A Primer.* Missouri: Real View Books.
Johnston, George A. 1923. *The Development of Berkeley's Philosophy.* New York: Macmillan; Russell & Russell, 1965; Garland, 1988.

———. 1930. *Berkeley's Commonplace Book*. London: Faber and Faber.

Jolley, Nicholas. 1990. *The Light of the Soul: Theories of Ideas in Leibniz, Malebranche, and Descartes*. Oxford: Oxford University Press.

Joly, Henri. 1901. *Malebranche*. Paris: F. Alcan.

Keeling, S. V. 1933. Review of Gilson 1930a. *Mind* 42:75–85.

1934a. *Descartes*. London: Edward Arnold, 1934; 2d ed. Oxford: Oxford University Press, 1968.

———. 1934b. Cartesian mechanism. *Philosophy* 9:51–66.

———. 1936. Philosophy in France: Recent interpretations of Cartesianism. *Philosophy* 2:336–40.

Kennedy, Leonard A., and Jack C. Marler, eds. 1986. *Thomistic Papers II*. Houston: Center for Thomistic Studies, University of St. Thomas.

Kennicott, Philip. 2001. Paul Weiss Turns 100 Today, but His Search for Meaning is far from Over. *The Washington Post* (19 May) C–1.

Kneebone, John T., et al., eds. 1998–. *Dictionary of Virginia Biography*. 2 vols. to date. Richmond: Library of Virginia. http://www.lva.lib.va.us/whatwedo/pubs/dvb/ (accessed 17 May 2006).

Laberthonnière, Lucien. 1935. *Études sur Descartes*. 2 vols. Ed. Louis Canet. Paris: J. Vrin.

Lacouture, Jean. 1990. *François Mauriac*. 2 vols. Paris: Seuil.

Laporte, Jean Marie Frédéric. 1937. La liberté selon Descartes. *Revue de métaphysique et de morale* (janvier) 101–64. Extract reprinted in Laporte 1951, 37–87.

———. 1951. *Études d'histoire de la philosophie française au XVIIe siècle*. Paris: J. Vrin.

Leprieur, François. 1989. *Quand Rome condamne: dominicains et prêtres-ouvriers*. Paris: Plon/Les Éditions du Cerf.

Lechalas, Georges. 1900–01. Review of Joly 1901. *Revue de philosophie*, 629–33.

Leclerc, Max. 1916. Nécrologie: Victor Delbos (1862–1916). *Revue de métaphysique et de morale* 23:657–58.

Leduc-Fayette, D., ed. 1999. *Le regard d'Henri Gouhier: Actes du colloque du C.E.P.F., 29–31 mai 1996*. Paris: J. Vrin.

Lefèvre, Frédéric. 1925. *Une heure avec . . . .* 3. série. Paris: Éditions Gallimard.

Lennon, Thomas M. 1980. Philosophical Commentary. In Malebranche 1980, 759–848. Reprinted in Chappell 1992, 11, *Nicolas Malebranche*, 167–256.

Levine, Thelma Z. 1998. Balz, Albert George Adam. In Kneebone 1998– , 1:311–12.

Lévy-Bruhl, Lucien. 1899. *History of Modern Philosophy in France*. Chicago: Open Court, reprinted 1924.

Loisy, Alfred. 1919a. *De la discipline intellectuelle*. Paris: E. Nourry.
———. 1919b. *La paix des nations et la religion de l'avenir*. Paris: E. Nourry.
———. 1925. Review of Rougier 1925. *Revue critique d'histoire et de littérature* (1 septembre).
Luce, A. A. 1934. *Berkeley & Malebranche: A Study in the Origins of Berkeley's Thought*. 2d. 1967. Oxford: Oxford University Press.
Lyons, Louis M. 1936. The World's Wise Men: Étienne Gilson, French Philosopher from Canada. *The Boston Globe* (7 July, morning edition) 14.
Mc Donald, William J., ed. in chief. 1967. *New Catholic Encyclopedia*. 15 vols. New York: McGraw Hill.
McGrath, Margaret. 1982. *Etienne Gilson: A Bibliography/Une Bibliographie*. Toronto: Pontifical Institute of Mediaeval Studies.
McInerny, Ralph., ed. 1991. *The Catholic Writer: Papers Presented at a Conference Sponsored by the Wethersfield Institute, New York City, September 29–30, 1989*. San Francisco: Ignatius Press.
McKeon, Richard. 1936. Review of Gilson 1934b. *Yale Review*, n.s., 26:396–7.
———. 1954. *Thought, Action, and Passion*. Chicago: The University of Chicago Press.
———. 1990. Spiritual Autobiography. In McKeon, Z. 1990, 3–36.
McKeon, Zahava K., ed. 1990. *Freedom and History and Other Essays: An Introduction to the Thought of Richard McKeon*. Chicago: The University of Chicago Press.
Malbreil, Germain. 1979. Notice to *Réponse à M. Régis*. In Malebranche 1992, 1:1616–17.
Malebranche, Nicolas. 1880. *De la recherche de la vérité*. 2 vols. Ed. Francisque Bouillier. Paris: Éditions Garnier Frères.
———. 1958–67. *Les oeuvres complètes de Malebranche*. Direction: André Robinet (Bibliothèque des textes philosophiques. Directeur: Henri Gouhier), 20 vols., plus two unnumbered volumes. Paris: J. Vrin and Centre National de la Recherche Scientifique.
———. 1980. *The Search after Truth*. Trans. and ed. by Thomas M. Lennon and Paul Olscamp. Columbus: Ohio State University Press.
———. 1992. *Oeuvres*. 2 vols. Eds. Geneviève Rodis-Lewis and Germain Malbreil. Paris: Éditions Gallimard (Pléiade).
Marion, Jean-Luc. 1980. L'instauration de la rupture: Gilson à la lecture de Descartes. In Couratier 1980, 13–34.
Marion, Mathieu. 2004a. Investigating Rougier. *Cahiers d'épistémologie* 2004–02 (n.314) 1–20.
———. 2004b. Une philosophie politique pour l'empirisme logique? In *Actes du colloque Louis Rougier (1889-1982). Vie et œuvre d'un philosophe engagé (Genève, 10/04)*. *Philosophia Scientiae* (forthcoming).

Maritain, Jacques. 1926. Grandeur et misère de la métaphysique. *Chroniques du roseau d'or* 1. Reprinted in Maritain 1982–1999, 4 (1982) 275–308.

———. 1935. *Science et Sagesse suivi d'éclaircissements sur la philosophie morale*. Paris: Labergerie.

——— and Raïssa. 1982–1999. *Œuvres complètes: Jacques et Raïssa Maritain*. 16 vols. Paris: Éditions Saint-Paul.

Marx, Jean. 1959. La quête manqué de Gauvain. In Denomy 1959, 415–36.

Maurer, Armand A. 1981. The Legacy of Étienne Gilson. In Brezik 1981, 28–45.

———. 1990. Gilson's Use of History in Philosophy. In Russman 1990, 25–48.

———. 2000. Introduction to Gilson 1949. *Logos* 3:1 (Winter 2000) 12–19.

Mercier, André and Maja Svilar, eds. 1978. *Philosophes critiques d'eux-mêmes*. 11 vols. Bern: Peter Lang.

Merton, Thomas. 1948. *The Seven Story Mountain*. New York: Harcourt Brace.

———. 1954. *The Last of the Fathers: Saint Bernard of Clairvaux and the Encyclical Letter, Docta Mellifluus*. New York: Harcourt Brace.

Michel, Florian. 2002. Jacques Maritain en Amérique du Nord – I:1933–40. *Cahiers Jacques Maritain* 45:27–86.

———. 2003. Yves Simon à la bataille de Chicago (1948–1961). *Cahiers Jacques Maritain* 47:40–56.

Murphy, Francesca Aran. 2004. *Art and Intellect in the Philosophy of Étienne Gilson*. Columbia: University of Missouri Press.

———, ed. 2005 Correspondance entre Marie-Dominique Chenu et Étienne Gilson, Un choix de lettres (1923–69) *Revue Thomiste* 105 (janvier–mars) 25–87.

Nadler, Steven. 1992. *Malebranche and Ideas*. New York: Oxford University Press.

Neveu, Bruno. 2002. Henri Gouhier et l'histoire philosophique du sentiment religieux. In Sacquin 2002, 19–38.

Noël, Marie (Rouget, Marie). 1933a. *Berceuse de la Mère-Dieu*. Paris: Sénart.

———. 1933b. *Cantique des Pâques*. Paris: Sénart.

———. 1933c. *La Complainte des trios poissons*. Paris: Sénart.

———. 1933d. *Notes intimes*. Paris: Stock.

Ollé-Laprune, Léon. 1870. *La Philosophie de Malebranche*. 2 vols. Paris: Ladrange.

Parys, Franz, ed. 1988. *La philosophie d'inspiration chrétienne en France*. Paris: Desclée de Brouwer.

Pegis, Anton C. 1946. Gilson and Thomism. *Thought* 21:435–54.

———., ed. 1949. *The Wisdom of Catholicism*. New York: Doubleday & Company.
———., ed. 1957. *A Gilson Reader: Selections from the Writings of Étienne Gilson*. New York: Doubleday & Company.
Petit, Annie. 2002. Henri Gouhier et Auguste Comte. In Sacquin 2002, 65–76.
Pomahac, Gertrude C. 2004. Louis Auguste Romanet Fonds Finding Aid http://archive1.lse.ualberta.ca/FindingAids/LouisRomanet/LouisRomanet.html (accessed 3 October 2006).
Prévotat, Jacques. 1997. Autour du parti de l'intelligence. In Colin and Fouilloux 1997, 169–93.
Prouvost, Géry., ed. 1991. *Étienne Gilson–Jacques Maritain, Deux approches de l'être, Correspondance 1923–1971*. Paris: J. Vrin.
———. 1994a. Les relations entre philosophie et théologie chez É. Gilson et les thomistes contemporains. *Revue Thomiste* 94 (juillet–septembre) 413–30.
———, ed. 1994b. Lettres d'Étienne Gilson à Henri Gouhier. *Revue Thomiste*, 94 (juillet–septembre) 460–78.
Pullen, Larry., proj. mgr. 2005. Gifford Lectures. http://giffordlectures.org (accessed 8 February 2006). Online database contains Adam Lord Gifford's biography, a comprehensive collection of books derived from the Gifford Lectures, a biography of each lecturer, and a summary of the lecture or book.
Redpath, Peter A., ed. 2003. *A Thomistic Tapestry: Essays in Memory of Étienne Gilson*. Amsterdam; New York: Rodopi.
Renan, Ernest. 1852. *Averroès et Averroisme: Essai historique*. Paris: Michel Lévy.
Robinet, André. 1961. Robinet's biographical synthesis of Malebranche's life. In Malebranche 1958–67, 18.
———. 1964. 3 October letter to É. Gilson (unpublished). Gilson Archives.
———. 1965. *Système et existence dans l'œuvre de Malebranche*. Paris: J. Vrin.
———. 1967. La Bibliographie des Études Malebranchistes. In Malebranche 1958–67, 20:333–441.
———. 1999. Variations sur l'"idée efficace'. In Leduc-Fayette 1999, 199–210.
Rodis-Lewis, Geneviève. 1963. *Nicolas Malebranche*. Paris: Presses Universitaires de France.
———. 1967. La connaissance par idée chez Malebranche & Échange de vues. In Delorme and Bastide 1967, 111–52.
———. 1984. *Descartes: textes et débats*. Paris: Librairie Générale Française.

Rolland, E. 1938. Le surnaturel dans la philosophie de Malebranche. *Archives de philosophie*, 14 (n.1) 1–101.

Rolland-Gosselin, M.-D. 1926. Review of Gouhier 1926a and b. *Revue des sciences philosophiques et théologiques* 15:574–75.

Rome, Beatrice K. 1963. *The Philosophy of Malebranche: A Study of His Integration of Faith, Reason, and Experimental Observation*. Chicago: Henry Regnery Company.

Rouget, Marie. See Noël, Marie, pseud.

Rougier, Louis. 1925. *Le scolastique et le thomisme*. Paris, Gauthier-Villars.

———. 1931a. L'affaire Pascal et la méthode littéraire de M. Brunschvicg. *Mercure de France* 231:513–53.

———. 1931b. Le thomisme et la critique sympathique de M. Gilson. *Mercure de France* 231 (15 octobre) 340–78.

———. 1936. De l'opinion dans les démocraties et dans les gouvernements autoritaires. In Anon. 1936, 593–600.

Roustan, Désiré. 1938a. L'édition des œuvres de Malebranche. *Bulletin de la société française de philosophie* 38:94–98.

———. 1938b. La première édition des œuvres complètes de Malebranche. *Revue philosophique* 125:129–41.

Russman, Thomas A., ed. 1990. *Thomistic Papers V*. Houston: Center for Thomistic Studies, University of St. Thomas.

Sacquin, Michèle., ed. 2002. *Henri Gouhier: Historien des philosophes français (1898–1994)*. Paris: Bibliothèque Nationale de France.

Sayer, Charles. 1901–02. Review of Joly 1901. *Annales de philosophie chrétienne* 143 (ns 45) (octobre 1901–mai 1902) 593–96.

Schwob, Philippe. 1934. *Protection ou exploitation de l'épargne; une expérience américaine, l'investment trust*. Paris: Librairie du Recueil Sirey.

Sebba, Gregor. 1964. *Bibliographia Cartesiana: A Critical Guide to the Descartes Literature 1800–1960*. The Hague: Martinus Nijhoff.

Sertillanges, A.-D. 1941. *Le Christianisme et les philosophies*. 2 vols. Paris: Aubier-Montaigne.

Shook, Laurence K., ed., 1968. *Theology of Renewal*. Vol. I. Renewal of Religious Thought. New York and Montreal: Palm.

———. 1984. *Étienne Gilson*. Toronto: Pontifical Institute of Mediaeval Studies.

———. 1986. Maritain and Gilson: Early Relations. In Kennedy and Marler 1986, 7–27.

Souday, Paul. 1924. Feuilleton. *Les Temps* 9 Octobre 1924.

Suprema Sacra Congregatio Sancti Officii. 1911. *Index librorum prohibitorum Leonis XIII sum. pont. auctoritate, recognitus ss. d.n. Pii p. X iussu*. Rome.

Geneviève Sutton. 1980. Marie Noël. In Alden and Brooks 1980, 6, Pt. 2, 857–61.

Swanson, Jenny. 2002. *John of Wales, A Study of the Works and Ideas of a Thirteenth-Century Friar*. Cambridge: Cambridge University Press.

Synan, Edward A. 1989. Institute Retrospective. In Dimnik 1989, 13–27.

———. 1991. Gilson Remembered. In McInerny 1991, 49–64.

———. 2000. Étienne Gilson. In Damico et al. 1995–2000, 3:75–87.

Marchand-Thébault, Marie-Louise, ed. 1973. *Histoire de l'Université de Paris*. Paris: Chancellerie des universités de Paris.

Théry, Gabriel. 1925. *Rougier et la critique historique*. Paris: Desclée de Brouwer.

Thieulloy, Guillaume de. 2005. *Le chevalier de l'absolu: Jacques Maritain entre mystique et politique*. Paris: Éditions Gallimard.

Thomas, Lowell. 1932. *Kabluk of the Eskimo*. Boston: Little Brown.

Thomas, P-Félix. 1889. *La philosophie de Gassendi*. Paris: F. Alcan, 1889. Reprinted New York: Burt Franklin, 1967.

Tilliette, Xavier. 1994. Le professeur Henri Gouhier (1898–1994). *Bulletin de la société Paul Claudel* no.136:7–9.

University of Virginia.1926. Summer Quarter. *The University of Virginia Record*, n.s., 12 (5) (1 March).

Vacant, Alfred, E. Mangenot and E. Amann., eds. 1923–1950. *Dictionnaire de théologie catholique*. 15 vols. Paris: Letouzey et Ané.

Vieillard-Baron, Jean-Louis, ed. 1985. *Jean Baruzi: L'intelligence mystique*. Paris: Berg International.

Weber, Eugen. 1962. *Action Française: Royalism and Reaction in the Twentieth Century*. Stanford: Stanford University Press.

Wehrlé, Joannès. 1927. Malebranche. In Vacant, et al. 1923–1950, 9:776–1804.

———. 1928. Malebranche et l'Abbaye de Persigne, *La Province de Maine*, Série 2, 8: 10–22.

———. 1932. *Victor Delbos*. Paris: Bloud et Gay.

Weiss, Paul. 1995. Lost in Thought: Alone with Others. In Hahn 1995, 3–45.

INDEX OF NAMES & SUBJECTS

Marquette Studies in Philosophy
Andrew Tallon, editor

Harry Klocker, S.J. *William of Ockham and the Divine Freedom*

Margaret Monahan Hogan. *Finality and Marriage*

Gerald A. McCool, S.J. *The Neo-Thomists*

Augustine Shutte. *Philosophy for Africa*

Howard P. Kainz. *Democracy and the Kingdom of God*

Knud Løgstrup. *Metaphysics.* Translated by Dr. Russell Dees

Max Scheler. *Ressentiment.* New Introduction by Manfred Frings

Manfred Frings. *Max Scheler: A Concise Introduction into the World of a Great Thinker*

G. Heath King. *Existence Thought Style: Perspectives of a Primary Relation, portrayed through the work of Søren Kierkegaard*

Paul Ricoeur. *Key to Husserl's **Ideas I.*** Translated by Bond Harris and Jacqueline Bouchard Spurlock. Edited and with an Introduction by Pol Vandevelde

Karl Jaspers. *Reason and Existenz.* With an new Introduction by Pol Vandevelde

Gregory R. Beabout. *Freedom and Its Misuses: Kierkegaard on Anxiety and Despair*

Manfred S. Frings. *The Mind of Max Scheler. The First Comprehensive Guide Based on the Complete Works*

Claude Pavur. *Nietzsche Humanist*

Pierre Rousselot. *Intelligence: Sense of Being, Faculty of God.* A New Translation of L'Intellectualisme de saint Thomas with a Foreword and Notes by Andrew Tallon. Volume 1 of Rousselot's Collected Philosophical Works

Immanuel Kant. *Critique of Practical Reason.* Translated by H.W. Cassirer. Edited by G. Heath King and Ronald Weitzman with an Introduction by D.M. MacKinnon

Gabriel Marcel's Perspectives on ***The Broken World.*** Translated by Katharine Rose Hanley. *The Broken World, A Four-Act* Play followed by "Concrete Approaches to Investigating the Ontological Mystery." Six original illustrations by Stephen Healy. Commentaries by Henri Gouhier and Marcel Belay. Eight Appendices. Introduction by Ralph McInerny

Christopher Kaczor, editor. *Proportionalism: For and Against*

Karl-Otto Apel. *Towards a Transformation of Philosophy.* Translated by Glyn Adey and David Fisby. New Foreword by Pol Vandevelde

Gene Fendt. *Is Hamlet a Religious Drama? An Essay on a Question in Kierkegaard*

Michael Gelven. *This Side of Evil*

William Sweet, editor. *The Bases of Ethics*

Pierre Rousselot. *The Problem of Love in the Middle Ages. A Historical Contribution.* Translated and with an Introduction by Alan Vincelette. Reviewed and corrected by Pol Vandevelde

Bernard Montagnes. *The Doctrine of the Analogy of Being according to St. Thomas Aquinas.* Translated by E. M. Macierowski. Translation reviewed & corrected by Pol Vandevelde. Edited with revisions by Andrew Tallon

Jules Toner. *Love and Friendship*. Book 1: *The Experience of Love*. Book 2: *Personal Friendship: The Experience and the Ideal.* Two books in 1 volume. Edited with an Introduction by Andrew Tallon

Gordon Marino. *Kierkegaard in the Present Age.* Preface by Philip Rieff

Jan Herman Brinks. *Paradigms of Political Change: Luther, Frederick II, and Bismarck. The GDR on Its Way to German Unity*

Roger Burggraeve. *The Wisdom of Love in the Service of Love Emmanuel Levinas on Justice, Peace, and Human Rights.* Translated and with an Afterword by Jeffrey Bloechl. Preface by David A. Boileau

Gabriel Marcel. *Awakenings.* [Gabriel Marcel's Autobiography] Translated by Peter S. Rogers. Introduction by Patrick Bourgeois

Margaret Monahan Hogan. *Marriage as a Relationship.* Foreword by Richard A. McCormick, S.J. Afterword by Sidney Callahan

Anton Pannekoek. *Lenin as Philosopher: A Critical Examination of the Philosophical Basis of Leninism.* Revised Edition. Edited, annotated, and with an Introduction by Lance Byron Richey

Gregor Malantschuk. *Kierkegaard's Concept of Existence.* Edited and Translated by Howard V. Hong and Edna H. Hong

John Cowburn. *Love*

Roger Alan Deacon. *Fabricating Foucault: Rationalising the Management of Individuals*

Gabriel Marcel. *Ghostly Mysteries: Existential Drama. A Mystery of Love & The Posthumous Joke. Translated with an introduction by K.R. Hanley*

John Cowburn, S.J. *Personalism & Scholasticism*

Julia Watkin. *God and the Modern World*

Gabriel Marcel. *Music & Philosophy.* Translated by Stephen Maddux & Robert E. Wood. Introduction by Robert E. Wood

Lodewijk Meyer. *Philosophy as the Interpreter of Holy Scripture (1666).* Translated by Samuel Shirley. Introduction and Notes by Lee C. Rice and Francis Pastijn

Fred Ablondi. *Gerauld de Cordemoy: Atomist, Occasionalist, Cartesian*

Roland J. Teske, S.J. *Studies in the Philosophy of William of Auvergne, Bishop of Paris (1228-1249)*

Stefan Lorenz Sorgner. *Metaphysics without Truth: On the Importance of Consistency within Nietzsche's Philosophy*

Pol Vandevelde, Editor. *Issues in Interpretation Theory*

Jos V.M. Welie. *Justice in Oral Health Care: Ethical and Educational Perspectives*

Thomas C. Anderson. *A Commentary on Gabriel Marcel's* ***The Mystery of Being***

RJ Snell. *Through a Glass Darkly: Bernard Lonergan & Richard Rorty on Knowing without a God's-Eye View*

www. marquette.edu/mupress